# GLEIM® Aviation

**SECOND EDITION**

# INSTRUMENT PILOT
## ACS & Oral Exam Guide

by
Irvin N. Gleim, Ph.D., CFII, and Garrett W. Gleim, CFII

**Gleim Publications, Inc.**
P.O. Box 12848 · University Station
Gainesville, Florida 32604
(352) 375-0772
(800) 87-GLEIM or (800) 874-5346
Fax: (352) 375-6940
Website: www.GleimAviation.com
Email: admin@gleim.com

---

For updates to the first printing of the second edition of

**Instrument Pilot ACS & Oral Exam Guide**

**Go To:** www.GleimAviation.com/updates

**Or:** Email update@gleim.com with **IPACS 2-1** in the subject line. You will receive our current update as a reply.

Updates are available until the next edition is published.

---

ISSN 2474-8293
ISBN 978-1-61854-137-6

This edition is copyright © 2017 by Gleim Publications, Inc. Portions of this manuscript are taken from *Instrument Pilot PTS and Oral Exam Guide* copyright © 2014 and *Instrument Pilot ACS and Oral Exam Guide* copyright © 2016 by Gleim Publications, Inc.

First Printing: October 2017

ALL RIGHTS RESERVED. No part of this material may be reproduced in any form whatsoever without express written permission from Gleim Publications, Inc. Reward is offered for information exposing violators. Contact copyright@gleim.com.

---

If you purchased this book without a cover, you should be aware that it is probably stolen property. Old editions of our books are reported to us as "unsold and destroyed," and neither the author nor the publisher has received any payment for this "stripped book." Please report the sale of books without covers by calling (800) 874-5346.

---

**Environmental Statement** -- This book is printed on recyclable, environmentally friendly groundwood paper, sourced from certified sustainable forests and produced either TCF (totally chlorine-free) or ECF (elementally chlorine-free).

---

This second edition is designed specifically for pilots or flight instructors who aspire to add the instrument rating to their certificates. Please submit any corrections and suggestions for subsequent editions to www.GleimAviation.com/Questions.

Two other volumes are also available to help you pass the practical exam. **Instrument Pilot Flight Maneuvers and Practical Test Prep** focuses on your flight training and the maneuvers. **Aviation Weather and Weather Services** combines all of the information from the FAA's *Aviation Weather* (AC 00-6), *Aviation Weather Services* (AC 00-45), and numerous other FAA publications into one easy-to-understand book. It will help you study all aspects of aviation weather and provide you with a single reference book.

---

If necessary, we will develop an update for **Instrument Pilot ACS and Oral Exam Guide**. Visit our website or email update@gleim.com for the latest updates. Updates for this edition will be available until the next edition is published. To continue providing our customers with first-rate service, we request that technical questions about our materials be submitted at www.GleimAviation.com/Questions. We will give each question thorough consideration and a prompt response. Questions concerning orders, prices, shipments, or payments will be handled via telephone by our competent and courteous customer service staff.

## ABOUT THE AUTHORS

Irvin N. Gleim earned his private pilot certificate in 1965 from the Institute of Aviation at the University of Illinois, where he subsequently received his Ph.D. He is a commercial pilot and flight instructor (instrument) with multi-engine and seaplane ratings and is a member of the Aircraft Owners and Pilots Association, American Bonanza Society, Civil Air Patrol, Experimental Aircraft Association, National Association of Flight Instructors, and Seaplane Pilots Association. He is the author of flight maneuvers and practical test prep books for the sport, private, instrument, commercial, and flight instructor certificates/ratings, and study guides for the remote, sport, private/recreational, instrument, commercial, flight/ground instructor, fundamentals of instructing, airline transport pilot, and flight engineer FAA knowledge tests. Three additional pilot training books are *Pilot Handbook*, *Aviation Weather and Weather Services*, and *FAR/AIM*.

Dr. Gleim has also written articles for professional accounting and business law journals and is the author of widely used review manuals for the CIA (Certified Internal Auditor) exam, the CMA (Certified Management Accountant) exam, the CPA (Certified Public Accountant) exam, and the EA (IRS Enrolled Agent) exam. He is Professor Emeritus, Fisher School of Accounting, University of Florida, and is a CFM, CIA, CMA, and CPA.

Garrett W. Gleim earned his private pilot certificate in 1997 in a Piper Super Cub. He is a commercial pilot (single and multi-engine), ground instructor (advanced and instrument), and flight instructor (instrument and multi-engine), and is a member of the Aircraft Owners and Pilots Association and National Association of Flight Instructors. Mr. Gleim is the author of study guides for the sport, private/recreational, instrument, commercial, flight/ground instructor, fundamentals of instructing, and airline transport pilot FAA knowledge tests. He received a Bachelor of Science in Economics from The Wharton School, University of Pennsylvania. Mr. Gleim is also a CPA (not in public practice).

## REVIEWERS AND CONTRIBUTORS

Paul Duty, CFII, MEI, AGI, Remote Pilot, is a graduate of Embry-Riddle Aeronautical University with a Master of Business Administration-Aviation degree. He is our aviation marketing specialist and an aviation editor. Mr. Duty is an active flight instructor and remote pilot. He researched questions, wrote and edited answer explanations, and incorporated revisions into the text.

Char Marissa Hajdaj, CFII, ATP, Glider, ASES, LTA, Remote Pilot, is the Gleim 141 Chief Ground Instructor and an aviation editor. Ms. Hajdaj has over 17 years of aviation experience with a background in flight instruction and as a corporate pilot. She researched questions, wrote and edited answer explanations, and incorporated revisions into the text.

The CFIs who have worked with us throughout the years to develop and improve our pilot training materials.

The many FAA employees who helped, in person or by telephone, primarily in Gainesville, Orlando, Oklahoma City, and Washington, DC.

The many pilots who have provided comments and suggestions during the past several decades.

## A PERSONAL THANKS

This manual would not have been possible without the extraordinary effort and dedication of Jacob Bennett, Julie Cutlip, Ethan Good, Blaine Hatton, Fernanda Martinez, Kelsey Olson, Bree Rodriguez, Teresa Soard, Justin Stephenson, Joanne Strong, Elmer Tucker, and Candace Van Doren, who typed the entire manuscript and all revisions and drafted and laid out the diagrams, illustrations, and cover for this book.

The authors also appreciate the production and editorial assistance of Steven Critelli, Jim Harvin, Jessica Hatker, Kristen Hennen, Belea Keeney, Katie Larson, Diana León, Bernadyn Nettles, Jake Pettifor, Shane Rapp, Drew Sheppard, and Alyssa Thomas.

Finally, we appreciate the encouragement, support, and tolerance of our families throughout this project.

---

Returns of books purchased from bookstores and other resellers should be made to the respective bookstore or reseller. For more information regarding the Gleim Return Policy, please contact our offices at (800) 874-5346 or visit www.GleimAviation.com/returnpolicy.

# TABLE OF CONTENTS

| | Page |
|---|---|
| **Preface** | vi |
| **FAA Instrument Rating Airman Certification Standards Reprinted** | 1 |
| **FAA Flight Instructor–Instrument Practical Test Standards Reprinted** | 51 |
|     Addition of an Instrument Instructor Rating to a Flight Instructor Certificate | 63 |
|     Renewal or Reinstatement of a Flight Instructor | 64 |
|     Applicant's Practical Test Checklist | 65 |
|     Examiner's Practical Test Checklist | 66 |
|     Areas of Operation | 68 |
| **Aircraft Information** | 92 |
| **FAA Instrument Rating Oral Exam Guide** | 93 |
|     <u>Part I: Single-Pilot Resource Management (SRM)</u> | 94 |
|         Aeronautical Decision Making | 94 |
|         Risk Management | 97 |
|         Task Management | 101 |
|         Situational Awareness | 101 |
|         Controlled Flight into Terrain Awareness | 103 |
|         Automation Management | 104 |
|     <u>Part II: Airman Certification Standards (ACS) Tasks</u> | 105 |
|         Preflight Preparation | 105 |
|         Preflight Procedures | 116 |
|         Air Traffic Control Clearances and Procedures | 129 |
|         Flight by Reference to Instruments | 134 |
|         Navigation Systems | 136 |
|         Instrument Approach Procedures | 143 |
|         Emergency Operations | 147 |
|         Postflight Procedures | 151 |
| **FAA Flight Instructor–Instrument Oral Exam Guide*** | 153 |
|     Fundamentals of Instructing | 154 |
|     Technical Subject Areas | 166 |
|     Preflight Lesson on a Maneuver to Be Performed in Flight | 170 |
|     Flight by Reference to Instruments | 171 |
| **Appendix A: Sources** | 175 |
| **Appendix B: Abbreviations and Acronyms** | 176 |
| **Index** | 179 |

*Includes only the CFII Tasks not covered in the Instrument Rating Oral Exam Guide.

# PREFACE

On June 15, 2016, the FAA released the Instrument Rating Airman Certification Standards (ACS), replacing the Practical Test Standards (PTS). The ACS enhances the PTS by integrating knowledge, risk management, and skills into each area of operation and task. At the time of this printing, Flight Instructor–Instrument applicants should follow their applicable PTS, but should be familiar with the ACS as well because it contains the standards instrument students must meet.

All pilots or flight instructors aspiring to add the instrument rating to their certificates should bring the following resources to refer to during the oral section of their practical test: their personal logbook, the aircraft's logbook, POH/AFM, Chart Supplement, approach plates, en route IFR charts, *FAR/AIM*, and *Aviation Weather and Weather Services*. Instrument rating applicants should also bring the Instrument Airman Certification Standards (ACS), while Flight Instructor–Instrument applicants should bring both the Instrument ACS and the Flight Instructor–Instrument Practical Test Standards (PTS). In addition, all students should have an Oral Exam Guide to prep for the assortment of questions they may face.

Unlike most publishers, Gleim combines the ACS, PTS, and an Oral Exam Guide into one convenient, easy-to use book, the *Instrument Pilot ACS and Oral Exam Guide*. The ACS portion comes first and includes a direct reprint of the current version of the FAA Instrument Rating Airman Certification Standards at the time of print. The ACS is followed by a reprint of the Flight Instructor–Instrument Practical Test Standards.

The Oral Exam Guide comes after the ACS and PTS portions. Most flight schools and many CFIs recommend that pilots preparing for their practical test study an Oral Exam Guide, and we agree. Your evaluator will ask a wide-ranging series of questions during the oral portion of your practical test. Those questions may pertain to any subject or task included in the ACS for the instrument rating. Most of the questions are grouped by the tasks in the Instrument Rating ACS. Because most of the Flight Instructor–Instrument (CFII) tasks overlap those in the Instrument Rating ACS, we have included CFII-specific tasks in a separate Oral Exam Guide section that follows the one for the instrument rating. By studying the series of potential questions in this book, you will gain a significant advantage as you prepare for your testing experience.

The convenient table of contents in the Gleim Oral Exam Guide cross references each question to the appropriate ACS Area of Operation, and Appendix A includes abbreviations and acronyms used by instrument pilots.

Think of this book as both an "ACS (or PTS) guide" and an "oral exam guide." It is a thoroughly researched tool that supports the entire Gleim Aviation system of oral and practical test preparation, which includes the following manuals: *Instrument Pilot FAA Knowledge Test Prep*, *Instrument Pilot Flight Maneuvers and Practical Test Prep*, *Instrument Pilot Syllabus*, *Aviation Weather and Weather Services*, *FAR/AIM*, and *Pilot Handbook*. These books contain all of the information you need to do well on your practical test.

Enjoy Flying -- Safely!

*Irvin N. Gleim*
*Garrett W. Gleim*

October 2017

# FAA INSTRUMENT RATING
# AIRMAN CERTIFICATION STANDARDS REPRINTED
# (FAA-S-ACS-8A)

## Table of Contents

Introduction...................................................................................................................... 2
   Airman Certification Standards Concept..................................................................... 2
   Using the ACS............................................................................................................ 2
I.   Preflight Preparation................................................................................................ 4
   A.  Pilot Qualifications............................................................................................ 4
   B.  Weather Information........................................................................................ 5
   C.  Cross-Country Flight Planning......................................................................... 6
II.  Preflight Procedures................................................................................................ 7
   A.  Aircraft Systems Related to IFR Operations.................................................... 7
   B.  Aircraft Flight Instruments and Navigation Equipment..................................... 8
   C.  Instrument Flight Deck Check.......................................................................... 9
III. Air Traffic Control Clearances and Procedures...................................................... 10
   A.  Compliance with Air Traffic Control Clearances............................................. 10
   B.  Holding Procedures....................................................................................... 11
IV. Flight by Reference to Instruments........................................................................ 12
   A.  Instrument Flight............................................................................................ 12
   B.  Recovery from Unusual Flight Attitudes........................................................ 13
V.  Navigation Systems............................................................................................... 14
   A.  Intercepting and Tracking Navigational Systems and Arcs........................... 14
   B.  Departure, En route and Arrival Operations.................................................. 15
VI. Instrument Approach Procedures.......................................................................... 16
   A.  Nonprecision Approach.................................................................................. 16
   B.  Precision Approach....................................................................................... 17
   C.  Missed Approach.......................................................................................... 18
   D.  Circling Approach.......................................................................................... 19
   E.  Landing from an Instrument Approach.......................................................... 20
VII. Emergency Operations.......................................................................................... 21
   A.  Loss of Communications............................................................................... 21
   B.  One Engine Inoperative during Straight-and-Level Flight and Turns (AMEL, AMES)............ 22
   C.  Instrument Approach and Landing with an Inoperative Engine (Simulated) (AMEL, AMES).. 23
   D.  Approach with Loss of Primary Flight Instrument Indicators.......................... 24
VIII. Postflight Procedures............................................................................................. 25
   A.  Checking Instruments and Equipment.......................................................... 25
Appendix Table of Contents........................................................................................... 26

# Introduction

## Airman Certification Standards Concept

The goal of the airman certification process is to ensure the applicant possesses knowledge, ability to manage risks, and skill consistent with the privileges of the certificate or rating being exercised, in order to act as Pilot-in-Command (PIC).

In fulfilling its responsibilities for the airman certification process, the Federal Aviation Administration (FAA) Flight Standards Service (AFS) plans, develops, and maintains materials related to airman certification training and testing. These materials have included several components. The FAA knowledge test measures mastery of the aeronautical knowledge areas listed in Title 14 of the Code of Federal Regulations (14 CFR) part 61. Other materials, such as handbooks in the FAA-H-8083 series, provide guidance to applicants on aeronautical knowledge, risk management, and flight proficiency.

Safe operations in today's National Airspace System (NAS) require integration of aeronautical knowledge, risk management, and flight proficiency standards. To accomplish these goals, the FAA drew upon the expertise of organizations and individuals across the aviation and training community to develop the Airman Certification Standards (ACS). The ACS integrates the elements of knowledge, risk management, and skill listed in 14 CFR part 61 for each airman certificate or rating. It thus forms a more comprehensive standard for what an applicant must know, consider, and do for the safe conduct and successful completion of each Task to be tested on both the qualifying FAA knowledge test and the oral and flight portions of the practical test.

Through the ground and flight portion of the practical test, the FAA expects evaluators to assess the applicant's mastery of the topic in accordance with the level of learning most appropriate for the specified Task. The oral questioning will continue throughout the entire practical test. For some topics, the evaluator will ask the applicant to describe or explain. For other items, the evaluator will assess the applicant's understanding by providing a scenario that requires the applicant to appropriately apply and/or correlate knowledge, experience, and information to the circumstances of the given scenario. The flight portion of the practical test requires the applicant to demonstrate knowledge, risk management, flight proficiency, and operational skill in accordance with the ACS.

*Note:* *As used in the ACS, an* evaluator *is any person authorized to conduct airman testing (e.g., an FAA Aviation Safety Inspector (ASI), Designated Pilot Examiner (DPE), or other individual authorized to conduct a test for a certificate or rating.)*

## Using the ACS

The ACS consists of **Areas of Operation** arranged in a logical sequence, beginning with Preflight Preparation and ending with Postflight Procedures. Each Area of Operation includes **Tasks** appropriate to that Area of Operation. Each Task begins with an **Objective** stating what the applicant should know, consider, and/or do. The ACS then lists the aeronautical knowledge, risk management, and skill elements relevant to the specific Task, along with the conditions and standards for acceptable performance. The ACS uses **Notes** to emphasize special considerations. The ACS uses the terms "will" and "must" to convey directive (mandatory) information. The term "may" denotes items that are recommended but not required. The **References** for each Task indicate the source material for Task elements. For example, in Tasks such as "Current and forecast weather for departure, arrival, and en route phases of flight" (IR.I.B.K1), the applicant should be prepared for questions on any weather product presented in the references for that Task.

The abbreviation(s) within parentheses immediately following a Task refer to the category and/or class aircraft appropriate to that Task. The meaning of each abbreviation is as follows.

    ASEL:  Airplane – Single-Engine Land
    ASES:  Airplane – Single-Engine Sea
    AMEL:  Airplane – Multiengine Land
    AMES:  Airplane – Multiengine Sea

*Note:* *When administering a test based on this ACS, the Tasks appropriate to the class airplane (ASEL, ASES, AMEL, or AMES) used for the test must be included in the plan of action. The absence of a class indicates the Task is for all classes.*

Each Task in the ACS is coded according to a scheme that includes four elements. For example:

**IR.I.C.K4:**

**IR** = Applicable ACS (Instrument Rating – Airplane)
**I** = Area of Operation (Preflight Preparation)
**C** = Task (Cross-Country Flight Planning)
**K4** = Task Element Knowledge 4 (Elements of an IFR flight plan.)

Knowledge test questions are linked to the ACS codes, which will soon replace the system of Learning Statement Codes (LSC). After this transition occurs, the Airman Knowledge Test Report (AKTR) will list an ACS code that correlates to a specific Task element for a given Area of Operation and Task. Remedial instruction and re-testing will be specific, targeted, and based on specified learning criteria. Similarly, a Notice of Disapproval for the practical test will use the ACS codes to identify the deficient Task elements.

The current knowledge test management system does not have the capability to print ACS codes. Until a new test management system is in place, the LSC (e.g., "PLT058") code will continue to be displayed on the AKTR. The LSC codes are linked to references leading to broad subject areas. By contrast, each ACS code is tied to a unique Task element in the ACS itself. Because of this fundamental difference, there is no one-to-one correlation between LSC codes and ACS codes.

Because all active knowledge test questions for the Instrument Rating Airplane (IRA) knowledge test have been aligned with the corresponding ACS, evaluators can continue to use LSC codes in conjunction with the ACS for the time being. The evaluator should look up the LSC code(s) on the applicant's AKTR in the Learning Statement Reference Guide. After noting the subject area(s), the evaluator can use the corresponding Area(s) of Operation/Task(s) in the ACS to narrow the scope of material for retesting, and to evaluate the applicant's understanding of that material in the context of the appropriate ACS Area(s) of Operation and Task(s).

Applicants for a combined Private Pilot Certificate with Instrument Rating, in accordance with 14 CFR part 61, section 61.65 (a) and (g), must pass all areas designated in the Private Pilot Airplane (PAR) ACS and the Instrument Rating Airplane (IRA) ACS. Examiners need not duplicate Tasks. For example, only one preflight demonstration would be required; however, the Preflight Task from the IRA ACS would be more extensive than the Preflight Task from the PAR ACS to ensure readiness for Instrument Flight Rules (IFR) flight.

A combined checkride should be treated as one practical test, requiring only one application and resulting in only one temporary certificate, disapproval notice, or letter of discontinuance, as applicable. Failure of any Task will result in a failure of the entire test and application. Therefore, even if the deficient maneuver was instrument related and the performance of all visual flight rules (VFR) Tasks was determined to be satisfactory, the applicant will receive a notice of disapproval.

The applicant must pass the IRA knowledge test before taking the instrument rating practical test. The practical test is conducted in accordance with the ACS that is current as of the date of the test. Further, the applicant must pass the ground portion of the practical test before beginning the flight portion.

The ground portion of the practical test allows the evaluator to determine whether the applicant is sufficiently prepared to advance to the flight portion of the practical test. The oral questioning will continue throughout the entire practical test.

The FAA encourages applicants and instructors to use the ACS when preparing for knowledge tests and practical tests. The FAA will revise the ACS as circumstances require.

## I. Preflight Preparation

| Task | A. Pilot Qualifications |
|---|---|
| References | 14 CFR part 61; FAA-H-8083-2, FAA-H-8083-15 |
| Objective | To determine the applicant exhibits satisfactory knowledge, risk management, and skills associated with the requirements to act as PIC under instrument flight rules. |
| Knowledge | The applicant demonstrates understanding of: |
| IR.I.A.K1 | Certification requirements, recency of experience, and record keeping. |
| IR.I.A.K2 | Privileges and limitations |
| Risk Management | The applicant demonstrates the ability to identify, assess and mitigate risks, encompassing: |
| IR.I.A.R1 | Failure to distinguish proficiency versus currency. |
| IR.I.A.R2 | Failure to set personal minimums. |
| IR.I.A.R3 | Failure to ensure fitness for flight and physiological factors that might affect the pilot's ability to fly under instrument conditions. |
| IR.I.A.R4 | Flying unfamiliar aircraft, or operating with unfamiliar flight display systems, and avionics. |
| Skills | The applicant demonstrates the ability to: |
| IR.I.A.S1 | Apply requirements to act as PIC under Instrument Flight Rules (IFR) in a scenario given by the evaluator. |

## I. Preflight Preparation

| Task | B. Weather Information |
|---|---|
| References | 14 CFR part 91; FAA-H-8083-25, AC 00-6; AC 00-45, AIM |
| Objective | To determine the applicant exhibits satisfactory knowledge, risk management, and skills associated with obtaining, understanding, and applying weather information for a flight under IFR. |
| Knowledge | The applicant demonstrates understanding of: |
| IR.I.B.K1 | Acceptable sources of weather data for flight planning purposes. |
| IR.I.B.K2 | Weather products and resources utilized for preflight planning, current and forecast weather for departure and en route operations and arrival phases of flight. |
| IR.I.B.K3 | Meteorology applicable to the departure, en route, alternate, and destination for flights conducted under IFR in Instrument Meteorological Conditions (IMC) to include expected climate and hazardous conditions such as: |
| IR.I.B.K3a | a. Atmospheric composition and stability |
| IR.I.B.K3b | b. Wind (e.g. crosswind, tailwind, wind shear, etc.) |
| IR.I.B.K3c | c. Temperature |
| IR.I.B.K3d | d. Moisture/precipitation |
| IR.I.B.K3e | e. Weather system formation, including air masses and fronts |
| IR.I.B.K3f | f. Clouds |
| IR.I.B.K3g | g. Turbulence |
| IR.I.B.K3h | h. Thunderstorms and microbursts |
| IR.I.B.K3i | i. Icing and freezing level information |
| IR.I.B.K3j | j. Fog |
| IR.I.B.K3k | k. Frost |
| IR.I.B.K4 | Flight deck displays of digital weather and aeronautical information. |
| Risk Management | The applicant demonstrates the ability to identify, assess and mitigate risks, encompassing: |
| IR.I.B.R1 | Factors involved in making a valid go/no-go decision, to include: |
| IR.I.B.R1a | a. Circumstances that would make diversion prudent |
| IR.I.B.R1b | b. Hazardous weather conditions to include known or forecast icing |
| IR.I.B.R1c | c. Personal weather minimums |
| IR.I.B.R2 | Limitations of: |
| IR.I.B.R2a | a. Onboard weather equipment |
| IR.I.B.R2b | b. Aviation weather reports and forecasts |
| IR.I.B.R2c | c. Inflight weather resources |
| Skills | The applicant demonstrates the ability to: |
| IR.I.B.S1 | Use available aviation weather resources to obtain an adequate weather briefing. |
| IR.I.B.S2 | Discuss the implications of at least three of the conditions listed in K3a through K3k above, using actual weather or weather conditions in a scenario provided by the evaluator. |
| IR.I.B.S3 | Correlate weather information to make a competent go/no-go decision. |
| IR.I.B.S4 | Determine whether an alternate airport is required, and, if required, whether the selected alternate airport meets regulatory requirements. |

## I. Preflight Preparation

| Task | *C. Cross-Country Flight Planning* |
|---|---|
| **References** | 14 CFR part 91; FAA-H-8083-2, FAA-H-8083-15, FAA-H-8083-16, FAA-H-8083-25; Navigation Charts, Chart Supplements; AIM; NOTAMs |
| **Objective** | To determine the applicant exhibits satisfactory knowledge, risk management, and skills associated with planning an IFR cross-country and filing an IFR flight plan. |
| **Knowledge** | The applicant demonstrates understanding of: |
| IR.I.C.K1 | Route planning, including consideration of special use airspace, preferred routes, and alternate airports. |
| IR.I.C.K2 | Altitude selection accounting for terrain and obstacles, glide distance of aircraft, IFR cruising altitudes, effect of wind, and oxygen requirements. |
| IR.I.C.K3 | Calculating: |
| IR.I.C.K3a | a. Time, climb and descent rates, course, distance, heading, true airspeed, and groundspeed |
| IR.I.C.K3b | b. Estimated time of arrival to include conversion to universal coordinated time (UTC) |
| IR.I.C.K3c | c. Fuel requirements, to include reserve |
| IR.I.C.K4 | Elements of an IFR flight plan. |
| IR.I.C.K5 | Procedures for activating and closing an IFR flight plan in controlled and non-controlled airspace. |
| **Risk Management** | The applicant demonstrates the ability to identify, assess and mitigate risks, encompassing: |
| IR.I.C.R1 | Pilot. |
| IR.I.C.R2 | Aircraft. |
| IR.I.C.R3 | Environment (e.g., weather, airports, airspace, terrain, obstacles). |
| IR.I.C.R4 | External pressures. |
| IR.I.C.R5 | Limitations of air traffic control (ATC) services. |
| IR.I.C.R6 | Limitations of electronic planning applications and programs. |
| IR.I.C.R7 | Improper fuel planning. |
| **Skills** | The applicant demonstrates the ability to: |
| IR.I.C.S1 | Prepare, present and explain a cross-country flight plan assigned by the evaluator including a risk analysis based on real time weather which includes calculating time en route and fuel considering factors such as power settings, operating altitude, wind, fuel reserve requirements, and weight and balance requirements. |
| IR.I.C.S2 | Recalculate fuel reserves based on a scenario provided by the evaluator. |
| IR.I.C.S3 | Create a navigation log and simulate filing an IFR flight plan. |
| IR.I.C.S4 | Interpret departure, arrival, en route, and approach procedures with reference to appropriate and current charts. |
| IR.I.C.S5 | Recognize simulated wing contamination due to airframe icing and demonstrate knowledge of the adverse effects of airframe icing during pre-takeoff, takeoff, cruise, and landing phases of flight as well as the corrective actions. |
| IR.I.C.S6 | Apply pertinent information from appropriate and current aeronautical charts, chart supplements; NOTAMs relative to airport, runway and taxiway closures; and other flight publications. |

## II. Preflight Procedures

| Task | A. Aircraft Systems Related to IFR Operations |
|---|---|
| References | 14 CFR parts 61, 91; FAA-H-8083-2, FAA-H-8083-15; AFM; AC 91-74 |
| Objective | To determine the applicant exhibits satisfactory knowledge, risk management, and skills associated with anti-icing and de-icing systems. |
| Knowledge | The applicant demonstrates understanding of: |
| IR.II.A.K1 | The general operational characteristics and limitations of applicable anti-icing and deicing systems, including airframe, propeller, intake, fuel, and pitot-static systems. |
| Risk Management | The applicant demonstrates the ability to identify, assess and mitigate risks, encompassing: |
| IR.II.A.R1 | Pilots with little or no experience with flight in icing conditions. |
| IR.II.A.R2 | Limitations of anti-icing and deicing systems. |
| Skills | The applicant demonstrates the ability to: |
| IR.II.A.S1 | Demonstrate familiarity with anti- or de-icing procedures and/or information published by the manufacturer that is specific to the aircraft used on the practical test. |

## II. Preflight Procedures

| Task | B. Aircraft Flight Instruments and Navigation Equipment |
|---|---|
| References | 14 CFR parts 61, 91; FAA-H-8083-15; AIM |
| Objective | To determine the applicant exhibits satisfactory knowledge, risk management, and skills associated with managing instruments appropriate for an IFR flight. |
| Knowledge | The applicant demonstrates understanding of: |
| IR.II.B.K1 | General operation of their aircraft's applicable flight instrument system(s) including: |
| IR.II.B.K1a | a. Pitot-static instrument system: altimeter, airspeed indicator, vertical speed indicator |
| IR.II.B.K1b | b. Gyroscopic/electric/vacuum instrument system: attitude indicator, heading indicator, turn-and-slip indicator/turn coordinator |
| IR.II.B.K1c | c. Electrical systems, electronic flight instrument displays (PFD, MFD), transponder |
| IR.II.B.K1d | d. Magnetic compass |
| IR.II.B.K2 | The general operation of their aircraft's applicable navigation system(s) including: |
| IR.II.B.K2a | a. VOR, DME, ILS, marker beacon receiver/indicators |
| IR.II.B.K2b | b. RNAV, GPS, Wide Area Augmentation System (WAAS), FMS, autopilot |
| Risk Management | The applicant demonstrates the ability to identify, assess and mitigate risks, encompassing: |
| IR.II.B.R1 | Failure to monitor and manage automated systems. |
| IR.II.B.R2 | The difference between approved and non-approved navigation devices. |
| IR.II.B.R3 | Common failure modes of flight and navigation instruments. |
| IR.II.B.R4 | The limitations of electronic flight bags. |
| IR.II.B.R5 | Failure to ensure currency of navigation databases. |
| Skills | The applicant demonstrates the ability to: |
| IR.II.B.S1 | Operate and manage installed instruments and navigation equipment. |

## II. Preflight Procedures

| Task | C. Instrument Flight Deck Check |
|---|---|
| References | 14 CFR part 91; FAA-8083-2, FAA-H-8083-3, FAA-H-8083-15, FAA-H-8083-25; AC 91.21-1; POH/AFM |
| Objective | To determine the applicant exhibits satisfactory knowledge, risk management, and skills associated with conducting a preflight check on the aircraft instruments necessary for an IFR flight. |
| Knowledge | The applicant demonstrates understanding of: |
| IR.II.C.K1 | Purpose of performing an instrument flight deck check and how to detect possible defects. |
| IR.II.C.K2 | IFR airworthiness, to include aircraft inspection requirements and required equipment for IFR flight. |
| IR.II.C.K3 | Required procedures, documentation, and limitations of flying with inoperative equipment. |
| Risk Management | The applicant demonstrates the ability to identify, assess and mitigate risks, encompassing: |
| IR.II.C.R1 | Operating with inoperative equipment. |
| IR.II.C.R2 | Operating with outdated navigation publications or databases. |
| Skills | The applicant demonstrates the ability to: |
| IR.II.C.S1 | Perform preflight inspection by following the checklist appropriate to the aircraft and determine that the aircraft is in a condition for safe instrument flight, to include communications equipment, navigation equipment, and databases appropriate to the aircraft flown, magnetic compass, heading indicator, attitude indicator, altimeter, turn-and-slip indicator/turn coordinator, vertical speed indicator, airspeed indicator, clock, power source for gyro instruments, pitot heat, electronic flight instrument display, traffic awareness/warning/avoidance system, terrain awareness/warning/alert system, FMS, and autopilot. |

## III. Air Traffic Control Clearances and Procedures

| Task | **A. Compliance with Air Traffic Control Clearances** |
|---|---|
| References | 14 CFR parts 61, 91; FAA-H-8083-15; AIM |
| Objective | To determine the applicant exhibits satisfactory knowledge, risk management, and skills associated with ATC clearances and procedures. |
| Knowledge | The applicant demonstrates understanding of: |
| IR.III.A.K1 | Elements and procedures related to ATC clearances and pilot/controller responsibilities for departure, en route, and arrival phases of flight including clearance void times. |
| IR.III.A.K2 | PIC emergency authority. |
| IR.III.A.K3 | Lost communication procedures and procedures for flights outside of radar environments. |
| Risk Management | The applicant demonstrates the ability to identify, assess and mitigate risks, encompassing: |
| IR.III.A.R1 | Failure to fully understand an ATC clearance. |
| IR.III.A.R2 | Inappropriate, incomplete, or incorrect ATC clearances. |
| IR.III.A.R3 | ATC clearance inconsistent with aircraft performance and/or navigation capability. |
| IR.III.A.R4 | ATC clearance intended for other aircraft with similar call signs. |
| Skills | The applicant demonstrates the ability to: |
| IR.III.A.S1 | Correctly copy, read back, interpret, and comply with simulated and/or actual ATC clearances in a timely manner using standard phraseology as provided in the Aeronautical Information Manual. |
| IR.III.A.S2 | Correctly set communication frequencies, navigation systems (identifying when appropriate), and transponder codes in compliance with the ATC clearance. |
| IR.III.A.S3 | Use the current and appropriate navigation publications. |
| IR.III.A.S4 | Perform the appropriate aircraft checklist items relative to the phase of flight. |
| IR.III.A.S4 | Intercept all courses, radials, and bearings appropriate to the procedure, route, or clearance in a timely manner. |
| IR.III.A.S5 | Maintain the applicable airspeed within ±10 knots; headings within ±10°; altitude within ±100 feet; and tracks a course, radial, or bearing within ¾-scale deflection of the CDI. |
| IR.III.A.S6 | Demonstrate single-pilot resource management skills (SRM). |

## III. Air Traffic Control Clearances and Procedures

| Task | *B. Holding Procedures* |
|---|---|
| References | 14 CFR parts 61, 91; FAA-H-8083-15, FAA-H-8083-16; AIM |
| Objective | To determine the applicant exhibits satisfactory knowledge, risk management, and skills associated with holding procedures. |
| Knowledge | The applicant demonstrates understanding of: |
| IR.III.B.K1 | Elements related to holding procedures, including reporting criteria, appropriate speeds, and recommended entry procedures. |
| Risk Management | The applicant demonstrates the ability to identify, assess and mitigate risks, encompassing: |
| IR.III.B.R1 | Recalculating fuel reserves if assigned an unanticipated expect further clearance (EFC) time. |
| IR.III.B.R2 | Scenarios and circumstances that could result in minimum fuel or the need to declare an emergency. |
| IR.III.B.R3 | Scenarios that could lead to holding, including deteriorating weather at the planned destination. |
| IR.III.B.R4 | Improper holding entry and improper wind correction while holding. |
| Skills | The applicant demonstrates the ability to: |
| IR.III.B.S1 | Explain and use an entry procedure that ensures the aircraft remains within the holding pattern airspace for a standard, nonstandard, published, or non-published holding pattern. |
| IR.III.B.S2 | Change to the holding airspeed appropriate for the altitude or aircraft when 3 minutes or less from, but prior to arriving at, the holding fix and set appropriate power as needed for fuel conservation. |
| IR.III.B.S3 | Recognize arrival at the holding fix and promptly initiate entry into the holding pattern. |
| IR.III.B.S4 | Maintain airspeed within ±10 knots; altitude within ±100 feet; headings within ±10°; and track a selected course, radial or bearing within ¾-scale deflection of the CDI. |
| IR.III.B.S5 | Use proper wind correction procedures to maintain the desired pattern and to arrive over the fix as close as possible to a specified time and maintain pattern leg lengths when specified. |
| IR.III.B.S6 | Use MFD and other graphical navigation displays, if installed, to monitor position in relation to the desired flightpath during holding. |
| IR.III.B.S7 | Comply with ATC reporting requirements and restrictions associated with the holding pattern. |
| IR.III.B.S8 | Demonstrate SRM. |

## IV. Flight by Reference to Instruments

| Task | *A. Instrument Flight* |
|---|---|
| References | 14 CFR part 61; FAA-8083-2, FAA-H-8083-15 |
| Objective | To determine the applicant exhibits satisfactory knowledge, risk management, and skills associated with performing basic instrument flight maneuvers. |
| Knowledge | The applicant demonstrates understanding of: |
| IR.IV.A.K1 | Elements related to attitude instrument flying during straight-and-level flight, climbs, turns, and descents while conducting various instrument flight procedures. |
| IR.IV.A.K2 | Interpretation, operation, and limitations of pitch, bank, and power instruments. |
| IR.IV.A.K3 | Normal and abnormal instrument indications and operations. |
| Risk Management | The applicant demonstrates the ability to identify, assess and mitigate risks, encompassing: |
| IR.IV.A.R1 | Situations that can affect physiology and degrade instrument cross-check. |
| IR.IV.A.R2 | Spatial disorientation and optical illusions. |
| IR.IV.A.R3 | Flying with unfamiliar flight display systems. |
| Skills | The applicant demonstrates the ability to: |
| IR.IV.A.S1 | Maintain altitude within ±100 feet during level flight, headings within ±10°, airspeed within ±10 knots, and bank angles within ±5° during turns. |
| IR.IV.A.S2 | Use proper instrument cross-check and interpretation, and apply the appropriate pitch, bank, power, and trim corrections when applicable. |

## IV. Flight by Reference to Instruments

| Task | *B. Recovery from Unusual Flight Attitudes* |
|---|---|
| References | 14 CFR part 61; FAA-H-8083-15 |
| Objective | To determine the applicant exhibits satisfactory knowledge, risk management, and skills associated with recovering from unusual flight attitudes. |
| Knowledge | The applicant demonstrates understanding of: |
| IR.IV.B.K1 | Procedures for recovery from unusual flight attitudes. |
| IR.IV.B.K2 | Unusual flight attitude causal factors, including physiological factors, system and equipment failures, and environmental factors. |
| Risk Management | The applicant demonstrates the ability to identify, assess and mitigate risks, encompassing: |
| IR.IV.B.R1 | Situations that could lead to loss of control or unusual flight attitudes (e.g., stress, task saturation, and distractions). |
| IR.IV.B.R2 | Failure to recognize an unusual flight attitude and follow the proper recovery procedure. |
| Skills | The applicant demonstrates the ability to: |
| IR.IV.B.S1 | Use proper instrument cross-check and interpretation to identify an unusual attitude (including both nose-high and nose-low), and apply the appropriate pitch, bank, and power corrections, in the correct sequence, to return to a stabilized level flight attitude. |

## V. Navigation Systems

| Task | A. Intercepting and Tracking Navigational Systems and Arcs |
|---|---|
| References | 14 CFR parts 61, 91; FAA-H-8083-15, FAA-H-8083-16; AFM; AIM<br>***Note:*** *The evaluator must reference the manufacturer's equipment supplement(s) as necessary for appropriate limitations, procedures, etc.* |
| Objective | To determine the applicant exhibits satisfactory knowledge, risk management, and skills associated with intercepting and tracking navigation aids and arcs. |
| Knowledge | The applicant demonstrates understanding of: |
| IR.V.A.K1 | Ground-based navigation (orientation, course determination, equipment, tests and regulations) including procedures for intercepting and tracking courses and arcs. |
| IR.V.A.K2 | Satellite-based navigation (orientation, course determination, equipment, tests and regulations, authorized use of databases, Receiver Autonomous Integrity Monitoring (RAIM), and Wide Area Augmentation System (WAAS)) including procedures for intercepting and tracking courses and arcs. |
| Risk Management | The applicant demonstrates the ability to identify, assess and mitigate risks, encompassing: |
| IR.V.A.R1 | Failure to manage automated navigation and autoflight systems. |
| IR.V.A.R2 | Distractions, loss of situational awareness, and/or improper task management. |
| IR.V.A.R3 | Limitations of the navigation system in use. |
| Skills | The applicant demonstrates the ability to: |
| IR.V.A.S1 | Tune and correctly identify the navigation facility/program the navigation system and verify system accuracy as appropriate for the equipment installed in the aircraft. |
| IR.V.A.S2 | Determine aircraft position relative to the navigational facility or waypoint. |
| IR.V.A.S3 | Set and correctly orient to the course to be intercepted. |
| IR.V.A.S4 | Intercept the specified course at appropriate angle, inbound to or outbound from a navigational facility or waypoint. |
| IR.V.A.S5 | Maintain airspeed within ±10 knots, altitude within ±100 feet, and selected headings within ±5°. |
| IR.V.A.S6 | Apply proper correction to maintain a course, allowing no more than ¾-scale deflection of the CDI. |
| IR.V.A.S7 | Recognize navigational system or facility failure, and when required, report the failure to ATC. |
| IR.V.A.S8 | Use an MFD and other graphical navigation displays, if installed, to monitor position, track wind drift, and other parameters to intercept and maintain the desired flightpath. |
| IR.V.A.S9 | Properly use the autopilot, if installed, to intercept courses. |

## V. Navigation Systems

| Task | **B. Departure, En route and Arrival Operations** |
|---|---|
| References | 14 CFR parts 61, 91; FAA-H-8083-15, FAA-H-8083-16; AC 91-74; AFM; AIM |
| Objective | To determine the applicant exhibits satisfactory knowledge, risk management, and skills associated with IFR departure, en route, and arrival operations. |
| Knowledge | The applicant demonstrates understanding of: |
| IR.V.B.K1 | Elements related to ATC routes, including departure procedures (DPs) and associated climb gradients; arrival procedures (STARs) and associated constraints; and instrument approach procedures (IAPs). |
| IR.V.B.K2 | Pilot/controller responsibilities, communication procedures, and ATC services available to pilots. |
| Risk Management | The applicant demonstrates the ability to identify, assess and mitigate risks, encompassing: |
| IR.V.B.R1 | Failure to communicate with ATC or follow published procedures. |
| IR.V.B.R2 | Failure to recognize limitations of traffic avoidance equipment. |
| IR.V.B.R3 | Failure to use see and avoid techniques when possible. |
| Skills | The applicant demonstrates the ability to: |
| IR.V.B.S1 | Select, identify (as necessary) and use the appropriate communication and navigation facilities associated with the proposed flight. |
| IR.V.B.S2 | Perform the appropriate aircraft checklist items relative to the phase of flight. |
| IR.V.B.S3 | Use the current and appropriate navigation publications for the proposed flight. |
| IR.V.B.S4 | Establish two-way communications with the proper controlling agency, use proper phraseology and comply, in a timely manner, with all ATC instructions and airspace restrictions as well as exhibit adequate knowledge of communication failure procedures. |
| IR.V.B.S5 | Intercept all courses, radials, and bearings appropriate to the procedure, route, or clearance in a timely manner. |
| IR.V.B.S6 | Comply with all applicable charted procedures. |
| IR.V.B.S7 | Maintain airspeed within ±10 knots, altitude within ±100 feet, and selected headings within ±10° and apply proper correction to maintain a course, allowing no more than ¾-scale deflection of the CDI. |
| IR.V.B.S8 | Update/interpret weather in flight. |
| IR.V.B.S9 | Explain and use flight deck displays of digital weather and aeronautical information, as applicable. |
| IR.V.B.S10 | Demonstrate SRM. |

## VI. Instrument Approach Procedures

| Task | *A. Nonprecision Approach* |
|---|---|
| References | 14 CFR parts 61, 91; FAA-H-8083-15, FAA-H-8083-16; IAP, AIM |
| Objective | To determine the applicant exhibits satisfactory knowledge, risk management, and skills associated with performing nonprecision approach procedures.<br>*Note:  See Appendix 7: Aircraft, Equipment, and Operational Requirements & Limitations for related considerations.* |
| Knowledge | The applicant demonstrates understanding of: |
| IR.VI.A.K1 | Procedures and limitations associated with a nonprecision approach, including the differences between Localizer Performance (LP) and Lateral Navigation (LNAV) approach guidance. |
| IR.VI.A.K2 | Navigation system annunciations expected during an RNAV approach. |
| Risk Management | The applicant demonstrates the ability to identify, assess and mitigate risks, encompassing: |
| IR.VI.A.R1 | Failure to follow prescribed procedures (e.g., to prevent descending below the minimum descent altitude (MDA) without proper visual references). |
| IR.VI.A.R2 | Deteriorating weather conditions on approach. |
| IR.VI.A.R3 | An unstable approach, including excessive descent rates. |
| IR.VI.A.R4 | Failure to ensure proper aircraft configuration during an approach and missed approach. |
| IR.VI.A.R5 | Failure to manage automated navigation and auto flight systems. |
| Skills | The applicant demonstrates the ability to: |
| IR.VI.A.S1 | Accomplish the appropriate nonprecision instrument approaches as selected by the evaluator. |
| IR.VI.A.S2 | Establish two-way communications with ATC, as appropriate, to the phase of flight or approach segment, and uses proper communication phraseology. |
| IR.VI.A.S3 | Select, tune, identify, and confirm the operational status of navigation equipment to be used for the approach. |
| IR.VI.A.S4 | Comply with all clearances issued by ATC or the evaluator. |
| IR.VI.A.S5 | Recognize if any flight instrumentation is inaccurate or inoperative, and take appropriate action. |
| IR.VI.A.S6 | Advise ATC or the evaluator of any inability to comply with a clearance. |
| IR.VI.A.S7 | Establish the appropriate aircraft configuration and airspeed considering turbulence and wind shear, and complete the aircraft checklist items appropriate to the phase of the flight. |
| IR.VI.A.S8 | Maintain altitude within ±100 feet, heading within ±10°, and maintain airspeed within ±10 knots prior to beginning the final approach segment. |
| IR.VI.A.S9 | Apply adjustments to the published MDA and visibility criteria for the aircraft approach category when required (e.g., by NOTAMs, inoperative aircraft and ground navigation equipment, inoperative visual aids associated with the landing environment, National Weather Service (NWS) reporting factors and criteria). |
| IR.VI.A.S10 | Establish a stabilized approach with a rate of descent and track that will ensure arrival at the MDA prior to reaching the missed approach point (MAP). |
| IR.VI.A.S11 | Maintain no more than a ¾-scale deflection of the CDI, and maintain airspeed within ±10 knots of desired value while on the final approach segment. |
| IR.VI.A.S12 | Maintain the MDA, when reached, within +100 feet, –0 feet to the MAP. |
| IR.VI.A.S13 | Execute the missed approach procedure when the required visual references for the intended runway are not distinctly visible and identifiable at the MAP. |
| IR.VI.A.S14 | Execute a normal landing from a straight-in or circling approach when instructed by the evaluator. |
| IR.VI.A.S15 | Use an MFD and other graphical navigation displays, if installed, to monitor position, track wind drift and other parameters to maintain desired flightpath. |

## VI. Instrument Approach Procedures

| Task | *B. Precision Approach* |
|---|---|
| **References** | 14 CFR parts 61, 91; FAA-H-8083-15, FAA-H-8083-16; IAP; AIM |
| **Objective** | To determine the applicant exhibits satisfactory knowledge, risk management, and skills associated with performing precision approach procedures.<br>***Note:*** *See Appendix 7: Aircraft, Equipment, and Operational Requirements & Limitations for related considerations.* |
| **Knowledge** | The applicant demonstrates understanding of: |
| IR.VI.B.K1 | Procedures and limitations associated with a precision approach, including determining required descent rates and adjusting minimums in the case of inoperative equipment. |
| **Risk Management** | The applicant demonstrates the ability to identify, assess and mitigate risks, encompassing: |
| IR.VI.B.R1 | Failure to immediately initiate the missed approach at Decision Altitude (DA)/Decision Height (DH) if the required visual references are not visible. |
| IR.VI.B.R2 | Deteriorating weather conditions on approach. |
| IR.VI.B.R3 | An unstable approach including excessive descent rates. |
| IR.VI.B.R4 | Failure to ensure proper aircraft configuration during an approach and missed approach. |
| IR.VI.B.R5 | Failure to manage automated navigation and auto flight systems. |
| **Skills** | The applicant demonstrates the ability to: |
| IR.VI.B.S1 | Conduct the precision instrument approach(es) selected by the examiner. |
| IR.VI.B.S2 | Establish two-way communications with ATC appropriate for the phase of flight or approach segment, and use proper communication phraseology. |
| IR.VI.B.S3 | Select, tune, identify, and confirm the operational status of navigation equipment to be used for the approach procedure. |
| IR.VI.B.S4 | Comply with all clearances issued by ATC or the evaluator. |
| IR.VI.B.S5 | Recognize if any flight instrumentation is inaccurate or inoperative, and take appropriate action. |
| IR.VI.B.S6 | Advise ATC or the evaluator of any inability to comply with a clearance. |
| IR.VI.B.S7 | Establish the appropriate aircraft configuration and airspeed considering turbulence and wind shear, and complete the aircraft checklist items appropriate to the phase of the flight. |
| IR.VI.B.S8 | Maintain altitude within ±100 feet, heading within ±10°, and maintain airspeed within ±10 knots prior to beginning the final approach segment. |
| IR.VI.B.S9 | Apply adjustments to the published DA/DH and visibility criteria for the aircraft approach category when required (e.g., by NOTAMs, Inoperative aircraft and ground navigation equipment, inoperative visual aids associated with the landing environment, NWS reporting factors and criteria). |
| IR.VI.B.S10 | Establish a predetermined rate of descent at the point where vertical guidance begins, which approximates that required for the aircraft to correctly follow the vertical guidance. |
| IR.VI.B.S11 | Maintain a stabilized final approach from the Final Approach Fix (FAF) to DA/DH allowing no more than ¾-scale deflection of either the vertical or lateral guidance indications and maintain the desired airspeed within ±10 knots. |
| IR.VI.B.S12 | Immediately initiate the missed approach when at the DA/DH, and the required visual references for the runway are not unmistakably visible and identifiable. |
| IR.VI.B.S13 | Transition to a normal landing approach (missed approach for seaplanes) only when the aircraft is in a position from which a descent to a landing on the runway can be made at a normal rate of descent using normal maneuvering. |
| IR.VI.B.S14 | Maintain vertical and lateral guidance within ¾-scale deflection of the indicators during the visual descent from DA/DH to a point over the runway where vertical or lateral guidance must be abandoned to accomplish a normal landing. |
| IR.VI.B.S15 | Use an MFD and other graphical navigation displays, if installed, to monitor position, track wind drift and other parameters to maintain desired flightpath. |

## VI. Instrument Approach Procedures

| Task | *C. Missed Approach* |
|---|---|
| **References** | 14 CFR parts 61, 91; FAA-H-8083-15; IAP; AIM |
| **Objective** | To determine the applicant exhibits satisfactory knowledge, risk management, and skills associated with performing a missed approach procedure. |
| **Knowledge** | The applicant demonstrates understanding of: |
| *IR.VI.C.K1* | Elements related to missed approach procedures and limitations associated with standard instrument approaches, including while using a FMS and/or autopilot, if equipped. |
| **Risk Management** | The applicant demonstrates the ability to identify, assess and mitigate risks, encompassing: |
| *IR.VI.C.R1* | Failure to follow prescribed procedures. |
| *IR.VI.C.R2* | Holding, diverting, or electing to fly the approach again. |
| *IR.VI.C.R3* | Failure to ensure proper aircraft configuration during an approach and missed approach. |
| *IR.VI.C.R4* | Factors that might lead to executing a missed approach procedure before the missed approach point or to a go-around below DA/MDA. |
| *IR.VI.C.R5* | Failure to manage automated navigation and auto flight systems. |
| **Skills** | The applicant demonstrates the ability to: |
| *IR.VI.C.S1* | Initiate the missed approach promptly by applying power, establishing a climb attitude, and reducing drag in accordance with the aircraft manufacturer's recommendations. |
| *IR.VI.C.S2* | Report to ATC upon beginning the missed approach procedure. |
| *IR.VI.C.S3* | Comply with the published or alternate missed approach procedure. |
| *IR.VI.C.S4* | Advise ATC or the evaluator of any inability to comply with a clearance, restriction, or climb gradient. |
| *IR.VI.C.S5* | Follow the recommended checklist items appropriate to the missed approach/go-around procedure. |
| *IR.VI.C.S6* | Request, if appropriate, ATC clearance to the alternate airport, clearance limit, or as directed by the evaluator. |
| *IR.VI.C.S7* | Maintain the recommended airspeed within ±10 knots; heading, course, or bearing within ±10°; and altitude(s) within ±100 feet during the missed approach procedure. |
| *IR.VI.C.S8* | Use an MFD and other graphical navigation displays, if installed, to monitor position and track to help navigate the missed approach. |
| *IR.VI.C.S9* | Demonstrate SRM. |

## VI. Instrument Approach Procedures

| Task | D. Circling Approach |
|---|---|
| References | 14 CFR parts 61, 91; FAA-H-8083-15; IAP; AIM |
| Objective | To determine the applicant exhibits satisfactory knowledge, risk management, and skills associated with performing a circling approach procedure. |
| Knowledge | The applicant demonstrates understanding of: |
| IR.VI.D.K1 | Elements related to circling approach procedures and limitations including approach categories and related airspeed restrictions. |
| Risk Management | The applicant demonstrates the ability to identify, assess and mitigate risks, encompassing: |
| IR.VI.D.R1 | Failure to follow prescribed circling approach procedures. |
| IR.VI.D.R2 | Executing a circling approach at night and/or with marginal visibility. |
| IR.VI.D.R3 | Losing visual contact with an identifiable part of the airport. |
| IR.VI.D.R4 | Failure to manage automated navigation and auto flight systems. |
| IR.VI.D.R5 | Failure to maintain an appropriate airspeed while circling. |
| IR.VI.D.R6 | Low altitude maneuvering/stall/spin. |
| IR.VI.D.R7 | Executing an improper missed approach after the MAP while circling. |
| Skills | The applicant demonstrates the ability to: |
| IR.VI.D.S1 | Select and comply with the circling approach procedure considering turbulence, wind shear, and the maneuvering capabilities of the aircraft. |
| IR.VI.D.S2 | Confirm the direction of traffic and adhere to all restrictions and instructions issued by ATC or the evaluator. |
| IR.VI.D.S3 | Avoid circling beyond visibility requirements and maintain the appropriate circling altitude until in a position from which a descent to a normal landing can be made. |
| IR.VI.D.S4 | Maneuver the aircraft after reaching the MDA on a flightpath that will permit a normal landing on a runway. |
| IR.VI.D.S5 | Maintain altitude +100 feet, -0 feet until a descent to a normal landing can be made. The runway selected must require at least a 90° change of direction from the final approach course to align the aircraft for landing. |
| IR.VI.D.S6 | Demonstrate SRM. |

## VI. Instrument Approach Procedures

| Task | E. Landing from an Instrument Approach |
|---|---|
| References | 14 CFR parts 61, 91; FAA-H-8083-15; AIM |
| Objective | To determine the applicant exhibits satisfactory knowledge, risk management, and skills associated with performing the procedures for a landing from an instrument approach. |
| Knowledge | The applicant demonstrates understanding of: |
| IR.VI.E.K1 | Elements related to the pilot's responsibilities, and the environmental, operational, and meteorological factors that affect landing from a straight-in or circling approach. |
| IR.VI.E.K2 | Airport signs, markings and lighting, to include approach lighting systems. |
| Risk Management | The applicant demonstrates the ability to identify, assess and mitigate risks, encompassing: |
| IR.VI.E.R1 | Attempting to land from an unstable approach. |
| IR.VI.E.R2 | Flying below the glidepath. |
| IR.VI.E.R3 | Transitioning from instrument to visual references for landing. |
| Skills | The applicant demonstrates the ability to: |
| IR.VI.E.S1 | Transition at the DA/DH, MDA, or visual descent point VDP to a visual flight condition, allowing for safe visual maneuvering and a normal landing. |
| IR.VI.E.S2 | Adhere to all ATC or evaluator advisories, such as NOTAMs, wind shear, wake turbulence, runway surface, braking conditions, and other operational considerations. |
| IR.VI.E.S3 | Complete the appropriate checklist items for the pre-landing and landing phase. |
| IR.VI.E.S4 | Maintain positive aircraft control throughout the complete landing maneuver. |
| IR.VI.E.S5 | Demonstrate SRM. |

## VII. Emergency Operations

| Task | A. Loss of Communications |
|---|---|
| References | 14 CFR parts 61, 91; AIM |
| Objective | To determine the applicant exhibits satisfactory knowledge, risk management, and skills associated with loss of communications. |
| Knowledge | The applicant demonstrates understanding of: |
| IR.VII.A.K1 | Procedures to be followed in the event of lost communication during various phases of flight, including techniques for reestablishing communications, when it is acceptable to deviate from an IFR clearance, and when to begin an approach at the destination. |
| Risk Management | The applicant demonstrates the ability to identify, assess and mitigate risks, encompassing: |
| IR.VII.A.R1 | Possible reasons for loss of communication. |
| IR.VII.A.R2 | Failure to follow procedures for lost communications. |
| Skills | The applicant demonstrates the ability to: |
| IR.VII.A.S1 | Recognize a simulated loss of communication. |
| IR.VII.A.S2 | Simulate actions to re-establish communication. |
| IR.VII.A.S3 | Determine whether to continue to flight plan destination or deviate. |
| IR.VII.A.S4 | Determine appropriate time to begin an approach. |

## VII. Emergency Operations

| Task | B. One Engine Inoperative during Straight-and-Level Flight and Turns (AMEL, AMES) |
|---|---|
| References | 14 CFR 61; FAA-H-8083-3, FAA-H-8083-15 |
| Objective | To determine the applicant exhibits satisfactory knowledge, risk management and skills associated the procedures for operating the aircraft with an inoperative engine during straight-and-level flight and in turns. |
| Knowledge | The applicant demonstrates understanding of: |
| IR.VII.B.K1 | Procedures used if engine failure occurs during straight-and-level flight and turns while on instruments. |
| Risk Management | The applicant demonstrates the ability to identify, assess and mitigate risks, encompassing: |
| IR.VII.B.R1 | Failure to correctly identify the inoperative engine. |
| IR.VII.B.R2 | Inability to climb or maintain altitude with an inoperative engine. |
| IR.VII.B.R3 | Low altitude maneuvering/stall/spin. |
| IR.VII.B.R4 | Distractions, loss of situational awareness, and/or improper task management. |
| Skills | The applicant demonstrates the ability to: |
| IR.VII.B.S1 | Promptly recognize an engine failure simulated by the evaluator during straight-and-level flight and turns. |
| IR.VII.B.S2 | Recognize engine failure and simulate feathering of the propeller on the inoperative engine. (Evaluator should then establish a zero-thrust on the inoperative engine). |
| IR.VII.B.S3 | Establish the best engine-inoperative airspeed and trim the aircraft. |
| IR.VII.B.S4 | Verify the accomplishment of prescribed checklist procedures for securing the inoperative engine. |
| IR.VII.B.S5 | Establish and maintain the recommended flight attitude necessary for best performance during straight-and-level and turning flight. |
| IR.VII.B.S6 | Attempt to determine and resolve the reason for the engine failure. |
| IR.VII.B.S7 | Monitor all engine control functions and make necessary adjustments. |
| IR.VII.B.S8 | Maintain the specified altitude within ±100 feet, or minimum sink as appropriate, airspeed ±10 knots, and the specified heading ±10°. |
| IR.VII.B.S9 | Assess the aircraft's performance capability and decide an appropriate action to ensure a safe landing. |
| IR.VII.B.S10 | Avoid loss of aircraft control, or attempted flight contrary to the engine-inoperative operating limitations of the aircraft. |
| IR.VII.B.S11 | Demonstrate SRM. |

## VII. Emergency Operations

| Task | **_C. Instrument Approach and Landing with an Inoperative Engine (Simulated) (AMEL, AMES)_** |
|---|---|
| References | 14 CFR parts 61,91; FAA-H-8083-3, FAA-H-8083-15 |
| Objective | To determine that the applicant exhibits satisfactory knowledge, risk management, and skills associated with executing a published instrument approach with one engine inoperative. |
| Knowledge | The applicant demonstrates understanding of: |
| IR.VII.C.K1 | Instrument approach procedures with one engine inoperative. |
| Risk Management | The applicant demonstrates the ability to identify, assess and mitigate risks, encompassing: |
| IR.VII.C.R1 | Failure to plan for engine failure during approach and landing. |
| IR.VII.C.R2 | Distractions, loss of situational awareness, and/or improper task management. |
| IR.VII.C.R3 | Single engine performance. |
| Skills | The applicant demonstrates the ability to: |
| IR.VII.C.S1 | Recognize engine failure, set the engine controls, reduce drag, identify and verify the inoperative engine, and simulate feathering of the propeller on the inoperative engine. (Evaluator should then establish a zero-thrust on the inoperative engine). |
| IR.VII.C.S2 | Reduce drag by establishing and maintaining a bank angle and inclinometer ball displacement toward the operating engine and configuring the aircraft, as required for best performance in straight-and-level flight and during the approach phase. |
| IR.VII.C.S3 | Follow the manufacturer's recommended emergency procedures. |
| IR.VII.C.S4 | Monitor the operating engine and make necessary adjustments. |
| IR.VII.C.S5 | Request and follow an actual or a simulated ATC clearance for an instrument approach. |
| IR.VII.C.S6 | Maintain altitude within 100 feet, airspeed within ±10 knots if within the aircraft's capability, and heading ±10°. |
| IR.VII.C.S7 | Establish a rate of descent that will ensure arrival at the MDA or DH/DA with the airplane in a position from which a descent to a landing on the intended runway can be made, either straight in or circling as appropriate. |
| IR.VII.C.S8 | On final approach segment, maintain vertical and lateral guidance within ¾-scale deflection. |
| IR.VII.C.S9 | Avoid loss of aircraft control, or attempted flight contrary to the engine-inoperative operating limitations of the aircraft. |
| IR.VII.C.S10 | Comply with the published criteria for the aircraft approach category when circling. |
| IR.VII.C.S11 | Complete the appropriate checklist. |

## VII. Emergency Operations

| Task | D. Approach with Loss of Primary Flight Instrument Indicators |
|---|---|
| References | 14 CFR parts 61, 91; FAA-H-8083-15; IAP |
| Objective | To determine the applicant exhibits satisfactory knowledge, risk management, and skills associated with performing an approach with the loss of primary flight control instruments. |
| Knowledge | The applicant demonstrates understanding of: |
| IR.VII.D.K1 | Recognizing if primary flight instruments are inaccurate or inoperative, and advising ATC or the evaluator. |
| IR.VII.D.K2 | Common failure modes of vacuum and electric attitude instruments and how to correct or minimize the effect of their loss. |
| Risk Management | The applicant demonstrates the ability to identify, assess and mitigate risks, encompassing: |
| IR.VII.D.R1 | Use of secondary flight displays when primary displays have failed. |
| IR.VII.D.R2 | Failure to maintain aircraft control. |
| IR.VII.D.R3 | Distractions, loss of situational awareness, and/or improper task management. |
| Skills | The applicant demonstrates the ability to: |
| IR.VII.D.S1 | Advise ATC or evaluator if unable to comply with a clearance. |
| IR.VII.D.S2 | Complete a nonprecision instrument approach without the use of the primary flight instruments using the skill elements of the nonprecision approach Task (See Area of Operation VI, Task A). |
| IR.VII.D.S3 | Demonstrate SRM. |

## VIII. Postflight Procedures

| Task | *A. Checking Instruments and Equipment* |
|---|---|
| References | 14 CFR parts 61, 91 |
| Objective | To determine the applicant exhibits satisfactory knowledge, risk management, and skills associated with checking flight instruments and equipment during postflight. |
| Knowledge | The applicant demonstrates understanding of: |
| *IR.VIII.A.K1* | Procedures for checking the functionality of all installed instruments and navigation equipment. |
| Risk Management | The applicant demonstrates the ability to identify, assess and mitigate risks, encompassing: |
| *IR.VIII.A.R1* | Failure to perform a proper postflight inspection and properly document aircraft discrepancies. |
| Skills | The applicant demonstrates the ability to: |
| *IR.VIII.A.S1* | Conduct a postflight inspection, and document discrepancies and servicing requirements, if any. |

## Appendix Table of Contents

| | |
|---|---|
| **Appendix 1: The Knowledge Test Eligibility, Prerequisites, and Testing Centers** | 27 |
| Knowledge Test Description | 27 |
| Knowledge Test Tables | 27 |
| Knowledge Test Blueprint | 27 |
| English Language Standard | 28 |
| Knowledge Test Requirements | 28 |
| Knowledge Test Centers | 28 |
| Knowledge Test Registration | 28 |
| **Appendix 2: Knowledge Test Procedures and Tips** | 29 |
| Acceptable Materials | 29 |
| Test Tips | 30 |
| Cheating or Other Unauthorized Conduct | 30 |
| Testing Procedures for Applicants Requesting Special Accommodations | 30 |
| **Appendix 3: Airman Knowledge Test Report** | 31 |
| FAA Knowledge Test Question Coding | 31 |
| **Appendix 4: The Practical Test – Eligibility and Prerequisites** | 32 |
| Additional Instrument Rating Desired | 32 |
| Removal of the "Airplane Multiengine VFR Only" Limitation | 32 |
| **Appendix 5: Practical Test Roles, Responsibilities, and Outcomes** | 33 |
| Applicant Responsibilities | 33 |
| Instructor Responsibilities | 33 |
| Evaluator Responsibilities | 33 |
| Possible Outcomes of the Test | 34 |
| Instrument Proficiency Check | 37 |
| **Appendix 6: Safety of Flight** | 38 |
| General | 38 |
| Stall and Spin Awareness | 38 |
| Use of Checklists | 38 |
| Use of Distractions | 38 |
| Positive Exchange of Flight Controls | 38 |
| Aeronautical Decision-Making, Risk Management, Crew Resource Management and Single-Pilot Resource Management | 39 |
| Multiengine Considerations | 39 |
| **Appendix 7: Aircraft, Equipment, and Operational Requirements & Limitations** | 40 |
| Aircraft Requirements & Limitations | 40 |
| Equipment Requirements & Limitations | 40 |
| Operational Requirements, Limitations, & Task Information | 40 |
| **Appendix 8: Use of Flight Simulation Training Devices (FSTD) and Aviation Training Devices (ATD): Airplane Single-Engine, Multi Engine Land and Sea** | 42 |
| Use of Flight Simulator Training Devices | 42 |
| Use of Aviation Training Devices | 42 |
| Credit for Time in an FSTD | 43 |
| Credit for Time in an ATD | 43 |
| Instrument Experience | 44 |
| Instrument Proficiency Check | 44 |
| Use of an FSTD on a Practical Test | 44 |
| **Appendix 9: References** | 46 |
| **Appendix 10: Abbreviations and Acronyms** | 47 |

## Appendix 1: The Knowledge Test Eligibility, Prerequisites, and Testing Centers

### Knowledge Test Description

The knowledge test is an important part of the airman certification process. Applicants must pass the knowledge test before taking the practical test.

The knowledge test consists of objective, multiple-choice questions. There is a single correct response for each test question. Each test question is independent of other questions. A correct response to one question does not depend upon, or influence, the correct response to another.

### Knowledge Test Tables

| Test Code | Test Name | Number of Questions | Age | Allotted Time | Passing Score |
|---|---|---|---|---|---|
| AIF | Flight Instructor Instrument Airplane (Added Rating)* | 20 | 16 | 1.0 | 70 |
| FIH | Flight Instructor Instrument Helicopter | 50 | 16 | 2.5 | 70 |
| FII | Flight Instructor Instrument Airplane | 50 | 16 | 2.5 | 70 |
| HIF | Flight Instructor Instrument Helicopter (Added Rating)* | 20 | 16 | 1.0 | 70 |
| ICH | Instrument Rating Helicopter *Canadian Conversion* | 40 | 15 | 2.0 | 70 |
| ICP | Instrument Rating Airplane *Canadian Conversion* | 40 | 15 | 2.0 | 70 |
| IFP | Instrument Rating Foreign Pilot | 50 | n/a | 2.5 | 70 |
| IGI | Ground Instructor Instrument | 50 | 16 | 2.5 | 70 |
| IRA | Instrument Rating Airplane | 60 | 15 | 2.5 | 70 |
| IRH | Instrument Rating Helicopter | 60 | 15 | 2.5 | 70 |

*See Rating Table Appendix 4.

### Knowledge Test Blueprint

| IRA Knowledge Areas Required by 14 CFR part 61, section 61.65 to be on the Knowledge Test | Percent of Questions Per Test |
|---|---|
| Regulations | 5 – 15% |
| IFR En Route and Approach Procedures | 5 – 15% |
| Air Traffic Control and Procedures | 5 – 20% |
| IFR Navigation | 5 – 20% |
| Weather Reports, Critical Weather, Wind shear and Forecasts | 10 – 20% |
| Safe and Efficient IFR Operations | 5 – 10% |
| Aeronautical Decision-Making | 5 – 10% |
| Crew Resource Management (CRM) | 5 – 10% |
| **Total Number of Questions** | 60 |

## English Language Standard

In accordance with the requirements of 14 CFR part 61 and the FAA Aviation English Language Proficiency standard, throughout the application and testing process the applicant must demonstrate the ability to read, write, speak, and understand the English language. English language proficiency is required to communicate effectively with Air Traffic Control (ATC), to comply with ATC instructions, and to ensure clear and effective crew communication and coordination. Normal restatement of questions as would be done for a native English speaker is permitted, and does not constitute grounds for disqualification.

## Knowledge Test Requirements

In order to take the IRA Knowledge Test, you must provide proper identification. To verify your eligibility to take the test, you must also provide one of the following in accordance with the requirements of 14 CFR part 61:

- 14 CFR part 61, section 61.35 lists the prerequisites for taking the knowledge test, to include the minimum age an applicant must be to sit for the test.
  - Received an endorsement, if required by this part, from an authorized instructor certifying that the applicant accomplished the appropriate ground-training or a home-study course required by this part for the certificate or rating sought and is prepared for the knowledge test;
  - Proper identification at the time of application that contains the applicant's—
    - i) Photograph;
    - ii) Signature;
    - iii) Date of birth;
    - iv) If the permanent mailing address is a post office box number, then the applicant must provide a government-issued residential address
- 14 CFR part 61, section 61.49 acceptable forms of retest authorization for **all** Instrument Rating tests:
  - An applicant retesting **after failure** is required to submit the applicable test report indicating failure, along with an endorsement from an authorized instructor who gave the applicant the required additional training. The endorsement must certify that the applicant is competent to pass the test. The test proctor must retain the original failed test report presented as authorization and attach it to the applicable sign-in/out log.

    *Note:* *If the applicant no longer possesses the original test report, he or she may request a duplicate replacement issued by the Airman Certification Branch (AFS-760).*
- Acceptable forms of authorization for Instrument Rating Airplane Canadian Conversion (ICP) only:
  - Confirmation of Verification Letter issued by AFS-760 (Knowledge Testing Authorization Requirements Matrix).
  - Requires **no** instructor endorsement or other form of written authorization.

## Knowledge Test Centers

The FAA authorizes hundreds of knowledge testing center locations that offer a full range of airman knowledge tests. For information on authorized testing centers and to register for the knowledge test, contact one of the providers listed at www.faa.gov.

## Knowledge Test Registration

When you contact a knowledge testing center to register for a test, please be prepared to select a test date, choose a testing center, and make financial arrangements for test payment when you call. You may register for test(s) several weeks in advance, and you may cancel in accordance with the testing center's cancellation policy.

## Appendix 2: Knowledge Test Procedures and Tips

Before starting the actual test, the testing center will provide an opportunity to practice navigating through the test. This practice or tutorial session may include sample questions to familiarize the applicant with the look and feel of the software. (e.g., selecting an answer, marking a question for later review, monitoring time remaining for the test, and other features of the testing software.)

**Acceptable Materials**

The applicant may use the following aids, reference materials, and test materials, as long as the material does not include actual test questions or answers:

| Acceptable Materials | Unacceptable Materials | Notes |
|---|---|---|
| Supplement book provided by proctor | Written materials that are handwritten, printed, or electronic | Testing centers may provide calculators and/or deny the use of personal calculators |
| All models of aviation-oriented calculators or small electronic calculators that perform only arithmetic functions | Electronic calculators incorporating permanent or continuous type memory circuits without erasure capability. | Unit Member (proctor) may prohibit the use of your calculator if he or she is unable to determine the calculator's erasure capability |
| Calculators with simple programmable memories, which allow addition to, subtraction from, or retrieval of one number from the memory; or simple functions, such as square root and percentages | Magnetic Cards, magnetic tapes, modules, computer chips, or any other device upon which pre-written programs or information related to the test can be stored and retrieved | Printouts of data must be surrendered at the completion of the test if the calculator incorporates this design feature. |
| Scales, straightedges, protractors, plotters, navigation computers, blank log sheets, holding pattern entry aids, and electronic or mechanical calculators that are directly related to the test | Dictionaries | Before, and upon completion of the test, while in the presence of the Unit Member, actuate the ON/OFF switch or RESET button, and perform any other function that ensures erasure of any data stored in memory circuits |
| Manufacturer's permanently inscribed instructions on the front and back of such aids, e.g., formulas, conversions, regulations, signals, weather data, holding pattern diagrams, frequencies, weight and balance formulas, and air traffic control procedures | Any booklet or manual containing instructions related to use of test aids | Unit Member makes the final determination regarding aids, reference materials, and test materials |

**Test Tips**

When taking a knowledge test, please keep the following points in mind:

- Carefully read the instructions provided with the test.
- Answer each question in accordance with the latest regulations and guidance publications.
- Read each question carefully before looking at the answer options. You should clearly understand the problem before trying to solve it.
- After formulating a response, determine which answer option corresponds with your answer. The answer you choose should completely solve the problem.
- Remember that only one answer is complete and correct. The other possible answers are either incomplete or erroneous.
- If a certain question is difficult for you, mark it for review and return to it after you have answered the less difficult questions. This procedure will enable you to use the available time to maximum advantage.
- When solving a calculation problem, be sure to read all the associated notes.
- For questions involving use of a graph, you may request a printed copy that you can mark in computing your answer. This copy and all other notes and paperwork must be given to the testing center upon completion of the test.

**Cheating or Other Unauthorized Conduct**

To avoid test compromise, computer testing centers must follow strict security procedures established by the FAA and described in FAA Order 8080.6 (as amended), Conduct of Airman Knowledge Tests. The FAA has directed testing centers to terminate a test at any time a test unit member suspects that a cheating incident has occurred.

The FAA will investigate and, if the agency determines that cheating or unauthorized conduct has occurred, any airman certificate or rating you hold may be revoked. You will also be prohibited from applying for or taking any test for a certificate or rating under 14 CFR part 61 for a period of 1 year.

**Testing Procedures for Applicants Requesting Special Accommodations**

An applicant with learning or reading disability may request approval from the Airman Testing Standards Branch (AFS-630) through the local Flight Standards District Office (FSDO) or International Field Office/International Field Unit (IFO/IFU) to take airman knowledge test using one of the three options listed below, in preferential order:

Option 1: Use current testing facilities and procedures whenever possible.

Option 2: Use a self-contained, electronic device which pronounces and displays typed-in words (e.g., the Franklin Speaking Wordmaster®) to facilitate the testing process.

*Note: The device should consist of an electronic thesaurus that audibly pronounces typed-in words and presents them on a display screen. The device should also have a built-in headphone jack in order to avoid disturbing others during testing.*

Option 3: Request the proctor's assistance in reading specific words or terms from the test questions and/or supplement book. To prevent compromising the testing process, the proctor must be an individual with no aviation background or expertise. The proctor may provide reading assistance only (i.e., no explanation of words or terms). When an applicant requests this option, the FSDO or IFO/IFU inspector must contact AFS-630 for assistance in selecting the test site and assisting the proctor. Before approving any option, the FSDO or IFO/IFU inspector must advise the applicant of the regulatory certification requirement to be able to read, write, speak, and understand the English language.

## Appendix 3: Airman Knowledge Test Report

Immediately upon completion of the knowledge test, the applicant receives a printed Airman Knowledge Test Report (AKTR) documenting the score with the testing center's raised, embossed seal. The applicant must retain the original AKTR. The instructor must provide instruction in each area of deficiency and provide a logbook endorsement certifying that the applicant has demonstrated satisfactory knowledge in each area. When taking the practical test, the applicant must present the original AKTR to the evaluator, who is required to assess the noted areas of deficiency during the oral portion of the practical test.

An AKTR expires 24 calendar months after the month the applicant completes the knowledge test. If the AKTR expires before completion of the practical test, the applicant must retake the knowledge test.

To obtain a duplicate AKTR due to loss or destruction of the original, the applicant can send a signed request accompanied by a check or money order for $12.00, payable to the FAA to:

Federal Aviation Administration
Airmen Certification Branch, AFS-760
P.O. Box 25082
Oklahoma City, OK 73125

To obtain a copy of the application form or a list of the information required, please see the Airman Certification Branch (AFS-760) web page.

**FAA Knowledge Test Question Coding**

Each Task in the ACS includes an ACS code. This ACS code will soon be displayed on the AKTR to indicate what Task element was proven deficient on the knowledge test. Instructors can then provide remedial training in the deficient areas, and evaluators can re-test this element during the practical test.

The ACS coding consists of four elements. For example, this code is interpreted as follows:

**IR.I.C.K4:**

- IR = Applicable ACS (Instrument Rating – Airplane)
- I = Area of Operation (Preflight Preparation)
- C = Task (Cross-Country Flight Planning)
- K4 = Task Element Knowledge 4 (Elements of an IFR flight plan.)

Knowledge test questions are linked to the ACS codes, which will soon replace the system of Learning Statement Codes (LSC). After this transition occurs, the Airman Knowledge Test Report (AKTR) will list an ACS code that correlates to a specific Task element for a given Area of Operation and Task. Remedial instruction and re-testing will be specific, targeted, and based on specified learning criteria. Similarly, a Notice of Disapproval for the practical test will use the ACS codes to identify the deficient Task elements.

The current knowledge test management system does not have the capability to print ACS codes. Until a new test management system is in place, the LSC (e.g., "PLT058") code will continue to be displayed on the AKTR. The LSC codes are linked to references leading to broad subject areas. By contrast, each ACS code is tied to a unique Task element in the ACS itself. Because of this fundamental difference, there is no one-to-one correlation between LSC codes and ACS codes.

Because all active knowledge test questions for the Instrument Rating Airplane (IRA) knowledge test have been aligned with the corresponding ACS, evaluators can continue to use LSC codes in conjunction with the ACS for the time being. The evaluator should look up the LSC code(s) on the applicant's AKTR in the Learning Statement Reference Guide. After noting the subject area(s), the evaluator can use the corresponding Area(s) of Operation/Task(s) in the ACS to narrow the scope of material for retesting, and to evaluate the applicant's understanding of that material in the context of the appropriate ACS Area(s) of Operation and Task(s).

## Appendix 4: The Practical Test – Eligibility and Prerequisites

The prerequisite requirements and general eligibility for a practical test and the specific requirements for the original issuance of an instrument rating in the airplane can be found in 14 CFR part 61, sections 61.39 and 61.65, respectively.

If an applicant holds both single-engine and multiengine class ratings on a pilot certificate and takes the instrument rating practical test in a single-engine airplane, the certificate issued must bear the limitation "Multiengine Limited to VFR Only." If the applicant takes the test in a multiengine airplane, the instrument privileges will be automatically conferred for the airplane single-engine rating.

**Additional Instrument Rating Desired**

If you hold an instrument rating in another category and adding Instrument – Airplane, you are required to complete the Task(s) indicated in the following table:

| Area of Operation | Required Task(s) |
|---|---|
| I | None |
| II | A,C |
| III | None |
| IV | All |
| V | None |
| VI | All |
| VII | All[1] |
| VIII | All |

**Removal of the "Airplane Multiengine VFR Only" Limitation**

The removal of the "Airplane Multiengine VFR Only" limitation, at the private pilot or commercial pilot certificate level, requires an applicant to satisfactorily perform the following Area of Operation and Tasks from the Instrument Rating– Airplane ACS in a multiengine airplane that has a manufacturer's published $V_{MC}$ speed.

*VII. Emergency Operations*

*Task B: One Engine Inoperative during Straight-and-Level Flight and Turns (AMEL, AMES)*

*Task C: Instrument Approach and Landing with an Inoperative Engine (Simulated) (AMEL, AMES)*

---

[1] TASK B and C are applicable *only* to *multiengine airplanes*.

## Appendix 5: Practical Test Roles, Responsibilities, and Outcomes

### Applicant Responsibilities

The applicant is responsible for mastering the established standards for knowledge, risk management, and skill elements in all Tasks appropriate to the certificate and rating sought. The applicant should use this ACS, its references, and the Applicant's Practical Test Checklist in this Appendix in preparation to take the practical test.

### Instructor Responsibilities

The instructor is responsible for training the applicant to meet the established standards for knowledge, risk management, and skill elements in all Tasks appropriate to the certificate and rating sought. The instructor should use this ACS and its references as part of preparing the applicant to take the practical test and, if necessary, in retraining the applicant to proficiency in all subject(s) missed on the knowledge test.

### Evaluator Responsibilities

An evaluator is:

- Aviation Safety Inspector (ASI);
- Pilot examiner (other than administrative pilot examiners);
- Training center evaluator (TCE);
- Chief instructor, assistant chief instructor or check instructor of pilot school holding examining authority; or
- Instrument Flight Instructor (CFII) conducting an instrument proficiency check (IPC).

The evaluator who conducts the practical test is responsible for determining that the applicant meets the established standards of aeronautical knowledge, skills (flight proficiency), and risk management for the Tasks in the appropriate ACS. This responsibility also includes verifying the experience requirements specified for a certificate or rating.

Prior to beginning the practical test, the evaluator must also determine that the applicant meets FAA Aviation English Language Proficiency Standard by verifying that he or she can understand ATC instructions and communicate in English at a level that is understandable to ATC and other pilots. The evaluator should use the procedures outlined in the AC 60-28, English Language Skill Standards required by 14 CFR parts 61, 63, and 65 (current version) when evaluating the applicant's ability to meet the standard.

The evaluator must develop a Plan of Action (POA), written in English, to conduct the practical test. It must include all of the required Areas of Operation and Tasks. The POA must include a scenario that evaluates as many of the required Areas of Operation and Tasks as possible. As the scenario unfolds during the test, the evaluator will introduce problems and emergencies that the applicant must manage. The evaluator has the discretion to modify the POA in order to accommodate unexpected situations as they arise. For example, the evaluator may elect to suspend and later resume a scenario in order to assess certain Tasks.

In the integrated ACS framework, the Areas of Operation contain Tasks that include "Knowledge" elements (such as K1), "risk management" elements (such as R1), and "skill" elements (such as S1). Knowledge and risk management elements are primarily evaluated during the knowledge testing phase of the airman certification process. The evaluator must assess the applicant on all skill elements for each Task included in each Area of Operation of the ACS, unless otherwise noted. The evaluator administering the practical test has the discretion to combine Tasks/elements as appropriate to testing scenarios.

The required minimum elements to include in the POA, unless otherwise noted, from each applicable Task are as follows:

- at least one knowledge element;
- at least one risk management element;
- all skill elements; and
- any Task elements in which the applicant was shown to be deficient on the knowledge test.

*Note: Task elements added to the POA on the basis of being listed on the AKTR may satisfy the other minimum Task element requirements. The missed items on the AKTR are not required to be added in addition to the minimum Task element requirements.*

There is no expectation for testing every knowledge element and risk management element in a Task, but the evaluator has discretion to sample as needed to ensure the applicant's mastery of that Task.

Unless otherwise noted in the Task, the evaluator must test each item in the skills section by asking the applicant to perform each one. As safety of flight conditions permit, the evaluator may use questions during flight to test knowledge and risk management elements not evident in the demonstrated skills. To the greatest extent practicable, evaluators must test the applicant's ability to apply and correlate information, and use rote questions only when they are appropriate for the material being tested. If the Task includes an element with sub-elements, the evaluator may choose the primary element and select at least one sub-element to satisfy the requirement that at least one knowledge element be selected. For example, if the evaluator chooses IR.I.B.K3, he or she must select a sub-element like IR.I.B.K3d to satisfy the requirement to select one knowledge element.

## Possible Outcomes of the Test

There are three possible outcomes of the practical test: (1) Temporary Airman Certificate (satisfactory), (2) Notice of Disapproval (unsatisfactory), or (3) Letter of Discontinuance.

If the evaluator determines that a Task is incomplete, or the outcome is uncertain, the evaluator may require the applicant to repeat that Task, or portions of that Task. This provision does not mean that instruction, practice, or the repetition of an unsatisfactory Task is permitted during the practical test.

If the evaluator determines the applicant's skill and abilities are in doubt, the outcome is unsatisfactory and the evaluator must issue a Notice of Disapproval.

### *Satisfactory Performance*

Satisfactory performance requires that the applicant:

- demonstrate the Tasks specified in the Areas of Operation for the certificate or rating sought within the established standards;
- demonstrate mastery of the aircraft by performing each Task successfully;
- demonstrate proficiency and competency in accordance with the approved standards;
- demonstrate sound judgment and exercise aeronautical decision-making/risk management; and
- demonstrate competence in crew resource management in aircraft certificated for more than one required pilot crew member, or single-pilot competence in an airplane that is certificated for single-pilot operations.

Satisfactory performance will result in the issuance of a temporary certificate.

### *Unsatisfactory Performance*

If, in the judgment of the evaluator, the applicant does not meet the standards for any Task, the applicant fails the Task and associated Area of Operation. The test is unsatisfactory, and the evaluator issues a Notice of Disapproval.

When the evaluator issues a Notice of Disapproval, he or she must list the ACS code associated with the Area of Operation in which the application did not meet the standard. The Notice of Disapproval must also list the Area(s) of Operation not tested, and the number of practical test failures. If the applicant's inability to meet English language requirements contributed to the failure of a Task, the evaluator should note "English Proficiency" on the Notice of Disapproval.

The evaluator or the applicant may end the test if the applicant fails a Task. The evaluator may continue the test only with the consent of the applicant, and the applicant is entitled to credit only for those Areas of Operation and the associated Tasks satisfactorily performed. Though not required, the evaluator has discretion to reevaluate any Task, including those previously passed, during the retest.

Typical areas of unsatisfactory performance and grounds for disqualification include:

- Any action or lack of action by the applicant that requires corrective intervention by the evaluator to maintain safe flight.
- Failure to use proper and effective visual scanning techniques to clear the area before and while performing maneuvers.
- Consistently exceeding tolerances stated in the skill elements of the Task.
- Failure to take prompt corrective action when tolerances are exceeded.
- Failure to exercise risk management.

## *Discontinuance*

When it is necessary to discontinue a practical test for reasons other than unsatisfactory performance (e.g., equipment failure, weather, illness), the evaluator must return all test paperwork to the applicant. The evaluator must prepare, sign, and issue a Letter of Discontinuance that lists those Areas of Operation the applicant successfully completed and the date the test must be completed. The evaluator should advise the applicant to present the Letter of Discontinuance to the evaluator when the practical test resumes in order to receive credit for the items successfully completed. The Letter of Discontinuance becomes part of the applicant's certification file.

# Practical Test Checklist (Applicant)
## Appointment with Evaluator

Evaluator's Name: _____

Location: _____

Date/Time: _____

**Acceptable Aircraft**

- ☑ Aircraft Documents:
    - ☑ Airworthiness Certificate
    - ☑ Registration Certificate
    - ☑ Operating Limitations
- ☑ Aircraft Maintenance Records:
    - ☑ Logbook Record of Airworthiness Inspections and AD Compliance
- ☑ Pilot's Operating Handbook, FAA-Approved Aircraft Flight Manual

**Personal Equipment**

- ☑ View-Limiting Device
- ☑ Current Aeronautical Charts (May be electronic)
- ☑ Computer and Plotter
- ☑ Flight Plan Form
- ☑ Flight Plan Form and Flight Logs (printed or electronic)
- ☑ Chart Supplements, Airport Diagrams and Appropriate Publications (regulations, AIM, etc.)

**Personal Records**

- ☑ Identification—Photo/Signature ID
- ☑ Pilot Certificate
- ☑ Current Medical Certificate
- ☑ Completed FAA Form 8710-1, Airman Certificate and/or Rating Application with Instructor's Signature or completed IACRA form
- ☑ Original Knowledge Test Report
- ☑ Pilot Logbook with appropriate Instructor Endorsements
- ☐ ~~FAA Form 8060-5, Notice of Disapproval (if applicable)~~
- ☐ ~~Letter of Discontinuance (if applicable)~~
- ☐ ~~Approved School Graduation Certificate (if applicable)~~
- ☐ Evaluator's Fee (if applicable)

**Instrument Proficiency Check**

14 CFR part 61, section 61.57(d) sets forth the requirements for an instrument proficiency check (IPC). Instructors and evaluators conducting an IPC must ensure the pilot meets the standards established in this ACS. A representative number of Tasks must be selected to assure the competence of the applicant to operate in the IFR environment. As a minimum, the applicant must demonstrate the ability to perform the Tasks listed in the table below. The person giving the check should develop a scenario that incorporates as many required Tasks as practical to assess the pilot's ADM and risk management skills.

Guidance on how to conduct an IPC is found in Advisory Circular 61-98, *Currency Requirements and Guidance for the Flight Review and Instrument Proficiency Check*. You may obtain a copy at: http://www.faa.gov.

| Area of Operation | IPC (Proficiency Check)[2] |
|---|---|
| I | None |
| II | None |
| III | B |
| IV | B |
| V | A |
| VI | All |
| VII[3] | B, C, D |
| VIII | All |

---

[2] AATDs can be utilized for the majority of the IPC as specified in the Letter of Authorization issued for the device. However, the circling approach, the landing Task, and the multiengine airplane Tasks must be accomplished in an aircraft or FFS (Level B, C, or D). A BATD cannot be used for any part of the IPC.

[3] Tasks B and C are applicable only to multiengine airplanes.

## Appendix 6: Safety of Flight

### General

Safety of flight must be the prime consideration at all times. The evaluator, applicant, and crew must be constantly alert for other traffic. If performing aspects of a given maneuver, such as emergency procedures, would jeopardize safety, the evaluator will ask the applicant to simulate that portion of the maneuver. The evaluator will assess the applicant's use of visual scanning and collision avoidance procedures throughout the entire test.

### Stall and Spin Awareness

During flight training and testing, the applicant and the instructor or evaluator must always recognize and avoid operations that could lead to an inadvertent stall or spin.

### Use of Checklists

Throughout the practical test, the applicant is evaluated on the use of an appropriate checklist.

Assessing proper checklist use depends upon the specific Task. In all cases, the evaluator should determine whether the applicant appropriately divides attention and uses proper visual scanning. In some situations, reading the actual checklist may be impractical or unsafe. In such cases, the evaluator should assess the applicant's performance of published or recommended immediate action "memory" items along with his or her review of the appropriate checklist once conditions permit.

In a single-pilot airplane, the applicant should demonstrate the crew resource management (CRM) principles described as single-pilot resource management (SRM). Proper use is dependent on the specific Task being evaluated. The situation may be such that the use of the checklist while accomplishing elements of an Objective would be either unsafe or impractical in a single-pilot operation. In this case, a review of the checklist after the elements have been accomplished is appropriate. Use of a checklist should also consider visual scanning and division of attention at all times.

### Use of Distractions

Numerous studies indicate that many accidents have occurred when the pilot has been distracted during critical phases of flight. The evaluator should incorporate realistic distractions during the flight portion of the practical test to evaluate the pilot's situational awareness and ability to utilize proper control technique while dividing attention both inside and outside the flight deck.

### Positive Exchange of Flight Controls

There must always be a clear understanding of who has control of the aircraft. Prior to flight, the pilots involved should conduct a briefing that includes reviewing the procedures for exchanging flight controls.

The FAA recommends a positive three-step process for exchanging flight controls between pilots:

- When one pilot seeks to have the other pilot take control of the aircraft, he or she will say, "You have the flight controls."
- The second pilot acknowledges immediately by saying, "I have the flight controls."
- The first pilot again says, "You have the flight controls," and visually confirms the exchange.

Pilots should follow this procedure during any exchange of flight controls, including any occurrence during the practical test. The FAA also recommends that both pilots use a visual check to verify that the exchange has occurred. There must never be any doubt as to who is flying the aircraft.

## Aeronautical Decision-Making, Risk Management, Crew Resource Management and Single-Pilot Resource Management

Throughout the practical test, the evaluator must assess the applicant's ability to use sound aeronautical decision-making procedures in order to identify hazards and mitigate risk. The evaluator must accomplish this requirement by reference to the risk management elements of the given Task(s), and by developing scenarios that incorporate and combine Tasks appropriate to assessing the applicant's risk management in making safe aeronautical decisions. For example, the evaluator may develop a scenario that incorporates weather decisions and performance planning.

In assessing the applicant's performance, the evaluator should take note of the applicant's use of CRM and, if appropriate, SRM. CRM/SRM is the set of competencies that includes situational awareness, communication skills, teamwork, task allocation, and decision-making within a comprehensive framework of standard operating procedures (SOP). SRM specifically refers to the management of all resources onboard the aircraft as well as outside resources available to the single pilot.

Deficiencies in CRM/SRM almost always contribute to the unsatisfactory performance of a Task. While evaluation of CRM/SRM may appear to be somewhat subjective, the evaluator should use the risk management elements of the given Task(s) to determine whether the applicant's performance of the Task(s) demonstrates both understanding and application of the associated risk management elements.

## Multiengine Considerations

For multiengine practical tests conducted in the airplane, the evaluator must discuss with the applicant during the required preflight briefing the methods for simulating an engine failure in accordance with the aircraft manufacturer's recommended procedures.

Practical tests conducted in an FSTD can only be accomplished as part of an approved curriculum or training program. Any limitations on powerplant failure will be noted in that program.

## Appendix 7: Aircraft, Equipment, and Operational Requirements & Limitations

### Aircraft Requirements & Limitations

14 CFR part 61, section 61.45 prescribes the required aircraft and equipment for a practical test. The regulation states the minimum aircraft registration and airworthiness requirements as well as the minimum equipment requirements, to include the minimum required controls.

An applicant may accomplish an instrument-airplane rating practical test in a multiengine airplane that is limited to center thrust. There is no need to place the "Limited to Center Thrust" limitation on the applicant's pilot certificate, provided the airplane multiengine land rating is not limited to center thrust. If the applicant's airplane multiengine land rating is limited to center thrust then the limitation will already be on the pilot certificate.

If the aircraft presented for the practical test has inoperative instruments or equipment, it must be addressed in accordance with 14 CFR part 91, section 91.213. If the aircraft can be operated in accordance with 14 CFR part 91, section 91.213, then it must be determined if the inoperative instruments or equipment are required to complete the practical test.

### Equipment Requirements & Limitations

The equipment examination should be administered before the flight portion of the practical test, but it must be closely coordinated and related to the flight portion. In a training core curriculum that has been approved under 14 CFR part 142, the evaluator may accept written evidence of the equipment exam, provided that the Administrator has approved the exam and authorized the individual who administers it.

Consistent with 14 CFR part 61, section 61.45 (b) and (d), the aircraft must have:

- the flight instruments necessary for controlling the aircraft without outside references,
- the radio equipment required for ATC communications, and
- the ability to perform instrument approach procedures
- GPS equipment must be instrument certified and contain the current database.

To assist in management of the aircraft during the practical test, the applicant is expected to demonstrate automation management skills by utilizing installed equipment such as autopilot, avionics and systems displays, and/or flight management system (FMS). The evaluator is expected to test the applicant's knowledge of the systems that are installed and operative during both the oral and flight portions of the practical test.

If the practical test is conducted in an aircraft, the applicant is required by 14 CFR part 61, section 61.45(d)(2) to provide an appropriate view limiting device acceptable to the evaluator. The applicant and the evaluator should establish a procedure as to when and how this device should be donned and removed, and brief this procedure before the flight. The device must be used during all testing that requires flight "solely by reference to instruments." This device must prevent the applicant from having visual reference outside the aircraft, but it must not restrict the evaluator's ability to see and avoid other traffic.

### Operational Requirements, Limitations, & Task Information

#### VI. Instrument Approach Procedures

A stabilized approach is characterized by a constant angle, constant rate of descent approach profile ending near the touchdown point, where the landing maneuver begins.

If the practical test is conducted in an airplane equipped with an approach-approved RNAV or GPS system or FSTD that is equipped to replicate an approved RNAV or GPS system, the applicant must demonstrate approach proficiency using that system. If the applicant has contracted for training in an approved course that includes GPS training, and the airplane/FSTD has a properly installed and operable GPS, the applicant must demonstrate GPS approach proficiency.

Localizer performance with vertical guidance (LPV) minimums with a decision altitude (DA) greater than 300 feet height above touchdown (HAT) may be used as a nonprecision approach; however, due to the precision of its glidepath and localizer-like lateral navigation characteristics, an LPV minimums can be used to demonstrate precision approach proficiency if the DA is equal to or less than 300 feet HAT.

The standard is to allow no more than a ¾ scale deflection of either the vertical or lateral deviation indications during the final approach. As markings on flight instruments vary, a ¾ scale deflection of either vertical or lateral guidance is deemed to occur when it is displaced three-fourths of the distance that it may be deflected from the indication representing that the aircraft is on the correct flight path.

*Task A. Nonprecision Approach*

The evaluator will select nonprecision approaches representative of the type that the applicant is likely to use. The choices must use at least two different types of navigational aids.

Examples of acceptable nonprecision approaches include: VOR, VOR/DME, LOC procedures on an ILS, LDA, RNAV (RNP) or RNAV (GPS) to LNAV, LNAV/VNAV or LPV line of minima as long as the LPV DA is greater than 300 feet HAT. The equipment must be installed and the database must be current and qualified to fly GPS-based approaches.

The applicant must accomplish at least two nonprecision approaches in simulated or actual weather conditions.

- One must include a procedure turn or, in the case of a GPS-based approach, a Terminal Arrival Area (TAA) procedure.
- At least one must be flown without the use of autopilot and without the assistance of radar vectors. The yaw damper and flight director are not considered parts of the autopilot for purposes of this Task.
- If the equipment allows, at least one should be conducted without vertical guidance.
- One is expected to be flown with reference to backup or partial panel instrumentation or navigation display, depending on the aircraft's instrument avionics configuration, representing the failure mode(s) most realistic for the equipment used.

*Task B. Precision Approach*

The applicant must accomplish a precision approach to the decision altitude (DA) using aircraft navigational equipment for centerline and vertical guidance in simulated or actual instrument conditions. Acceptable instrument approaches for this part of the practical test are the ILS and GLS. In addition, if the installed equipment and database is current and qualified for IFR flight and approaches to LPV minima, an LPV minima approach can be flown to demonstrate precision approach proficiency if the LPV DA is equal to or less than 300 feet HAT.

## Appendix 8: Use of Flight Simulation Training Devices (FSTD) and Aviation Training Devices (ATD): Airplane Single-Engine, Multi Engine Land and Sea

**Use of Flight Simulator Training Devices**

14 CFR part 61, section 61.4, *Qualification and approval of flight simulators and flight training devices*, states in paragraph (a) that each full flight simulator (FFS) and flight training device (FTD) used for training, and for which an airman is to receive credit to satisfy any training, testing, or checking requirement under this chapter, must be qualified and approved by the Administrator for—

> *(1) the training, testing, and checking for which it is used;*
>
> *(2) each particular maneuver, procedure, or crewmember function performed; and*
>
> *(3) the representation of the specific category and class of aircraft, type of aircraft, particular variation within the type of aircraft, or set of aircraft for certain flight training devices.*

14 CFR part 60 prescribes the rules governing the initial and continuing qualification and use of all Flight Simulator Training Devices (FSTD) used for meeting training, evaluation, or flight experience requirements for flight crewmember certification or qualification.

An FSTD is defined in 14 CFR part 60 as an FFS or FTD:

> ***Full Flight Simulator (FFS)***—*a replica of a specific type, make, model, or series aircraft. It includes the equipment and computer programs necessary to represent aircraft operations in ground and flight conditions, a visual system providing an out-of-the-flight deck view, a system that provides cues at least equivalent to those of a three-degree-of-freedom motion system, and has the full range of capabilities of the systems installed in the device as described in part 60 of this chapter and the qualification performance standard (QPS) for a specific FFS qualification level. (part 1)*
>
> ***Flight Training Device (FTD)***—*a replica of aircraft instruments, equipment, panels, and controls in an open flight deck area or an enclosed aircraft flight deck replica. It includes the equipment and computer programs necessary to represent aircraft (or set of aircraft) operations in ground and flight conditions having the full range of capabilities of the systems installed in the device as described in part 60 of this chapter and the QPS for a specific FTD qualification level. (part 1)*

The FAA National Simulator Program (NSP) qualifies Level A-D FFSs and Level 4 – 7[4] FTDs. In addition, each operational rule part identifies additional requirements for the approval and use of FSTDs in a training program[5]. Use of an FSTD for the completion of the instrument-airplane rating practical test is permitted only when accomplished in accordance with an FAA approved curriculum or training program. Use of an FSTD for the completion of an instrument proficiency check is also permitted when accomplished in accordance with an FAA approved curriculum or training program.

**Use of Aviation Training Devices**

14 CFR part 61, section 61.4(c) states the Administrator may approve a device other than an FFS or FTD for specific purposes. Under this authority, the FAA's General Aviation and Commercial Division provide approval for aviation training devices (ATD).

---

[4] The FSTD qualification standards in effect prior to part 60 defined a Level 7 FTD for airplanes (see Advisory Circular 120-45A, Airplane Flight Training Device Qualification, 1992). This device required high fidelity, airplane specific aerodynamic and flight control models similar to a Level D FFS, but did not require a motion cueing system or visual display system. In accordance with the "grandfather rights" of 14 CFR part 60, section 60.17, these previously qualified devices will retain their qualification basis as long as they continue to meet the standards under which they were originally qualified. There is only one airplane Level 7 FTD with grandfather rights that remains in the U.S. As a result of changes to part 60 that were published in the Federal Register in March 2016, the airplane Level 7 FTD was reinstated with updated evaluation standards. The new Level 7 FTD will require a visual display system for qualification. The minimum qualified Tasks for the Level 7 FTD are described in Table B1B of Appendix B of part 60.

[5] 14 CFR part 121, section 121.407; part 135, section 135.335; part 141, section 141.41; and part 142, section 142.59.

Advisory Circular (AC) 61-136A, *FAA Approval of Aviation Training Devices and Their Use for Training and Experience*, provides information and guidance for the required function, performance, and effective use of ATDs for pilot training and aeronautical experience (including currency). FAA issues a letter of authorization (LOA) to an ATD manufacturer approving an ATD as a basic aviation training device (BATD) or an advanced aviation training device (AATD). The LOA will be valid for a five year period with a specific expiration date and include the amount of credit a pilot may take for training and experience.

> *Aviation Training Device (ATD)—a training device, other than an FFS or FTD, that has been evaluated, qualified, and approved by the Administrator. In general, this includes a replica of aircraft instruments, equipment, panels, and controls in an open flight deck area or an enclosed aircraft cockpit. It includes the hardware and software necessary to represent a category and class of aircraft (or set of aircraft) operations in ground and flight conditions having the appropriate range of capabilities and systems installed in the device as described within the AC for the specific basic or advanced qualification level.*
>
> *Basic Aviation Training Device (BATD)—provides an adequate training platform for both procedural and operational performance Tasks specific to instrument experience and the ground and flight training requirements for the Private Pilot Certificate and instrument rating per 14 CFR parts 61 and 141.*
>
> *Advanced Aviation Training Device (AATD)—provides an adequate training platform for both procedural and operational performance Tasks specific to the ground and flight training requirements for the Private Pilot Certificate, Instrument Rating, Commercial Pilot Certificate, Airline Transport Pilot (ATP) Certificate, and Flight Instructor Certificate per 14 CFR parts 61 and 141. It also provides an adequate platform for Tasks required for instrument experience and the instrument proficiency check.*

*Note:* *ATDs cannot be used for practical tests, aircraft type specific training, or for an aircraft type rating; therefore the use of an ATD for the instrument – airplane rating practical test is not permitted. An AATD, however, may be used for some of the required Tasks of an instrument proficiency check as further explained in this appendix.*

### Credit for Time in an FSTD

14 CFR part 61, section 61.65 specifies the minimum aeronautical experience requirements for a person applying for an instrument rating. Paragraph (d) specifies the time requirements for an instrument-airplane rating, which includes specific experience requirements that must be completed in an airplane. Paragraph (h) of this section specifies the amount of credit a pilot can take for time in an FFS or FTD. For those that received training in programs outside of 14 CFR part 142, section 61.65(h)(2)[6] applies. For those pilots that received training through a 14 CFR part 142 program, section 61.65(h)(1) applies.

### Credit for Time in an ATD

14 CFR part 61, section 61.65 specifies the minimum aeronautical experience requirements for a person applying for an instrument rating. Paragraph (d) specifies the time requirements for an instrument-airplane rating, which includes specific experience requirements that must be completed in an airplane. Paragraph (i) specifies the maximum instrument time in an ATD a pilot may credit towards the instrument rating aeronautical experience requirements. Paragraph (j) specifies the maximum instrument time a pilot may credit in any combination of an FFS, FTD, and ATD.

---

[6] As part of program approval, 14 CFR part 141 training providers must also adhere to the requirements for permitted time in an FFS, FTD, or ATD per Appendix C to 14 CFR part 141.

In order to credit the time, the ATD must be FAA-approved and the instrument time must be provided by an authorized instructor. AC 61-136A, states the LOA for each approved ATD will indicate the credit allowances for pilot training and experience, as provided under 14 CFR parts 61 and 141. Time with an instructor in a BATD and an AATD may be credited towards the aeronautical experience requirements for the instrument-airplane rating as specified in the LOA for the device used. It is recommended that applicants who intend to take credit for time in a BATD or an AATD towards the aeronautical experience requirements for the instrument-airplane rating obtain a copy of the LOA for each device used so they have a record for how much credit may be taken. For additional information on the logging of ATD time reference AC 61-136A, see Appendix 4.

## Instrument Experience

14 CFR part 61, section 61.57 provides the recent flight experience requirements to serve as a PIC. Paragraph (c) specifies the necessary instrument experience required to serve as a PIC under IFR. The experience may be gained in an airplane, an FSTD, or an ATD. Refer to the subparagraphs of 14 CFR part 61, section 61.57(c) to determine the experience needed, which varies depending upon whether an airplane, FSTD, ATD, or combination of airplane and training devices are used.

## Instrument Proficiency Check

If a person fails to meet the experience requirements of 14 CFR part 61, section 61.57(c), a pilot may only establish instrument currency through an instrument proficiency check as described in 14 CFR section 61.57(d). An FSTD may be used as part of an approved curriculum to accomplish all or portions of this check. If specified in its LOA, an AATD may be used to complete most of the required Tasks. However, the circling approach, the landing Task, and the multiengine airplane Tasks must be accomplished in an aircraft or FFS (Level B, C, or D). A BATD cannot be used for an instrument proficiency check. See the Instrument Proficiency Check table in Appendix 5 for additional information.

## Use of an FSTD on a Practical Test

14 CFR part 61, section 61.45 specifies the required aircraft and equipment that must be provided for a practical test unless permitted to use an FFS or FTD for the flight portion. 14 CFR part 61, section 61 64 provides the criteria for using an FSTD for a practical test. Specifically, paragraph (a) states –

> *If an applicant for a certificate or rating uses a flight simulator or flight training device for training or any portion of the practical test, the flight simulator and flight training device—*
>
> *(1) Must represent the category, class, and type (if a type rating is applicable) for the rating sought; and*
>
> *(2) Must be qualified and approved by the Administrator and used in accordance with an approved course of training under 14 CFR part 141 or 142 of this chapter; or under 14 CFR part 121 or part 135 of this chapter, provided the applicant is a pilot employee of that air carrier operator.*

Therefore, practical tests or portions thereof, when accomplished in an FSTD, may only be conducted by FAA aviation safety inspectors (ASI), aircrew program designees (APD) authorized to conduct such tests in FSTDs in 14 CFR parts 121 or 135, qualified personnel and designees authorized to conduct such tests in FSTDs for 14 CFR part 141 pilot school graduates, or appropriately authorized 14 CFR part 142 Training Center Evaluators (TCE).

In addition, 14 CFR part 61, section 61.64(b) states if an airplane is not used during the practical test for a type rating for a turbojet airplane (except for preflight inspection), an applicant must accomplish the entire practical test in a Level C or higher FFS and the applicant must meet the specific experience criteria listed. If the experience criteria cannot be met, the applicant can either—

> *(f)(1) [...] complete the following Tasks on the practical test in an aircraft appropriate to category, class, and type for the rating sought: Preflight inspection, normal takeoff, normal instrument landing system approach, missed approach, and normal landing; or*
>
> *(f)(2) The applicant's pilot certificate will be issued with a limitation that states: "The [name of the additional type rating] is subject to pilot-in-command limitations," and the applicant is restricted from serving as pilot-in-command in an aircraft of that type.*

When flight Tasks are accomplished in an airplane, certain Task elements may be accomplished through "simulated" actions in the interest of safety and practicality. However, when accomplished in an FFS or FTD, these same actions would not be "simulated." For example, when in an airplane, a simulated engine fire may be addressed by retarding the throttle to idle, simulating the shutdown of the engine, simulating the discharge of the fire suppression agent, if applicable, and simulating the disconnection of associated electrical, hydraulic, and pneumatics systems. However, when the same emergency condition is addressed in an FSTD, all Task elements must be accomplished as would be expected under actual circumstances.

Similarly, safety of flight precautions taken in the airplane for the accomplishment of a specific maneuver or procedure (such as limiting altitude in an approach to stall or setting maximum airspeed for an engine failure expected to result in a rejected takeoff) need not be taken when an FSTD is used. It is important to understand that, whether accomplished in an airplane or FSTD, all Tasks and elements for each maneuver or procedure must have the same performance standards applied equally for determination of overall satisfactory performance.

## Appendix 9: References

This ACS is based on the following 14 CFR parts, FAA guidance documents, manufacturer's publications, and other documents.

| Reference | Title |
| --- | --- |
| 14 CFR part 61 | Certification: Pilots, Flight Instructors, and Ground Instructors |
| 14 CFR part 68 | Requirements for Operating Certain Small Aircraft Without a Medical Certificate |
| 14 CFR part 91 | General Operating and Flight Rules |
| AC 00-6 | Aviation Weather |
| AC 00-45 | Aviation Weather Services |
| AC 60-28 | English Language Skill Standards Required by 14 CFR parts 61, 63 and 65 |
| AC 91-74 | Pilot Guide: Flight in Icing Conditions |
| AC 91.21-1 | Use of Portable Electronic Devices Aboard Aircraft |
| AFM | Airplane Flight Manual |
| AIM | Aeronautical Information Manual |
| FAA-H-8083-2 | Risk Management Handbook |
| FAA-H-8083-3 | Airplane Flying Handbook |
| FAA-H-8083-15 | Instrument Flying Handbook |
| FAA-H-8083-16 | Instrument Procedures Handbook |
| FAA-H-8083-25 | Pilot's Handbook of Aeronautical Knowledge |
| IAP | Instrument Approach Procedures |
| POH/AFM | Pilot's Operating Handbook/FAA-Approved Airplane Flight Manual |
| Other | Chart Supplements |
|  | Navigation Charts |
|  | NOTAMs |

*Note:* Users should reference the current edition of the reference documents listed above. The current edition of all FAA publications can be found at www.faa.gov.

## Appendix 10: Abbreviations and Acronyms

The following abbreviations and acronyms are used in the ACS.

| Abb./Acronym | Definition |
|---|---|
| 14 CFR | Title 14 of the Code of Federal Regulations |
| AATD | Advanced Aviation Training Device |
| AC | Advisory Circular |
| ACS | Airman Certification Standards |
| AD | Airworthiness Directive |
| ADF | Automatic Direction Finder |
| ADM | Aeronautical Decision-Making |
| AELP | Aviation English Language Proficiency |
| AFM | Airplane Flight Manual |
| AFS | Flight Standards Service |
| AGL | Above Ground Level |
| AIM | Aeronautical Information Manual |
| AKTR | Airman Knowledge Test Report |
| ALD | Available Landing Distance |
| AMEL | Airplane Multiengine Land |
| AMES | Airplane Multiengine Sea |
| AOA | Angle of Attack |
| AOO | Area of Operation |
| ASEL | Airplane Single-Engine Land |
| ASES | Airplane Single-Engine Sea |
| ASI | Aviation Safety Inspector |
| ATC | Air Traffic Control |
| ATD | Aviation Training Device |
| ATP | Airline Transport Pilot |
| BATD | Basic Aviation Training Device |
| CDI | Course Deviation Indicator |
| CFIT | Controlled Flight Into Terrain |
| CFR | Code of Federal Regulations |
| CG | Center of Gravity |
| CP | Completion Phase |
| CRM | Crew Resource Management |
| CTP | Certification Training Program |
| DA | Decision Altitude |
| DH | Decision Height |
| DME | Distance Measuring Equipment |
| DP | Departure Procedures |
| DPE | Designated Pilot Examiner |
| ELT | Emergency Locator Transmitter |
| FAA | Federal Aviation Administration |
| FADEC | Full Authority Digital Engine Control |

| Abb./Acronym | Definition |
|---|---|
| FFS | Full Flight Simulator |
| FMS | Flight Management System |
| FSB | Flight Standardization Board |
| FSDO | Flight Standards District Office |
| FSTD | Flight Simulation Training Device |
| FTD | Flight Training Device |
| GBAS | Ground Based Augmentation System |
| GBAS GLS | Ground Based Augmentation Landing System |
| GNSS | Global Navigation Satellite System |
| GPS | Global Positioning System |
| HAT | Height Above Threshold (Touchdown) |
| HSI | Horizontal Situation Indicator |
| IA | Inspection Authorization |
| IAP | Instrument Approach Procedure |
| IFO | International Field Office |
| IFR | Instrument Flight Rules |
| IFU | International Field Unit |
| ILS | Instrument Landing System |
| IMC | Instrument Meteorological Conditions |
| IPC | Instrument Rating Airplane *Canadian Conversion* |
| IPC | Instrument Proficiency Check |
| IR | Instrument Rating |
| IRA | Instrument Rating Airplane |
| KOEL | Kinds of Operation Equipment List |
| LAHSO | Land and Hold Short Operations |
| LDA | Localizer-Type Directional Aid |
| LOA | Letter of Authorization |
| LOC | ILS Localizer |
| LPV | Localizer Performance with Vertical Guidance |
| LSC | Learning Statement Codes |
| MAP | Missed Approach Point |
| MDA | Minimum Descent Altitude |
| MEL | Minimum Equipment List |
| MFD | Multi-functional Displays |
| NAS | National Airspace System |
| NOD | Notice of Disapproval |
| NOTAMs | Notices to Airmen |
| NSP | National Simulator Program |
| NTSB | National Transportation Safety Board |
| NWS | National Weather System |
| PA | Private Airplane |
| PAR | Private Pilot Airplane |
| PAT | Private Pilot Airplane/Recreational Pilot – Transition |

| Abb./Acronym | Definition |
|---|---|
| PCP | Private Pilot Canadian Conversion |
| PFD | Primary Flight Display |
| PIC | Pilot-in-Command |
| POA | Plan of Action |
| POH | Pilot's Operating Handbook |
| PTS | Practical Test Standards |
| QPS | Qualification Performance Standard |
| RAIM | Receiver Autonomous Integrity Monitoring |
| RMP | Risk Management Process |
| RNAV | Area Navigation |
| RNP | Required Navigation Performance |
| SAE | Specialty Aircraft Examiner |
| SFRA | Special Flight Rules Area |
| SIAP | Standard Instrument Approach Procedure |
| SMS | Safety Management System |
| SOP | Standard Operating Procedures |
| SRM | Single-Pilot Resource Management |
| SRM | Safety Risk Management |
| STAR | Standard Terminal Arrival |
| SUA | Special Use Airspace |
| TAF | Terminal Forecast |
| TAS | True Airspeed |
| TCH | Threshold Crossing Height |
| TEM | Threat and Error Management |
| TFR | Temporary Flight Restrictions |
| UTC | Coordinated Universal Time |
| $V_A$ | Maneuvering speed |
| VDP | Visual Descent Point |
| $V_{FE}$ | Maximum flap extended speed |
| VFR | Visual Flight Rules |
| VMC | Visual Meteorological Conditions |
| $V_{MC}$ | Minimum Control Speed with the Critical Engine Inoperative |
| $V_{NE}$ | Never exceed speed |
| VOR | Very High Frequency Omnidirectional Range |
| $V_S$ | Stall Speed |
| $V_X$ | Best Angle of Climb Speed |
| $V_Y$ | Best Rate of Climb Speed |
| $V_{SSE}$ | Safe, intentional one-engine-inoperative speed. Originally known as safe single-engine speed |
| $V_{XSE}$ | Best angle of climb speed with one engine inoperative |
| $V_{YSE}$ | Best rate of climb speed with one engine inoperative |
| $V_{SO}$ | Stalling Speed or the Minimum Steady Flight Speed in the Landing Configuration |
| WAAS | Wide Area Augmentation System |

# Multi-Engine Add-on Rating Course

- Preparation for adding a multi-engine rating to your pilot certificate
- Comprehensive oral exam guide
- Review for all multi-engine pilots

**GLEIM WINGS CREDIT**
EARN CREDITS IN THE FAA'S PILOT PROFICIENCY PROGRAM

## GLEIM® | Aviation
Excellence in Aviation Training

800.874.5346
GleimAviation.com/MARC

# FAA FLIGHT INSTRUCTOR–INSTRUMENT PRACTICAL TEST STANDARDS REPRINTED (FAA-S-8081-9D)

### Introduction

*General Information*

The Flight Standards Service of the Federal Aviation Administration (FAA) has developed this practical test book as the standard that must be used by FAA examiners[1] when conducting flight instructor–instrument (airplane and helicopter) practical tests. Flight instructors are expected to use this book when preparing applicants for practical tests. Applicants should be familiar with this book and become familiar with these standards during their training.

It is important to note that pilot training must not be limited solely to meeting the TASKS and Objectives in this book. TASKS and Objectives are simply means to determine if an applicant meets the regulatory standards for the certificate or rating sought. Applicants should be trained using the references cited in this book.

The FAA gratefully acknowledges the valuable assistance provided by many industry participants who contributed their time and talent in assisting with the revision of these practical test standards.

This practical test standard (PTS) may be purchased from the Superintendent of Documents, U.S. Government Printing Office (GPO), Washington, DC 20402-9325, or from http://bookstore.gpo.gov. This PTS is also available for download, in pdf format, from the Flight Standards Service web site at www.faa.gov.

This PTS is published by the U.S. Department of Transportation, Federal Aviation Administration, Airman Testing Standards Branch, AFS-630, P.O. Box 25082, Oklahoma City, OK 73125. Comments regarding this book should be sent in e-mail form to AFS630comments@faa.gov.

*Practical Test Standard Concept*

Title 14 of the Code of Federal Regulations (14 CFR) part 61 specifies the areas in which knowledge and skill must be demonstrated by the applicant before the issuance of a flight instructor certificate with the associated category and class ratings. The CFRs provide the flexibility to permit the FAA to publish practical test standards containing the AREAS OF OPERATION and specific TASKS in which competency shall be demonstrated. The FAA will revise this book whenever it is determined that changes are needed in the interest of safety. **Adherence to the provisions of the regulations and the practical test standards is mandatory for the evaluation of flight instructor applicants.**

*Flight Instructor Practical Test Book Description*

This test book contains the practical test standards for flight instructor–instrument (airplane and helicopter).

The flight instructor practical test standards include the AREAS OF OPERATION and TASKS required for the issuance of an initial flight instructor certificate and for the addition of a category and/or class rating to that certificate.

AREAS OF OPERATION are phases of the practical test arranged in a logical sequence within each standard. They begin with Fundamentals of Instructing and end with Postflight Procedures. The examiner, however, may conduct the practical test in any sequence that will result in a complete and efficient test; however, **the ground portion of the practical test must be completed prior to the flight portion.**

---

[1] The word "examiner" denotes either the FAA inspector, FAA designated pilot examiner, or other authorized person who conducts the practical test.

TASKS are titles of knowledge areas, flight procedures, or maneuvers appropriate to an AREA OF OPERATION.

NOTE is used to emphasize special considerations required in the AREA OF OPERATION or TASK.

REFERENCE(S) identifies the publication(s) that describe(s) the TASK. Descriptions of TASKS and maneuver tolerances are not included in these standards because this information can be found in the current issue of the listed references. Publications other than those listed may be used for references if their content conveys substantially the same meaning as the referenced publications.

These practical test standards are based on the following references:

| | |
|---|---|
| **14 CFR Part 1** | Definitions and Abbreviations |
| **14 CFR Part 23** | Airworthiness Standards: Normal, Utility, Acrobatic, and Commuter Category Airplanes |
| **14 CFR Part 39** | Airworthiness Directives |
| **14 CFR Part 43** | Maintenance, Preventive Maintenance, Rebuilding, and Alteration |
| **14 CFR Part 61** | Certification: Pilots, Flight Instructors, and Ground Instructors |
| **14 CFR Part 67** | Medical Standards and Certification |
| **14 CFR Part 71** | Designation of Class A, B, C, D, and E Airspace Areas; Air Traffic Service Routes, and Reporting Points |
| **14 CFR Part 91** | General Operating and Flight Rules |
| **14 CFR Part 95** | IFR Altitudes |
| **14 CFR Part 97** | Standard Instrument Procedures |
| **NTSB Part 830** | Notification and Reporting of Aircraft Accidents and Incidents |
| **AC 00-2** | Advisory Circular Checklist |
| **AC 00-6** | Aviation Weather for Pilots and Flight Operations Personnel |
| **AC 00-45** | Aviation Weather Services |
| **AC 60-22** | Aeronautical Decision Making |
| **AC 60-28** | English Language Skill Standards Required by 14 CFR Parts 61, 63, and 65 |
| **AC 61-65** | Certification: Pilots and Flight Instructors |
| **AC 61-84** | Role of Preflight Preparation |
| **AC 61-98** | Currency and Additional Qualification Requirements for Certificated Pilots |
| **AC 90-42** | Traffic Advisory Practices at Airports Without Operating Control Towers |
| **AC 90-48** | Pilots' Role in Collision Avoidance |
| **AC 90-66** | Recommended Standard Traffic Patterns for Aeronautical Operations at Airports Without Operating Control Towers |
| **AC 90-105** | Approval of Guidance for RNP Operations and Barometric Vertical Navigation in the U.S. National Airspace System |
| **AC 120-51** | Crew Resource Management Training |
| **FAA-H-8083-1** | Weight and Balance Handbook |
| **FAA-H-8083-9** | Aviation Instructor's Handbook |
| **FAA-H-8083-15** | Instrument Flying Handbook |
| **FAA-H-8083-25** | Pilot's Handbook of Aeronautical Knowledge |
| **FAA-S-8081-4** | Instrument Rating Practical Test Standards |
| **FAA Order 8080.6** | Conduct of Airman Knowledge Tests |
| **AIM** | Aeronautical Information Manual |
| **AFD** | Airport/Facility Directory |
| **IAPs** | Instrument Approach Procedures |
| **DPs** | Departure Procedures |
| **STARs** | Standard Terminal Arrivals |
| **NOTAMs** | Notices to Airmen |
| **Others** | Enroute Low Altitude Charts |
| | Appropriate aircraft flight manuals |
| | FAA-approved flight manual supplements |

The Objective lists the important elements that must be satisfactorily performed to demonstrate competency in a TASK. The Objective includes:

1. Specifically what the applicant should be able to do,
2. Conditions under which the TASK is to be performed, and
3. Acceptable performance standards.

The examiner determines that the applicant meets the TASK Objective through the demonstration of competency in various elements of knowledge and/or skill. The Objectives of TASKS in certain AREAS OF OPERATION, such as Fundamentals of Instructing and Technical Subjects, include only knowledge elements. Objectives of TASKS in AREAS OF OPERATION that include elements of skill, as well as knowledge, also include common errors, which the applicant shall be able to describe, recognize, analyze, and correct.

The Objective of a TASK that involves pilot skill consists of four parts. The four parts include determination that the applicant exhibits:

1. Instructional knowledge of the elements of a TASK. This is accomplished through descriptions, explanations, and simulated instruction;
2. Instructional knowledge of common errors related to a TASK, including their recognition, analysis, and correction;
3. The ability to demonstrate and simultaneously explain the key elements of a TASK. The TASK demonstration must be to the INSTRUMENT PILOT skill level; the teaching techniques and procedures should conform to those set forth in FAA-H-8083-9, Aviation Instructor's Handbook, and FAA-H-8083-15, Instrument Flying Handbook; and
4. The ability to analyze and correct common errors related to a TASK.

## *Abbreviations*

| | |
|---|---|
| **14 CFR** | Title 14 of the Code of Federal Regulations |
| **ADF** | Automatic Direction Finder |
| **ADM** | Aeronautical Decision Making |
| **AFD** | Airport/Facility Directory |
| **AIRMET** | Airman's Meteorological Information |
| **AM** | Automation Management |
| **APV** | Approach With Vertical Guidance |
| **ATC** | Air Traffic Control |
| **ATIS** | Automatic Terminal Information Service |
| **ATS** | Air Traffic Service |
| **CDI** | Course Deviation Indicator |
| **CFIT** | Controlled Flight Into Terrain |
| **CRM** | Crew Resource Management |
| **DA/DH** | Decision Altitude/Decision Height |
| **DH** | Decision Height |
| **DME** | Distance Measuring Equipment |
| **DP** | Departure Procedures |
| **EGPWS** | Enhanced Ground Proximity Warning System |
| **FAA** | Federal Aviation Administration |
| **FDC** | Flight Data Center |
| **FITS** | FAA-Industry Training Standards |
| **FMS** | Flight Management System |
| **FSDO** | Flight Standards District Office |
| **GLS** | GNSS Landing System |
| **GNSS** | Global Navigation Satellite System |

| | |
|---|---|
| **GPO** | Government Printing Office |
| **GPS** | Global Positioning System |
| **GPWS** | Ground Proximity Warning System |
| **IAP** | Instrument Approach Procedures |
| **IFR** | Instrument Flight Rules |
| **ILS** | Instrument Landing System |
| **IMC** | Instrument Meteorological Conditions |
| **LAHSO** | Land and Hold Short Operations |
| **LCD** | Liquid Crystal Display |
| **LDA** | Localizer-Type Directional Aid |
| **LED** | Light-Emitting Diode |
| **LNAV** | Lateral Navigation |
| **LOC** | Localizer |
| **LORAN** | Long Range Navigation |
| **LPV** | Localizer Performance With Vertical Guidance |
| **MAP** | Missed Approach Point |
| **MDA** | Minimum Descent Altitude |
| **MLS** | Microwave Landing System |
| **NAS** | National Airspace System |
| **NAVAID** | Navigation Aid |
| **NDB** | Nondirectional Beacon |
| **NOTAM** | Notice to Airmen |
| **NPA** | Nonprecision Approach |
| **NWS** | National Weather Service |
| **OCS** | Obstacle Clearance Surface |
| **OEA** | Obstacle Evaluation Area |
| **PA** | Precision Approach |
| **PC** | Proficiency Check |
| **PTS** | Practical Test Standard |
| **RAIM** | Receiver Autonomous Integrity Monitoring |
| **RM** | Risk Management |
| **RMI** | Radio Magnetic Indicator |
| **RNAV** | Area Navigation |
| **RNP** | Required Navigation Performance |
| **SA** | Situational Awareness |
| **SAAAR** | Special Aircraft and Aircrew Authorization Required |
| **SAS** | Stability Augmentation System |
| **SDF** | Simplified Directional Facility |
| **SIGMETS** | Significant Meteorological Advisory |
| **SRM** | Single Pilot Resource Management |
| **STAR** | Standard Terminal Arrival |
| **TAWS** | Terrain Awareness and Warning System |
| **TCAS** | Traffic Alert and Collision Avoidance System |
| **TM** | Task Management |
| **VDP** | Visual Descent Point |
| **VHF** | Very High Frequency |
| **VNAV** | Vertical Navigation |
| **VOR** | Very High Frequency Omnidirectional Range |

## Use of the Practical Test Standards

The FAA requires that all flight instructor practical tests be conducted in accordance with the appropriate flight instructor practical test standards and the policies set forth in the INTRODUCTION.

All of the procedures and maneuvers in the instrument rating practical test standards have been included in the flight instructor practical test standards; however, to permit completion of the practical test for initial certification within a reasonable time-frame, the examiner shall select one or more TASKS in each AREA OF OPERATION. In certain AREAS OF OPERATION, there are required TASKS that the examiner must select. These required TASKS are identified by a **NOTE** immediately following each AREA OF OPERATION title.

In preparation for each practical test, the examiner shall prepare a written "plan of action." The plan of action includes a scenario. The examiner must develop a scenario that allows the evaluation of most of the AREAS OF OPERATIONS and TASKS required in the practical tests with minimum disruptions. During the mission, the examiner interjects problems and emergencies that the applicant must handle. It should be structured so that most of the AREAS OF OPERATIONS and TASKS are accomplished within the mission. The examiner must maintain the flexibility to change the plan due to unexpected situations as they arise and still result in an efficient and valid test. Some tasks (e.g., unusual attitudes) are not normally done during routine flight operations or may not fit into the scenario. These maneuvers still must be demonstrated. It is preferable that these maneuvers be demonstrated after the scenario is completed. But, the practical test scenario can be suspended to do maneuvers, and resumed if the situation, due to time and efficiency of the practical test, dictates so. *Any TASK selected for evaluation during a practical test shall be evaluated in its entirety*.

*Applicant shall be expected to perform TASK H in AREA OF OPERATION VI, Recovery from Unusual Attitudes and TASK A in AREA OF OPERATION VIII, Nonprecision Instrument Approach using a view-limiting device.*

The flight instructor applicant shall be prepared in *all* knowledge and skill areas and demonstrate the ability to instruct effectively in *all* TASKS included in the AREAS OF OPERATION of this practical test standard. Throughout the flight portion of the practical test, the examiner shall evaluate the applicant's ability to demonstrate and simultaneously explain the selected procedures and maneuvers, and to give flight instruction to students at various stages of flight training and levels of experience.

The term "instructional knowledge" means that the flight instructor applicant's discussions, explanations, and descriptions should follow the recommended teaching procedures and techniques explained in FAA-H-8083-9, Aviation Instructor's Handbook. This includes the development of scenario-based lessons, the ability to evaluate single pilot resource management (SRM) skills, and the ability to use learner-centered grading.

The purpose of including common errors in certain TASKS is to assist the examiner in determining that the flight instructor applicant has the ability to recognize, analyze, and correct such errors. The examiner will not simulate any condition that may jeopardize safe flight or result in possible damage to the aircraft. The common errors listed in the TASKS objective may or may not be found in the TASK References. However, the FAA considers their frequency of occurrence justification for inclusion in the TASK Objectives.

## Use of the Judgment Assessment Matrix

Most fatal accidents include a lack of SRM skills (task management (TM), risk management (RM), automation management (AM), aeronautical decision making (ADM), controlled flight into terrain (CFIT), and situational awareness (SA)) as a causal factor. Consequently, examiners must evaluate the applicant to ensure that he or she has the appropriate level of these skills. A Judgment Assessment Matrix is provided as a tool to evaluate the applicant's SRM skills objectively. The examiner will use the Judgment Assessment Matrix during the practical test. Since examiners give multiple tests, it is recommended that examiners make photocopies of the matrix.

### Special Emphasis Areas

Examiners shall place special emphasis upon areas of aircraft operations considered critical to flight safety. Among these are:

1. Positive aircraft control;
2. Positive exchange of the flight controls procedure (who is flying the aircraft);
3. Stall/spin awareness;
4. Collision avoidance;
5. Wake turbulence avoidance;
6. Land and Hold Short Operations (LAHSO);
7. Runway incursion avoidance;
8. CFIT;
9. ADM and RM;
10. Checklist usage;
11. SRM;
12. Icing condition operational hazards, anti-icing and deicing equipment, differences, and approved use and operations;
13. Required navigation performance (RNP);
14. Crew resource management (CRM) for multi-pilot aircraft; and
15. Other areas deemed appropriate to any phase of the practical test.

With the exception of SRM, any given area may not be addressed specifically under a TASK, but all areas are essential to flight safety and will be evaluated during the practical test.

### Aircraft and Equipment Required for the Practical Test

The flight instructor–instrument applicant is required by 14 CFR part 61 to provide an airworthy, certificated aircraft for use during the practical test. Its operating limitations must not prohibit the TASKS required on the practical test. This section further requires that the aircraft must:

1. Have fully functioning dual controls, and;
2. Be capable of performing all AREAS OF OPERATION appropriate for the instructor rating sought and have no operating limitations, which prohibit its use in any of the AREAS OF OPERATION, required for the practical test.

Flight instruments are those required for controlling the aircraft without outside references. The required radio equipment is that which is necessary for communications with air traffic control (ATC), and for the performance of two of the following nonprecision approaches: very high frequency omnidirectional range (VOR), nondirectional beacon (NDB), global positioning system (GPS) without vertical guidance, localizer (LOC), localizer-type directional aid (LDA), simplified directional facility (SDF), or area navigation (RNAV) and one precision approach: instrument landing system (ILS), GNSS landing system (GLS), localizer performance with vertical guidance (LPV) or microwave landing system (MLS). GPS equipment must be instrument certified and contain the current database. Note: An LPV approach is technically a nonprecision approach, however, due to the precision of its glidepath and localizer-like lateral navigation characteristics, an LPV can be used to demonstrate precision approach proficiency (AOA VIII TASK B). Also, although LPV and LNAV/VNAV approaches are nonprecision approaches, they cannot be used to demonstrate nonprecision approach proficiency (AOA VIII TASK A) due to the presence of a glidepath.

Modern technology has introduced into aviation a new method of displaying flight instruments, such as Electronic Flight Instrument Systems, Integrated Flight Deck displays, and others. For the purpose of the practical test standards, any flight instrument display that utilizes liquid crystal display (LCD) or picture-tube-like displays will be referred to as "Electronic Flight Instrument Display." Aircraft equipped with this technology may or may not have separate backup flight instruments installed. The abnormal or emergency procedure for loss of the electronic flight instrument display appropriate to the aircraft will be evaluated in the Loss of Primary Instruments TASK. The loss of the primary electronic flight instrument display must be tailored to failures that would normally be encountered in the aircraft. If the aircraft is capable, total failure of the electronic flight instrument display, or a supporting component, with access only to the standby flight instruments or backup display shall be evaluated.

The applicant is required to provide an appropriate view limiting device that is acceptable to the examiner. This device shall be used during all testing that requires testing "solely by reference to instruments." This device must prevent the applicant from having visual reference outside the aircraft, but not prevent the examiner from having visual reference outside the aircraft. A procedure should be established between the applicant and the examiner as to when and how this device should be donned and removed and this procedure should be briefed before the flight.

The applicant is expected to utilize an autopilot and/or flight management system (FMS), if properly installed, during the flight instructor–instrument practical test to assist in the management of the aircraft. The examiner is expected to test the applicant's knowledge of the systems that are installed and operative during the oral and flight portions of the practical test. The applicant will be required to demonstrate the use of the autopilot and/or FMS during one of the nonprecision approaches. The applicant is expected to demonstrate satisfactory automation management skills.

If the practical test is conducted in the aircraft, and the aircraft has an operable and properly installed GPS, the examiner will require and the applicant must demonstrate GPS approach proficiency. If the applicant has contracted for training in an approved course that includes GPS training in the system that is installed in the airplane/simulator/FTD and the airplane/simulator/FTD used for the checking/testing has the same system properly installed and operable, the applicant must demonstrate GPS approach proficiency.

**Note:** For GPS, add RNP when applicable.

**Note:** If any avionics/navigation unit, including GPS, in the aircraft used for the practical test is placarded inoperative, the examiner will review the maintenance log to verify that the discrepancy has been properly documented.

### *Use of FAA-Approved Flight Simulation Training Device (FSTD)*

An airman applicant for instrument rating certification is authorized to use a full flight simulator (FFS) qualified by the National Simulator Program as levels A-D and/or a flight training device (FTD) qualified by the National Simulator Program as levels 4-7 to complete certain flight TASK requirements listed in this practical test standard.

In order to do so, such devices must be used pursuant to and in accordance with a curriculum approved for use at a 14 CFR part 141 pilot school or 14 CFR part 142 training center. Practical tests or portions thereof, when accomplished in an FSTD, may only be conducted by FAA aviation safety inspectors, designees authorized to conduct such tests in FSTDs for part 141 pilot school graduates, or appropriately authorized part 142 Training Center Evaluators (TCE).

When flight TASKS are accomplished in an aircraft, certain TASK elements may be accomplished through "simulated" actions in the interest of safety and practicality, but when accomplished in a flight simulator or flight training device, these same actions would not be "simulated." For example, when in an aircraft, a simulated engine fire may be addressed by retarding the throttle to idle, simulating the shutdown of the engine, simulating the discharge of the fire suppression agent, if applicable, simulating the disconnection of associated electrical, hydraulic, and pneumatics systems. However, when the same emergency condition is addressed in a FSTD, all TASK elements must be accomplished as would be expected under actual circumstances.

Similarly, safety of flight precautions taken in the aircraft for the accomplishment of a specific maneuver or procedure (such as limiting altitude in an approach to stall or setting maximum airspeed for an engine failure expected to result in a rejected takeoff) need not be taken when a FSTD is used.

It is important to understand that, whether accomplished in an aircraft or FSTD, all TASKS and elements for each maneuver or procedure shall have the same performance standards applied equally for determination of overall satisfactory performance.

The applicant must demonstrate all of the instrument approach procedures required by 14 CFR part 61. At least one instrument approach procedure must be demonstrated in an airplane, helicopter, or powered lift as appropriate. One precision and one nonprecision approach not selected for actual flight demonstration may be performed in FSTDs that meet the requirements of Appendix 1 of this practical test standard.

### Flight Instructor Responsibility

An appropriately rated flight instructor is responsible for training the flight instructor applicant to acceptable standards in **all** subject matter areas, procedures, and maneuvers included in the TASKS within each AREA OF OPERATION in the appropriate flight instructor practical test standard.

Because of the impact of their teaching activities in developing safe, proficient pilots, flight instructors should exhibit a high level of knowledge, skill, and the ability to impart that knowledge and skill to students. The flight instructor shall certify that the applicant is:

1. Able to make a practical application of the fundamentals of instructing;
2. Competent to teach the subject matter, procedures, and maneuvers included in the standards to students with varying backgrounds and levels of experience and ability;
3. Able to perform the procedures and maneuvers included in the standards to the INSTRUMENT PILOT skill level while giving effective flight instruction; and
4. Competent to pass the required practical test for the issuance of the flight instructor certificate with the associated category and class ratings or the addition of a category and/or class rating to a flight instructor certificate.

Throughout the applicant's training, the flight instructor is responsible for emphasizing the performance of, and the ability to teach, **effective visual scanning, runway incursion avoidance, collision avoidance procedures, and LAHSO**. The flight instructor applicant should develop and use scenario based teaching methods particularly on special emphasis areas. These areas are covered in AC 90-48, Pilot's Role in Collision Avoidance; FAA-H-8083-3, Airplane Flying Handbook; FAA-H-8083-25, Pilot's Handbook of Aeronautical Knowledge; and the current Aeronautical Information Manual.

### Examiner Responsibility

The examiner conducting the practical test is responsible for determining that the applicant meets acceptable standards of teaching ability, knowledge, and skill in the selected TASKS. The examiner makes this determination by accomplishing an Objective that is appropriate to each selected TASK, and includes an evaluation of the applicant's:

1. Ability to apply the fundamentals of instructing;
2. Knowledge of, and ability to teach, the subject matter, procedures, and maneuvers covered in the TASKS;
3. Ability to perform the procedures and maneuvers included in the standards to the INSTRUMENT PILOT skill level while giving effective flight instruction;
4. Ability to analyze and correct common errors related to the procedures and maneuvers covered in the TASKS;
5. Ability to develop scenario-based instruction that meets lesson objectives;
6. Ability to teach and evaluate SRM and CRM, to include multi-pilot aircraft; and
7. Ability to use learner-centered grading and debriefing techniques appropriately.

It is intended that oral questioning be used at any time during the ground or flight portion of the practical test to determine that the applicant can instruct effectively and has a comprehensive knowledge of the TASKS and their related safety factors.

During the flight portion of the practical test, the examiner shall act as a student during selected maneuvers. This will give the examiner an opportunity to evaluate the flight instructor applicant's ability to analyze and correct simulated common errors related to these maneuvers. The examiner will also evaluate the applicant's use of visual scanning and collision avoidance procedures, and the applicant's ability to teach those procedures.

Examiners should, to the greatest extent possible, test the applicant's application and correlation skills. When possible, scenario based questions should be used.

The examiner shall place special emphasis on the applicant's demonstrated ability to teach precise aircraft control and sound judgment in aeronautical decision making. Evaluation of the applicant's ability to teach judgment shall be accomplished by asking the applicant to describe the oral discussions and the presentation of practical problems that would be used in instructing students in the exercise of sound judgment. The examiner shall also emphasize the evaluation of the applicant's demonstrated ability to teach spatial disorientation, wake turbulence and low-level wind shear avoidance, checklist usage, positive exchange of flight controls, and any other directed special emphasis areas.

### Satisfactory Performance

The practical test is passed if, in the judgment of the examiner, the applicant demonstrates satisfactory performance with regard to:

1. Knowledge of the fundamentals of instructing;
2. Knowledge of the technical subject areas;
3. Knowledge of the flight instructor's responsibilities concerning the pilot certification process;
4. Knowledge of the flight instructor's responsibilities concerning logbook entries and pilot certificate endorsements;
5. Ability to demonstrate the procedures and maneuvers selected by the examiner to the instrument instructor pilot skill level while giving effective instruction;
6. Competence in teaching the procedures and maneuvers selected by the examiner;
7. Competence in describing, recognizing, analyzing, and correcting common errors simulated by the examiner; and
8. Knowledge of the development and effective use of a course of training, a syllabus, and a lesson plan, including scenario-based training and collaborative assessment (learner centered grading).

### Unsatisfactory Performance

If, in the judgment of the examiner, the applicant does not meet the standards of performance of any TASK performed, the associated AREA OF OPERATION is failed and therefore, the practical test is failed. The examiner or applicant may discontinue the test at any time when the failure of an AREA OF OPERATION makes the applicant ineligible for the certificate or rating sought. **The test may be continued ONLY with the consent of the applicant.** If the test is discontinued, the applicant is entitled to credit for only those AREAS OF OPERATION and TASKS satisfactorily performed; however, during the retest and at the discretion of the examiner, any TASK may be re-evaluated, including those previously passed. Specific reasons for disqualification are:

1. Failure to perform a procedure or maneuver to the instrument pilot skill level while giving effective flight instruction;
2. Failure to provide an effective instructional explanation while demonstrating a procedure or maneuver (explanation during the demonstration must be clear, concise, technically accurate, and complete with no prompting from the examiner);
3. Any action or lack of action by the applicant which requires corrective intervention by the examiner to maintain safe flight; and
4. Failure to use proper and effective visual scanning techniques to clear the area before and while performing maneuvers.
5. Failure to incorporate SRM principles throughout the practical test.

When a notice of disapproval is issued, the examiner shall record the applicant's unsatisfactory performance in terms of AREAS OF OPERATION.

### Letter of Discontinuance

When a practical test is discontinued for reasons other than unsatisfactory performance (e.g., equipment failure, weather, or illness), FAA Form 8710-1, Airman Certificate and/or Rating Application, and, if applicable, the Airman Knowledge Test Report, shall be returned to the applicant. The examiner at that time shall prepare, sign, and issue a Letter of Discontinuance to the applicant. The Letter of Discontinuance should identify the AREAS OF OPERATION of the practical test that were successfully completed.

The applicant shall be advised that the Letter of Discontinuance shall be presented to the examiner when the practical test is resumed, and made part of the certification file.

*Single-Pilot Resource Management*

The examiner shall evaluate the applicant's ability throughout the practical test to use good aeronautical decision-making procedures in order to evaluate risks. The evaluation will be recorded on the Judgment Assessment Matrix (see Appendix 3). The examiner shall accomplish this requirement by developing a scenario that incorporates as many TASKS as possible to evaluate the applicant's risk management in making safe aeronautical decisions. For example, the examiner may develop a scenario that incorporates weather decisions and performance planning.

The applicant's ability to utilize all the assets available in making a risk analysis to determine the safest course of action is essential for satisfactory performance. The scenario should be realistic and within the capabilities of the aircraft used for the practical test.

Single-Pilot Resource Management (SRM) is defined as the art and science of managing all the resources (both on-board the aircraft and from outside sources) available to a single-pilot (prior and during flight) to ensure that the successful outcome of the flight is never in doubt. Single-Pilot Resource Management available resources can include human resources, hardware, and information. Human resources "...includes all other groups routinely working with the pilot who are involved in decisions that are required to operate a flight safely. These groups include, but are not limited to: dispatchers, weather briefers, maintenance personnel, and air traffic controllers." Single Pilot Resource Management is a set of skill competencies that must be evident in all TASKS in this practical test standard as applied to single-pilot operation.

The following six items are areas of SRM.

### 1. Aeronautical Decision Making

*References:* FAA-H-8083-25, AC 60-22, FAA-H-8083-15.

**Objective:** To determine the applicant exhibits sound aeronautical decision making during the planning and execution of the planned flight. The applicant should:

1. Use a sound decision-making process, such as the DECIDE model, 3P model, or similar process when making critical decisions that will have an effect on the outcome of the flight. The applicant should be able to explain the factors and alternative courses of action that were considered while making the decision.
2. Recognize and explain any hazardous attitudes that may have influenced any decision.
3. Determine and execute an appropriate course of action to handle any situation that arises that may cause a change in the original flight plan, in such a way that leads to a safe and successful conclusion of the flight.
4. Explain how the elements of risk management, CFIT awareness, overall situational awareness, use of automation, and task management influenced the decisions made and the resulting course of action.

### 2. Risk Management

*References:* FAA-H-8083-25; FITS document: *Managing Risk through Scenario Based Training, Single Pilot Resource Management, and Learner Centered Grading.*

**Objective:** To determine the applicant can utilize risk management tools and models to assess the potential risk associated with the planned flight during preflight planning and while in flight. The applicant should:

1. Explain the four fundamental risk elements associated with the flight being conducted in the given scenario and how each one was assessed.
2. Use a tool, such as the PAVE checklist, to help assess the four risk elements.
3. Use a personal checklist, such as the I'MSAFE checklist, to determine personal risks.
4. Use weather reports and forecasts to determine weather risks associated with the flight.
5. Explain how to recognize risks and how to mitigate those risks throughout the flight.
6. Use the 5P model to assess the risks associated with each of the five factors.

### 3. Task Management

*Reference:*         *FAA-H-8083-15.*

**Objective:**         To determine the applicant can prioritize the various tasks associated with the planning and execution of the flight. The applicant should:

1. Explain how to prioritize tasks in such a way to minimize distractions from flying the aircraft.
2. Complete all tasks in a timely manner considering the phase of flight without causing a distraction from flying.
3. Execute all checklists and procedures in a manner that does not increase workload at critical times, such as intercepting the final approach course.

### 4. Situational Awareness

*References:*        *FAA-H-8083-25, FAA-H-8083-15.*

**Objective:**         To determine the applicant can maintain situational awareness during all phases of the flight. The applicant should:

1. Explain the concept of situational awareness and associated factors.
2. Explain the dangers associated with becoming fixated on a particular problem to the exclusion of other aspects of the flight.
3. State the current situation at any time during the flight in such a way that displays an accurate assessment of the current and future status of the flight, including weather, terrain, traffic, ATC situation, fuel status, and aircraft status.
4. Uses the navigation displays, traffic displays, terrain displays, weather displays, and other features of the aircraft to maintain a complete and accurate awareness of the current situation and any reasonably anticipated changes that may occur.

### 5. Controlled Flight Into Terrain Awareness

*Reference:*         *Controlled Flight Into Terrain Training Aid website: http://www.faa.gov/ training_testing/training/media/cfit/volume1/titlepg.pdf.*

**Objective:**         To determine the applicant can accurately assess risks associated with terrain and obstacles, maintain accurate awareness of terrain and obstacles, and can use appropriate techniques and procedures to avoid controlled flight into terrain or obstacles by using all resources available. The applicant should:

1. Use current charts and procedures during the planning of the flight to ensure the intended flightpath avoids terrain and obstacles.
2. Be aware of potential terrain and obstacle hazards along the intended route.
3. Explain the terrain display, such as TAWS or display installed in the aircraft.
4. Use the terrain display, such as TAWS or display installed in the aircraft, for navigation, to maintain situational awareness, and to avoid terrain and obstacles.
5. Plan departures and arrivals to avoid terrain and obstacles.
6. Alter flight as necessary to avoid terrain.
7. Plan any course diversion, for whatever reason, in a way that ensures proper terrain and obstruction clearance to the new destination.
8. Explain and understand aircraft performance limitations associated with CFIT accidents.

### 6. Automation Management

*Reference:* FAA-H-8083-15.

*Objective:* To determine the applicant can effectively use the automation features of the aircraft, including autopilot and flight management systems, in such a way to manage workload and can remain aware of the current and anticipated modes and status of the automation. The applicant must:

1. Explain how to recognize the current mode of operation of the autopilot/FMS.
2. Explain how to recognize anticipated and unanticipated mode or status changes of the autopilot/FMS.
3. State at any time during the flight the current mode or status and what the next anticipated mode or status will be.
4. Use the autopilot/FMS to reduce workload as appropriate for the phase of flight, during emergency or abnormal operations.
5. Recognize unanticipated mode changes in a timely manner and promptly return the automation to the correct mode.

### *Applicant's Use of Checklists*

Throughout the practical test, the applicant is evaluated on the use of an appropriate checklist. Proper use is dependent on the specific TASK being evaluated. The situation may be such that the use of the checklist, while accomplishing elements of an Objective, would be either unsafe or impracticable, especially in a single-pilot operation. In this case, a review of the checklist after the elements have been accomplished would be appropriate. Division of attention and proper visual scanning should be considered when using a checklist.

### *Use of Distractions During Practical Tests*

Numerous studies indicate that many accidents have occurred when the pilot has been distracted during critical phases of flight. To evaluate the pilot's ability to utilize proper control technique while dividing attention both inside and/or outside the cockpit, the examiner shall cause a realistic distraction during the flight portion of the practical test to evaluate the applicant's ability to divide attention while maintaining safe flight.

### *Positive Exchange of Flight Controls*

During flight, there must always be a clear understanding between the pilots of who has control of the aircraft. Prior to flight, a briefing should be conducted that includes the procedure for the exchange of flight controls. Some operators have established a two-step procedure for exchange of flight controls. A popular three-step process in the exchange of flight controls between pilots is explained below. Any safe procedure agreed to by the applicant and the examiner is acceptable.

When one pilot wishes to give the other pilot control of the aircraft, he or she will say, "You have the flight controls." The other pilot acknowledges immediately by saying, "I have the flight controls." The first pilot again says, "You have the flight controls." When control is returned to the first pilot, follow the same procedure. A visual check is recommended to verify that the exchange has occurred. There should never be any doubt as to who is flying the aircraft.

### *Emphasis on Attitude Instrument Flying and Partial Panel Skills*

The FAA is concerned about numerous fatal accidents involving spatial disorientation of instrument rated pilots who have attempted to control and maneuver their aircraft in clouds with inoperative primary flight instruments (gyroscopic heading and/or attitude indicators) or loss of the primary electronic flight instruments display.

The FAA has stressed that it is imperative for instrument pilots to acquire and maintain adequate instrument skills and that they be capable of performing instrument flight with the use of the backup systems installed in the aircraft. Many light aircraft operated in IMC are not equipped with dual, independent gyroscopic heading and/or attitude indicators and in many cases are equipped with only a single vacuum source. Technically advanced aircraft may be equipped with backup flight instruments or an additional electronic flight display that is not located directly in front of the pilot.

FAA-S-8081-4, Instrument Rating Practical Test Standards, and FAA-S-8081-9, Flight Instructor–Instrument Practical Test Standards, place increased emphasis on and require the demonstration of a nonprecision instrument approach without the use of the primary flight instruments or electronic flight instrument display. This practical test book, FAA-S-8081-9, emphasizes this area from an instructional standpoint.

AREA OF OPERATION VI requires the applicant to demonstrate the ability to teach basic instrument flight TASKS under both full panel and reference to backup primary flight instruments/electronic flight instrument displays. These maneuvers are described in detail in FAA-H-8083-15, Instrument Flying Handbook. Examiners should determine that the applicant demonstrates and fully understands either the PRIMARY and SUPPORTING or the CONTROL and PERFORMANCE CONCEPT method of attitude instrument flying. Both attitude instrument flying methods are described in FAA-H-8083-15, Instrument Flying Handbook. The TASKS require the applicant to exhibit instructional knowledge of instrument flying techniques and procedures and to demonstrate the ability to teach basic instrument maneuvers with both full panel and partial panel or reference to backup primary flight instruments/electronic flight instrument displays.

### Addition of an Instrument Instructor Rating to a Flight Instructor Certificate

| Area of Operation | AP | RTR | IA or H |
|---|---|---|---|
| I | N | N | N |
| II | A & C | A & C | C |
| III | B & C | B & C | C |
| IV | N | N | N |
| V | Y | Y | N |
| VI | Y | Y | Y |
| VII | Y | Y | N |
| VIII | Y | Y | * A or B |
| IX | Y | Y | Y |
| X | Y | Y | Y |

Flight Instructor Certificate and Rating Held

**Legend:**
- AP — Airplane
- RTR — Helicopter/Gyroplane
- IA or H — Instrument Airplane or Helicopter

**Note:** N indicates that the AREA OF OPERATION is not required. Y indicates that the AREA OF OPERATION is to be performed or based on the note in the AREA OF OPERATION. If a TASK (or TASKS) is listed for an AREA OF OPERATION, that TASK (or TASKS) is mandatory.

* Combine with C, D, or E.

**Renewal or Reinstatement of a Flight Instructor**

| Required Areas of Operation | Number of Tasks |
|---|---|
| II | TASK "D" and one other TASK |
| III | 1 |
| IV | 1 |
| V | 1 |
| VI | 2 |
| VII | 1 |
| VIII | A or B combined with TASK C, D, or E |
| IX | 1 |

The Renewal or reinstatement of one rating on a Flight Instructor Certificate renews or reinstates all privileges existing on the certificate. (14 CFR part 61, sections 61.197 and 61.199)

## Applicant's Practical Test Checklist

## Flight Instructor–Instrument

### Appointment with Inspector or Examiner:

**Name:** _____

**Date/Time:** _____

- ☐ View-Limiting Device
- ☐ Aircraft Documents: Airworthiness Certificate, Registration Certificate, and Operating Limitations
- ☐ Aircraft Maintenance Records: Logbook Record of Airworthiness Inspections and AD Compliance
- ☐ Pilot's Operating Handbook and FAA-Approved Flight Manual

**Personal Equipment**

- ☐ Practical Test Standards
- ☐ Lesson Plan Library
- ☐ Current Aeronautical Charts
- ☐ Computer and Plotter
- ☐ Flight Plan and Flight Log Forms
- ☐ Current AIM, Airport Facility Directory, and Appropriate Publications

**Personal Records**

- ☐ Identification–Photo/Signature ID
- ☐ Pilot Certificate
- ☐ Current and Appropriate Medical Certificate
- ☐ Completed FAA Form 8710-1, Airman Certificate and/or Rating Application
- ☐ Airman Knowledge Test Report
- ☐ Pilot Logbook with Appropriate Instructor Endorsements
- ☐ FAA Form 8060-5, Notice of Disapproval (if applicable)
- ☐ Approved School Graduation Certificate (if applicable)
- ☐ Examiner's Fee (if applicable)

## Examiner's Practical Test Checklist
## Flight Instructor–Instrument

**Applicant's Name:** _____

**Location:** _____

**Date/Time:** _____

I. **Fundamentals of Instructing**
- ☐ A. The Learning Process
- ☐ B. Human Behavior and Effective Communication
- ☐ C. The Teaching Process
- ☐ D. Teaching Methods
- ☐ E. Critique and Evaluation
- ☐ F. Flight Instructor Characteristics and Responsibilities
- ☐ G. Planning Instructional Activity

II. **Technical Subject Areas**
- ☐ A. Aircraft Flight Instruments and Navigation Equipment
- ☐ B. Aeromedical Factors
- ☐ C. Regulations and Publications Related to IFR Operations
- ☐ D. Logbook Entries Related to Instrument Instruction

III. **Preflight Preparation**
- ☐ A. Weather Information
- ☐ B. Cross-Country Flight Planning
- ☐ C. Instrument Cockpit Check

IV. **Preflight Lesson on a Maneuver to Be Performed in Flight**
- ☐ A. Maneuver Lesson

V. **Air Traffic Control Clearances and Procedures**
- ☐ A. Air Traffic Control Clearances
- ☐ B. Compliance with Departure, En Route, and Arrival Procedures and Clearances

## VI. Flight by Reference to Instruments
- ☐ A. Straight-and-Level Flight
- ☐ B. Turns
- ☐ C. Change of Airspeed in Straight-and-Level and Turning Flight
- ☐ D. Constant Airspeed Climbs and Descents
- ☐ E. Constant Rate Climbs and Descents
- ☐ F. Timed Turns to Magnetic Compass Headings
- ☐ G. Steep Turns
- ☐ H. Recovery from Unusual Flight Attitudes

## VII. Navigation Systems
- ☐ A. Intercepting and Tracking Navigational Systems and DME Arcs
- ☐ B. Holding Procedures

## VIII. Instrument Approach Procedures
- ☐ A. Nonprecision Instrument Approach
- ☐ B. Precision Instrument Approach
- ☐ C. Missed Approach
- ☐ D. Circling Approach (Airplane)
- ☐ E. Landing From a Straight-In Approach

## IX. Emergency Operations
- ☐ A. Loss of Communications
- ☐ B. Loss of Gyro Attitude and Heading Indicators
- ☐ C. Engine Failure During Straight-and-Level Flight and Turns
- ☐ D. Instrument Approach–One Engine Inoperative

## X. Postflight Procedures
- ☐ A. Checking Instruments and Equipment

**Areas of Operation:**

**I. Fundamentals of Instructing**

**Note:** *The examiner shall select at least TASK E, F, and G and one other task.*

### Task A: Learning Process

*Reference:* FAA-H-8083-9.

**Objective:** To determine that the applicant exhibits instructional knowledge of the elements of the learning process by describing:

1. Learning theories.
2. Characteristics of learning.
3. Principles of learning.
4. Levels of learning.
5. Learning physical skills.
6. Memory.
7. Transfer of learning.

### Task B: Human Behavior and Effective Communication

*Reference:* FAA-H-8083-9.

**Objective:** To determine that the applicant exhibits instructional knowledge of the elements of human behavior and effective communication as it applies to the teaching/learning process by describing:

1. Human behavior–
   a. control of human behavior.
   b. human needs.
   c. defense mechanisms.
   d. the flight instructor as a practical psychologist.
2. Effective communication
   a. basic elements of communication.
   b. barriers of effective communication.
   c. developing communication skills.

### Task C: Teaching Process

*Reference:* FAA-H-8083-9.

**Objective:** To determine that the applicant exhibits instructional knowledge of the elements of the teaching process by describing:

1. Preparation of a lesson for a ground or flight instructional period.
2. Presentation methods.
3. Application, by the student, of the material or procedure that was presented.
4. Review and evaluation of student performance.
5. Problem-based learning.

### Task D:  Teaching Methods

*Reference:* FAA-H-8083-9.

**Objective:** To determine that the applicant exhibits instructional knowledge of the elements of teaching methods by describing:

1. Material organization.
2. The lecture method.
3. The cooperative or group learning method.
4. The guided discussion method.
5. The demonstration-performance method.
6. Computer-based training method.
7. Scenario-based training method.

### Task E:  Critique and Evaluation

*Reference:* FAA-H-8083-9.

**Objective:** To determine that the applicant exhibits instructional knowledge of the elements of critique and evaluation by explaining:

1. Critique—
   a. purpose and characteristics of an effective critique.
   b. methods and ground rules for a critique.

2. Evaluation—
   a. characteristics of effective oral questions and what types to avoid.
   b. responses to student questions.
   c. characteristics and development of effective written test.
   d. characteristics and uses of performance tests, specifically, the FAA Practical Test Standards.
   e. collaborative assessment (or learner-centered grading (LCG)).

### Task F:  Flight Instructor Characteristics and Responsibilities

*Reference:* FAA-H-8083-9.

**Objective:** To determine that the applicant exhibits instructional knowledge of the elements of instructor responsibilities and professionalism by describing:

1. Aviation instructor responsibilities in—
   a. providing adequate instruction.
   b. establishing standards of performance.
   c. emphasizing the positive.

2. Flight instructor responsibilities in—
   a. providing student pilot evaluation and supervision.
   b. preparing practical test recommendations and endorsements.
   c. determining requirements for conducting additional training and endorsement requirements.

3. Professionalism as an instructor by—
   a. explaining important personal characteristics.
   b. describing methods to minimize student frustration.

### Task G: Planning Instructional Activity

**Reference:** FAA-H-8083-9.

**Objective:** To determine that the applicant exhibits instructional knowledge of the elements of planning instructional activity by describing:

1. Developing objectives and standards for a course of training.
2. Theory of building blocks of learning.
3. Requirements for developing a training syllabus.
4. Purpose and characteristics of a lesson plan.
5. How a scenario-based lesson is developed.

## II. Technical Subject Areas

**Note:** The examiner shall select TASKs A and D and at least one other TASK.

### Task A: Aircraft Flight Instruments and Navigation Equipment

**References:** FAA-H-8083-15, FAA-S-8081-4.

**Objective:** To determine that the applicant exhibits instructional knowledge of aircraft:

1. Flight instrument systems and their operating characteristics to include—
   a. pitot-static system.
   b. attitude indicator.
   c. heading indicator/horizontal situation indicator/radio magnetic indicator.
   d. magnetic compass.
   e. turn-and-slip indicator/turn coordinator.
   f. electrical system.
   g. vacuum system.
   h. electronic engine instrument display.
   i. primary flight display, if installed.

2. Navigation equipment and their operating characteristics to include—
   a. VHF omnirange (VOR).
   b. distance measuring equipment (DME).
   c. instrument landing system (ILS).
   d. marker beacon receiver/indicators.
   e. automatic direction finder (ADF).
   f. transponder/altitude encoding.
   g. electronic flight instrument display.
   h. global positioning system (GPS).
   i. automatic pilot.
   j. flight management system (FMS).
   k. multifunction display, if installed.

3. Anti-ice/deicing and weather detection equipment and their operating characteristics to include—
   a. airframe.
   b. propeller or rotor.
   c. air intake.
   d. fuel system.
   e. pitot-static system.
   f. radar/lightning detection system.
   g. other inflight weather systems.

**Task B: Aeromedical Factors**

*References:* FAA-H-8083-25; AIM.

*Objective:* To determine that the applicant exhibits instructional knowledge of the elements related to aeromedical factors by describing the effects, corrective action, and safety considerations of:

1. Hypoxia.
2. Hyperventilation.
3. Middle ear and sinus problems.
4. Spatial disorientation.
5. Motion sickness.
6. Alcohol and drugs.
7. Carbon monoxide poisoning.
8. Evolved gases from scuba diving.
9. Stress and fatigue.

**Task C: Regulations and Publications Related to IFR Operations**

*References:* 14 CFR parts 61, 71, 91, 95, and 97; FAA-H-8083-15; AIM.

*Objective:* To determine that the applicant exhibits instructional knowledge of the elements related to regulations and publications, (related to instrument flight and instrument flight instruction) their purpose, general content, availability, and method of revision by describing:

1. 14 CFR parts 61, 71, 91, 95, and 97.
2. FAA-H-8083-15, Instrument Flying Handbook.
3. Aeronautical Information Manual.
4. Practical Test Standards.
5. Airport Facility Directory.
6. Standard Instrument Departures/Terminal Arrivals.
7. En Route Charts.
8. Standard Instrument Approach Procedure Charts.

**Task D: Logbook Entries Related to Instrument Instruction**

*References:* 14 CFR part 61; AC 61-65; AC 61-98.

*Objective:* To determine that the applicant exhibits instructional knowledge of logbook entries related to instrument instruction by describing:

1. Logbook entries or training records for instrument flight/instrument flight instruction or ground instruction given.
2. Preparation of a recommendation for an instrument rating practical test, including appropriate logbook entry.
3. Required endorsement of a pilot logbook for satisfactory completion of an instrument proficiency check.
4. Required flight instructor records.

### III. Preflight Preparation

*Note:* *The examiner shall select at least one TASK.*

### Task A: Weather Information

*Note:* *If the current weather reports, forecasts, or other pertinent information is not available, or if the current weather is not appropriate for the practical test scenario, then weather reports, forecasts, and other pertinent information shall be simulated by the examiner in a manner to adequately measure the applicant's competence.*

**References:** AC 00-6, AC 00-45; FAA-S-8081-4; AIM.

**Objective:** To determine that the applicant exhibits instructional knowledge related to IFR weather information.

1. Sources of weather—
   a. AWOS, ASOS, and ATIS reports.
   b. PATWAS and TIBS.
   c. TWEB.

2. Weather reports and charts—
   a. METAR, TAF, FA, and radar reports.
   b. inflight weather advisories.
   c. surface analysis, weather depiction, and radar summary charts.
   d. significant weather prognostic charts.
   e. winds and temperatures aloft charts.
   f. pilot weather reports (PIREPS).
   g. freezing level charts.
   h. stability charts.
   i. severe weather outlook charts.
   j. SIGMETS and AIRMETS.

### Task B: Cross-Country Flight Planning

**References:** 14 CFR part 91; FAA-H-8083-15, FAA-S-8081-4; AIM.

**Objective:** To determine that the applicant exhibits instructional knowledge of cross-country flight planning by describing the:

1. Regulatory requirements for instrument flight within various types of airspace.
2. Computation of estimated time en route and total fuel requirement for an IFR cross-country flight.
3. Selection and correct interpretation of the current and applicable en route charts, RNAV, DPs, STARs, and standard instrument approach procedure charts (IAP).
4. Procurement and interpretation of the applicable NOTAM information.
5. Completes and files an IFR flight plan that accurately reflects the conditions of the proposed flight. (Does not have to be filed with ATC.)
6. Demonstrates adequate knowledge of GPS and RAIM capability, when aircraft is so equipped.
7. Demonstrates the ability to recognize wing contamination due to airframe icing.
8. Demonstrates adequate knowledge of the adverse effects of airframe icing during landing phases of flight and corrective actions: pretakeoff, takeoff, and cruise.
9. Demonstrates familiarity with any icing procedures and/or information published by the manufacturer that is specific to the aircraft used on the practical test.

### Task C: Instrument Cockpit Check

*References:* 14 CFR part 91; FAA-H-8083-15, FAA-S-8081-4.

**Objective:** To determine that the applicant exhibits instructional knowledge of an instrument cockpit check by describing the reasons for the check and the detection of defects that could affect safe instrument flight. The check shall include:

1. Communications equipment.
2. Navigation equipment.
3. Magnetic compass.
4. Heading indicator/horizontal situation indicator/remote magnetic indicator.
5. Attitude indicator.
6. Altimeter.
7. Turn-and-slip indicator/turn coordinator.
8. Vertical-speed indicator.
9. Airspeed indicator.
10. Outside air temperature.
11. Clock.
12. Pilot heat.
13. Electronic flight instrument display.
14. Traffic awareness/warning/avoidance system.
15. Terrain awareness/warning/alert system.
16. Flight management system (FMS).
17. Automatic pilot.

## IV. Preflight Lesson on a Maneuver to Be Performed in Flight

*Note:* The examiner shall select at least one maneuver from AREAS OF OPERATION VI through IX and ask the applicant to present a preflight lesson on the selected maneuver as the lesson would be taught to a student. Previously developed lesson plans from the applicant's library may be used.

### Task A: Maneuver Lesson

*References:* FAA-H-8083-9, FAA-H-8083-15; FAA-S-8081-4.

**Objective:** To determine that the applicant exhibits instructional knowledge of the selected maneuver by:

1. Using a lesson plan that includes all essential items to make an effective and organized presentation.
2. Stating the objective.
3. Giving an accurate, comprehensive oral description of the maneuver, including the elements and associated common errors.
4. Using instructional aids, as appropriate.
5. Describing the recognition, analysis, and correction of common errors.

## V. Air Traffic Control Clearances and Procedures

*Note:* *The examiner shall select at least one TASK.*

### Task A: Air Traffic Control Clearances

*References:*     *14 CFR part 91; FAA-H-8083-15; FAA-S-8081-4.*

**Objective:** To determine that the applicant exhibits instructional knowledge of air traffic control clearances by describing:

1. Pilot and controller responsibilities to include tower, en route control, and clearance void times.
2. Correct and timely copying of an ATC clearance.
3. Ability to comply with the clearance.
4. Correct and timely read-back of an ATC clearance, using standard phraseology.
5. Correct interpretation of an ATC clearance and, when necessary, request for clarification, verification, or change.
6. Setting of communication and navigation frequencies in compliance with an ATC clearance.

### Task B: Compliance with Departure, En Route, and Arrival Procedures and Clearances

*References:*     *14 CFR part 91; FAA-H-8083-15; FAA-S-8081-4; AIM.*

**Objective:** To determine that the applicant exhibits instructional knowledge of the elements related to compliance with departure, en route, and arrival procedures and clearances by describing:

1. Selection and use of current and appropriate navigation publications.
2. Pilot and controller responsibilities with regard to DPs, En Route Low and High Altitude Charts, and STARs.
3. Selection and use of appropriate communications frequencies.
4. Selection and identification of the navigation aids.
5. Accomplishment of the appropriate checklist items.
6. Pilot's responsibility for compliance with vectors and also altitude, airspeed, climb, descent, and airspace restrictions.
7. Pilot's responsibility for the interception of courses, radials, and bearings appropriate to the procedure, route, or clearance.
8. Procedures to be used in the event of two-way communications failure.
9. The uses of the multifunction display and other graphical navigational displays, if installed, to monitor position track, wind drift, and other parameters to maintain situational awareness and desired flightpath.

## VI. Flight by Reference to Instruments

*Note:* *The examiner shall select TASK H and at least one other TASK. The applicant shall select either the primary and supporting or the control and performance method for teaching this AREA OF OPERATION.*

### Task A: Straight-and-Level Flight

**References:** FAA-H-8083-9, FAA-H-8083-15; FAA-S-8081-4.

**Objective:** To determine that the applicant:

1. Exhibits instructional knowledge of teaching straight-and-level flight by describing–
   a. the relationship of pitch, bank, and power in straight-and-level flight.
   b. procedure using full panel and partial panel.
   c. coordination of controls and trim.

2. Exhibits instructional knowledge of common errors related to straight-and-level flight by describing–
   a. slow or improper cross-check during straight-and-level flight.
   b. improper power control.
   c. failure to make smooth, precise corrections, as required.
   d. uncoordinated use of controls.
   e. improper trim control.

3. Demonstrates and simultaneously explains straight-and-level flight from an instructional standpoint.
4. Analyzes and corrects simulated common errors related to straight-and-level flight.

### Task B: Turns

**References:** FAA-H-8083-9, FAA-H-8083-15; FAA-S-8081-4.

**Objective:** To determine that the applicant:

1. Exhibits instructional knowledge of teaching turns by describing–
   a. the relationship of true airspeed and angle of bank to a standard rate turn.
   b. technique and procedure using full panel and partial panel for entry and recovery of a constant rate turn, including the performance of a half-standard rate turn.
   c. coordination of controls and trim.

2. Exhibits instructional knowledge of common errors related to turns by describing–
   a. improper cross-check procedures.
   b. improper bank control during roll-in and roll-out.
   c. failure to make smooth, precise corrections, as required.
   d. uncoordinated use of controls.
   e. improper trim technique.

3. Demonstrates and simultaneously explains turns from an instructional standpoint.
4. Analyzes and corrects simulated common errors related to turns.

**Task C: Change of Airspeed in Straight-and-Level and Turning Flight**

*References:* FAA-H-8083-9, FAA-H-8083-15; FAA-S-8081-4.

**Objective:** To determine that the applicant:

1. Exhibits instructional knowledge of teaching change of airspeed in straight-and-level flight and turns by describing–

    a. procedure using full panel and partial panel for maintaining altitude and changing airspeed in straight-and-level and turning flight.
    b. coordination of controls and trim technique.

2. Exhibits instructional knowledge of common errors related to changes of airspeed in straight-and-level and turning flight by describing–

    a. slow or improper cross-check during straight-and-level flight and turns.
    b. improper power control.
    c. failure to make smooth, precise corrections, as required.
    d. uncoordinated use of controls.
    e. improper trim technique.

3. Demonstrates and simultaneously explains changes of airspeed in straight-and-level and turning flight from an instructional standpoint.
4. Analyzes and corrects simulated common errors related to changes of airspeed in straight-and-level and turning flight.

**Task D: Constant Airspeed Climbs and Descents**

*References:* FAA-H-8083-9, FAA-H-8083-15; FAA-S-8081-4.

**Objective:** To determine that the applicant:

1. Exhibits instructional knowledge of constant airspeed climbs and descents by describing–

    a. procedure using full panel and partial panel for an entry into a straight climb or climbing turn, from either cruising or climbing airspeed.
    b. a stabilized straight climb or climbing turn.
    c. a level-off from a straight climb or climbing turn, at either cruising or climbing airspeed.
    d. procedure using full panel and partial panel for an entry into a straight descent or descending turn from either cruising or descending airspeed.
    e. a stabilized straight descent or descending turn.
    f. a level-off from a straight descent or descending turn, at either cruising or descending airspeed.

2. Exhibits instructional knowledge of common errors related to constant airspeed climbs and descents by describing–

    a. failure to use a proper power setting and pitch attitude.
    b. improper correction of vertical rate, airspeed, heading, or rate-of-turn errors.
    c. uncoordinated use of controls.
    d. improper trim control.

3. Demonstrates and simultaneously explains a constant airspeed climb and a constant airspeed descent from an instructional standpoint.
4. Analyzes and corrects simulated common errors related to constant airspeed climbs and descents.

### Task E: Constant Rate Climbs and Descents

**References:** FAA-H-8083-9, FAA-H-8083-15; FAA-S-8081-4.

**Objective:** To determine that the applicant:

1. Exhibits instructional knowledge of constant rate climbs and descents by describing–
   a. procedure using full panel and partial panel for an entry into a constant rate climb or descent.
   b. a stabilized constant rate straight climb or climbing turn, using the vertical speed indicator.
   c. a level-off from a constant rate straight climb or climbing turn.
   d. an entry into a constant rate straight descent or descending turn.
   e. a stabilized constant rate straight descent or descending turn using the vertical speed indicator.
   f. level-off from a constant rate straight descent or descending turn.

2. Exhibits instructional knowledge of common errors related to constant rate climbs and descents by describing–
   a. failure to use a proper power setting and pitch attitude.
   b. improper correction of vertical rate, airspeed, heading, or rate-of-turn errors.
   c. uncoordinated use of controls.
   d. improper trim control.

3. Demonstrates and simultaneously explains a constant rate climb and a constant rate descent from an instructional standpoint.
4. Analyzes and corrects simulated common errors related to constant rate climbs and descents.

### Task F: Timed Turns to Magnetic Compass Headings

**References:** FAA-H-8083-9, FAA-H-8083-15; FAA-S-8081-4.

**Objective:** To determine that the applicant:

1. Exhibits instructional knowledge of timed turns to magnetic compass headings by describing–
   a. operating characteristics and errors of the magnetic compass.
   b. calibration of the miniature aircraft of the turn coordinator[2], both right and left, using full panel and the clock.
   c. procedures using full panel and partial panel performing compass turns to a specified heading.

2. Exhibits instructional knowledge of common errors related to timed turns to magnetic compass headings by describing–
   a. incorrect calibration procedures.
   b. improper timing.
   c. uncoordinated use of controls.
   d. improper trim control.

3. Demonstrates and simultaneously explains timed turns to magnetic compass headings from an instructional standpoint.
4. Analyzes and corrects simulated common errors related to timed turns to magnetic compass headings.

---

[2] If the aircraft used for the practical test has a turn needle, substitute turn needle for miniature aircraft of turn coordinator.

### Task G: Steep Turns

**References:** FAA-H-8083-9, FAA-H-8083-15; FAA-S-8081-4.

**Objective:** To determine that the applicant:

1. Exhibits instructional knowledge of steep turns by describing–
   a. procedure using full panel and partial panel for entry and recovery of a steep turn.
   b. the need for a proper instrument cross-check.
   c. roll-in/roll-out procedure.
   d. coordination of control and trim.

2. Exhibits instructional knowledge of common errors related to steep turns by describing–
   a. failure to recognize and make proper corrections for pitch, bank, or power errors.
   b. failure to compensate for precession of the horizon bar of the attitude indicator.
   c. uncoordinated use of controls.
   d. improper trim technique.

3. Demonstrates and simultaneously explains steep turns from an instructional standpoint.
4. Analyzes and corrects simulated common errors related to steep turns.

### Task H: Recovery from Unusual Flight Attitudes

**References:** FAA-H-8083-9, FAA-H-8083-15; FAA-S-8081-4.

**Objective:** To determine that the applicant:

1. Exhibits instructional knowledge of recovery from unusual flight attitudes by describing–
   a. conditions or situations which contribute to the development of unusual flight attitudes.
   b. procedure using full panel and partial panel for recovery from nose-high and nose-low unusual flight attitudes.

2. Exhibits instructional knowledge of common errors related to recovery from unusual flight attitudes by describing–
   a. incorrect interpretation of the flight instruments.
   b. inappropriate application of controls.

3. Demonstrates and simultaneously explains recovery from unusual flight attitudes, solely by reference to instruments, from an instructional standpoint.
4. Analyzes and corrects simulated common errors related to recovery from unusual flight attitudes.

## VII. Navigation Systems

***Note:*** *The examiner shall select TASK A and B. If aircraft is not DME equipped, performance of DME arcs shall be tested orally.*

### Task A: *Intercepting and Tracking Navigational Systems and DME Arcs*

**References:** 14 CFR part 91; FAA-H-8083-9, FAA-H-8083-15; FAA-S-8081-4; AIM.

**Objective:** To determine that the applicant:

1. Exhibits instructional knowledge of the elements of intercepting and tracking navigational systems and DME arcs by describing–
   a. tuning and identification of a navigational facility.
   b. setting of a selected course on the navigation selector or the correct identification of a selected bearing on the RMI.
   c. method for determining aircraft position relative to a facility.
   d. procedure for intercepting and maintaining a selected course.
   e. procedure for intercepting and maintaining a DME arc.
   f. procedure for intercepting a course or localizer from a DME arc.
   g. recognition of navigation facility or waypoint passage.
   h. recognition of navigation receiver or facility failure.

2. Exhibits instructional knowledge of common errors related to intercepting and tracking navigational systems and DME arcs by describing–
   a. incorrect tuning and identification procedures.
   b. failure to properly set the navigation selector on the course to be intercepted.
   c. failure to use proper procedures for course or DME arc interception and tracking.
   d. improper procedures for intercepting a course or localizer from a DME arc.

3. Demonstrates and simultaneously explains intercepting and tracking navigational systems and DME arcs from an instructional standpoint.
4. Analyzes and corrects simulated common errors related to intercepting and tracking navigational systems and DME arcs.
5. Exhibits instructional knowledge on the uses of the MFD and other graphical navigational displays, if installed, to monitor position in relation to the desired flightpath during holding.

### Task B: Holding Procedures

**References:** 14 CFR part 91; FAA-H-8083-9, FAA-H-8083-15; FAA-S-8081-4; AIM.

**Objective:** To determine that the applicant:

1. Exhibits instructional knowledge of holding procedures by describing–
   a. setting of aircraft navigation equipment.
   b. requirement for establishing the appropriate holding airspeed for the aircraft and altitude.
   c. recognition of arrival at the holding fix and the prompt initiation of entry into the holding pattern.
   d. timing procedure.
   e. correction for wind drift.
   f. use of DME in a holding pattern.
   g. compliance with ATC reporting requirements.

2. Exhibits instructional knowledge of common errors related to holding procedures by describing–
   a. incorrect setting of aircraft navigation equipment.
   b. inappropriate altitude, airspeed, and bank control.
   c. improper timing.
   d. improper wind drift correction.
   e. failure to recognize holding fix passage.
   f. failure to comply with ATC instructions.

3. Demonstrates and simultaneously explains holding procedures from an instructional standpoint.
4. Analyzes and corrects simulated common errors related to holding procedures.
5. Exhibits instructional knowledge on the use of the MFD and other graphical navigational displays, if installed, to monitor position in relation to the desired flightpath during holding.

## VIII. Instrument Approach Procedures

***Note:*** *The examiner shall select TASKS A and B, to be combined with TASK C, D, or E. At least one nonprecision approach procedure shall be accomplished without the use of the gyroscopic heading and attitude indicators under simulated instrument conditions. Circling approaches are not applicable to helicopters.*

### Task A: Nonprecision Instrument Approach (NPA)

**References:** 14 CFR part 91; FAA-H-8083-9, FAA-H-8083-15; FAA-S-8081-4; IAP; AIM.

**Objective:** To determine that the applicant:

1. Exhibits instructional knowledge of the elements of a nonprecision instrument approach by describing–
   a. selection of the appropriate instrument approach procedure chart.
   b. pertinent information on the selected instrument approach chart.
   c. radio communications with ATC and compliance with ATC clearances, instructions, and procedures.
   d. appropriate aircraft configuration, airspeed, and checklist items.
   e. selection, tuning, identification, and determination of operational status of ground and aircraft navigation equipment.
   f. adjustments applied to the published MDA and visibility criteria for the aircraft approach category.
   g. maintenance of altitude, airspeed, and track, where applicable.
   h. establishment and maintenance of an appropriate rate of descent during the final approach segment.
   i. factors that should be considered in determining whether:
      (1) the approach should be continued straight-in to a landing;
      (2) a circling approach to a landing should be made; or
      (3) a missed approach should be performed.

2. Exhibits instructional knowledge of common errors related to a nonprecision instrument approach by describing–
   a. failure to have essential knowledge of the information on the instrument approach chart.
   b. incorrect communications procedures or noncompliance with ATC clearances or instructions.
   c. failure to accomplish checklist items.
   d. faulty basic instrument flying technique.
   e. inappropriate descent below the MDA.

3. Demonstrates and simultaneously explains a nonprecision instrument approach from an instructional standpoint.
4. Analyzes and corrects simulated common errors related to a nonprecision instrument approach.
5. Exhibits instructional knowledge on the uses of the MFD and other graphical navigational displays, if installed, to monitor position, track, wind drift, and other parameters to maintain desired flightpath.

**Task B: Precision Instrument Approach (PA)**

**References:** 14 CFR part 91; FAA-H-8083-9, FAA-H-8083-15; FAA-S-8081-4; IAP; AIM.

**Objective:** To determine that the applicant:

1. Exhibits instructional knowledge of a precision instrument approach by describing–
    a. selection of the appropriate instrument approach chart.
    b. pertinent information on the selected instrument approach chart.
    c. selection, tuning, identification, and determination of operational status of ground and aircraft navigation equipment.
    d. radio communications with ATC and compliance with ATC clearances, instructions, and procedures.
    e. appropriate aircraft configuration, airspeed, and checklist items.
    f. adjustments applied to the published DH/DA and visibility criteria for the aircraft approach category.
    g. maintenance of altitude, airspeed, and track, where applicable.
    h. establishment and maintenance of an appropriate rate of descent during the final approach segment.
    i. factors that should be considered in determining whether:

        (1) the approach should be continued straight-in to a landing;
        (2) a circling approach to a landing should be made; or
        (3) a missed approach should be performed.

2. Exhibits instructional knowledge of common errors related to a precision instrument approach by describing–
    a. failure to have essential knowledge of the information on the instrument approach chart.
    b. incorrect communications procedures or noncompliance with ATC clearances.
    c. failure to accomplish checklist items.
    d. faulty basic instrument flying technique.
    e. inappropriate application of DH/DA.

3. Demonstrates and simultaneously explains a precision instrument approach from an instructional standpoint.
4. Analyzes and corrects simulated common errors related to a precision instrument approach.
5. Exhibits instructional knowledge on the uses of the MFD and other parameters to maintain desired flightpath.

### Task C: Missed Approach

**References:** 14 CFR part 91; FAA-H-8083-9, FAA-H-8083-15; FAA-S-8081-4; IAP; AIM.

**Objective:** To determine that the applicant:

1. Exhibits instructional knowledge of a missed approach procedure by describing–
   a. pertinent information on the selected instrument approach chart.
   b. conditions requiring a missed approach.
   c. initiation of the missed approach, including the prompt application of power, establishment of a climb attitude, and reduction of drag.
   d. required report to ATC.
   e. compliance with the published or alternate missed approach procedure.
   f. notification of ATC if the aircraft is unable to comply with a clearance, instruction, restriction, or climb gradient.
   g. performance of recommended checklist items appropriate to the go-around procedure.
   h. importance of positive aircraft control.

2. Exhibits instructional knowledge of common errors related to a missed approach by describing–
   a. failure to have essential knowledge of the information on the instrument approach chart.
   b. failure to recognize conditions requiring a missed approach.
   c. failure to promptly initiate a missed approach.
   d. failure to make the required report to ATC.
   e. failure to comply with the missed approach procedure.
   f. faulty basic instrument flying technique.
   g. descent below the MDA prior to initiating a missed approach.

3. Demonstrates and simultaneously explains a missed approach from an instructional standpoint.
4. Analyzes and corrects simulated common errors related to a missed approach.
5. Exhibits instructional knowledge on the uses of the MFD and other graphical navigational displays, if installed, to monitor position and track to help navigate the missed approach.

**Task D: Circling Approach (Airplane)**

*References:* 14 CFR part 91; FAA-H-8083-9, FAA-H-8083-15; FAA-S-8081-4; IAP; AIM.

**Objective:** To determine that the applicant:

1. Exhibits instructional knowledge of the elements of a circling approach procedure by describing–
   a. selection of the appropriate circling approach maneuver considering the maneuvering capabilities of the aircraft.
   b. circling approach minimums on the selected instrument approach chart.
   c. compliance with advisories, clearance instructions, and/or restrictions.
   d. importance of flying a circling approach pattern that does not exceed the published visibility criteria.
   e. maintenance of an altitude no lower than the circling MDA until in a position from which a descent to a normal landing can be made.

2. Exhibits instructional knowledge of common errors related to a circling approach by describing–
   a. failure to have essential knowledge of the circling approach information on the instrument approach chart.
   b. failure to adhere to the published MDA and visibility criteria during the circling approach maneuver.
   c. inappropriate pilot technique during transition from the circling maneuver to the landing approach.

3. Demonstrates and simultaneously explains a circling approach from an instructional standpoint.
4. Analyzes and corrects simulated common errors related to a circling approach.

**Task E: Landing from a Straight-In Approach**

*References:* 14 CFR part 91; FAA-H-8083-9, FAA-H-8083-15; FAA-S-8081-4; IAP; AIM.

**Objective:** To determine that the applicant:

1. Exhibits instructional knowledge of the elements related to landing from a straight-in approach by describing–
   a. effect of specific environmental, operational, and meteorological factors.
   b. transition to, and maintenance of, a visual flight condition.
   c. adherence to ATC advisories, such as NOTAMs, wind shear, wake turbulence, runway surface, and braking conditions.
   d. completion of appropriate checklist items.
   e. maintenance of positive aircraft control.

2. Exhibits instructional knowledge of common errors related to landing from a straight-in approach by describing–
   a. inappropriate division of attention during the transition from instrument to visual flight conditions.
   b. failure to complete required checklist items.
   c. failure to properly plan and perform the turn to final approach.
   d. improper technique for wind shear, wake turbulence, and crosswind.
   e. failure to maintain positive aircraft control throughout the complete landing maneuver.

3. Demonstrates and simultaneously explains a landing from a straight-in approach from an instructional standpoint.
4. Analyzes and corrects simulated common errors related to landing from a straight-in approach.

## IX. Emergency Operations

*Note:* *The examiner shall select at least one TASK. The examiner shall omit TASKS C and D unless the applicant furnishes a multiengine airplane for the practical test, then TASK C or D is mandatory.*

### Task A: Loss of Communications

**References:** 14 CFR part 91; FAA-H-8083-9, FAA-H-8083-15; FAA-S-8081-4; IAP; AIM.

**Objective:** To determine that the applicant exhibits instructional knowledge of the elements related to loss of communications by describing:

1. Recognition of loss of communication.
2. When to continue with flight plan as filed or when to deviate.
3. How to determine the time to begin an approach at destination.

### Task B: Approach with Loss of Primary Flight Instrument Indicators

**References:** 14 CFR part 91; FAA-H-8083-9, FAA-H-8083-15; FAA-S-8081-4; IAP; AIM.

**Objective:** To determine that the applicant:

1. Exhibits instructional knowledge of the elements related to loss of primary flight instrument indicators by describing—
   a. recognition of inaccurate or inoperative primary instrument indicators and advising ATC and the examiner.
   b. notification of ATC or examiner anytime that the aircraft is unable to comply with an ATC clearance or whether able to continue the flight.
   c. importance of utilizing navigation equipment in an emergency situation and demonstrating a nonprecision approach without the use of primary flight instruments.
2. Exhibits instructional knowledge of common errors related to loss of primary flight instrument indicators by describing—
   a. recognition of failed system components that relate to primary flight instrument indication(s).
   b. failure to notify ATC of situation.
   c. failure to transition to emergency mode/standby instrumentation.
3. Demonstrates and simultaneously explains loss of primary flight instrument indicators by conducting a non-precision approach without the use of these indicators.
4. Analyzes and corrects common errors related to loss of primary flight instrument indicators.

**Task C: Engine Failure during Straight-and-Level Flight and Turns**

**References:** 14 CFR part 91; FAA-H-8083-9; FAA-S-8081-4; FAA-S-8081-12; FAA-S-8081-14; Aircraft Flight Manual.

**Objective:** To determine that the applicant:

1. Exhibits instructional knowledge of the elements related to engine failure during straight-and-level flight and turns, solely by reference to instruments, by describing–

    a. appropriate methods to be used for identifying and verifying the inoperative engine.
    b. technique for maintaining positive aircraft control by reference to instruments.
    c. importance of accurately assessing the aircraft's performance capability with regard to action that maintains altitude or minimum sink rate considering existing conditions.

2. Exhibits instructional knowledge of common errors related to engine failure during straight-and-level flight and turns, solely by reference to instruments, by describing–

    a. failure to recognize an inoperative engine.
    b. hazards of improperly identifying and verifying the inoperative engine.
    c. failure to properly adjust engine controls and reduce drag.
    d. failure to establish and maintain the best engine inoperative airspeed.
    e. failure to follow the prescribed checklist.
    f. failure to establish and maintain the recommended flight attitude for best performance.
    g. failure to maintain positive aircraft control while maneuvering.
    h. hazards of exceeding the aircraft's operating limitations.
    i. faulty basic instrument flying technique.

3. Demonstrates and simultaneously explains straight-and-level flight and turns after engine failure, solely by reference to instruments, from an instructional standpoint.
4. Analyzes and corrects simulated common errors related to straight-and-level flight and turns after engine failure, solely by reference to instruments.

### Task D: Instrument Approach–One Engine Inoperative (Multiengine)

*References:* 14 CFR part 91; FAA-H-8083-9; FAA-S-8081-4; FAA-S-8081-12; FAA-S-8081-14; Aircraft Flight Manual.

**Objective:** To determine that the applicant:

1. Exhibits instructional knowledge of the elements related to an instrument approach with one engine inoperative by describing–
   a. maintenance of altitude, airspeed and track appropriate to the phase of flight or approach segment.
   b. procedure if unable to comply with an ATC clearance or instruction.
   c. application of necessary adjustments to the published MDA and visibility criteria for the aircraft approach category.
   d. establishment and maintenance of an appropriate rate of descent during the final approach segment.
   e. factors that should be considered in determining whether:
      (1) the approach should be continued straight-in to a landing; or
      (2) a circling approach to a landing should be performed.

2. Exhibits instructional knowledge of common errors related to an instrument approach with one engine inoperative by describing–
   a. failure to have essential knowledge of the information that appears on the selected instrument approach chart.
   b. failure to use proper communications procedures.
   c. noncompliance with ATC clearances.
   d. incorrect use of navigation equipment.
   e. failure to identify and verify the inoperative engine and to follow the emergency checklist.
   f. inappropriate procedure in the adjustment of engine controls and the reduction of drag.
   g. inappropriate procedure in the establishment and maintenance of the best engine inoperative airspeed.
   h. failure to establish and maintain the proper flight attitude for best performance.
   i. failure to maintain positive aircraft control.
   j. faulty basic instrument flying technique.
   k. inappropriate descent below the MDA or DH.
   l. faulty technique during roundout and touchdown.

3. Demonstrates and simultaneously explains an instrument approach with one engine inoperative from an instructional standpoint.
4. Analyzes and corrects simulated common errors related to an instrument approach with one engine inoperative.

## X. Postflight Procedures

### Task A: Checking Instruments and Equipment

*References:* FAA-S-8081-4; Aircraft Flight Manual.

**Objective:** To determine that the applicant exhibits instructional knowledge of the elements related to checking instruments and equipment by describing:

1. Importance of noting instruments and navigation equipment for improper operation.
2. Reasons for making a written record of improper operation or failure and/or calibration of instruments prior to next IFR flight.

## Appendix 1: Flight Simulation Training Device (FSTD) Credit

### Task vs. Flight Simulation Training Device (FSTD) Credit

Examiners conducting the instrument rating practical tests with Flight Simulation Training Devices (FSTDs) should consult appropriate documentation to ensure that the device has been approved for training, testing, or checking, and assigned the appropriate qualification level in accordance with the requirements of 14 CFR part 60.

The FAA must approve the device for training, testing, and checking the specific flight TASKS listed in this appendix.

The device must continue to support the level of student or applicant performance required by this practical test standard.

If an FSTD is used for the practical test, the instrument approach procedures conducted in that FSTD are limited to one precision and one nonprecision approach procedure.

### Use of Chart

**X**     Creditable
**A**     Creditable if appropriate systems are installed and operating

**NOTE:** Users of the following chart are cautioned that use of the chart alone is incomplete. The description and objective of each TASK as listed in the body of the practical test standard, including all NOTES, must also be incorporated for accurate FSTD use.

"Postflight Procedures" means closing flight plans, checking for discrepancies and malfunctions, and noting them on a log or maintenance form.

## Flight Task Areas of Operation

| Flight Task Areas of Operation | 1 | 2 | 3 | 4 | 5 | 6 | 7 | A | B | C | D |
|---|---|---|---|---|---|---|---|---|---|---|---|
| **Preflight Procedures** | | | | | | | | | | | |
| C. Instrument Cockpit Check * | | | | A | A | X | X | X | X | X | X |
| **Air Traffic Control Clearances and Procedures** | | | | | | | | | | | |
| A. Air Traffic Control Clearances * | | | | A | A | X | X | X | X | X | X |
| B. Departure, En Route and Arrival Clearances * | | | | — | — | X | X | X | X | X | X |
| C. Holding Procedures | | | | — | — | X | X | X | X | X | X |
| **Flight by Reference to Instruments** | | | | | | | | | | | |
| A. Basic Instrument Flight Maneuvers | | | | — | — | X | X | X | X | X | X |
| B. Recovery from Unusual Flight Attitudes | | | | — | — | — | X | X | X | X | X |
| **Navigation Systems** | | | | | | | | | | | |
| A. Intercepting and Tracking Navigational Systems and DME ARCS | | | | — | A | X | X | X | X | X | X |
| **Instrument Approach Procedures** | | | | | | | | | | | |
| A. Nonprecision Approach (NPA) | | | | — | — | X | X | X | X | X | X |
| B. Precision Approach (PA) | | | | — | — | X | X | X | X | X | X |
| C. Missed Approach | | | | — | — | X | X | X | X | X | X |
| D. Circling Approach | | | | — | — | — | — | X | X | X | X |
| E. Landing from a Straight-in or Circling Approach | | | | — | — | — | — | — | X | X | X |
| **Emergency Operations** | | | | | | | | | | | |
| A. Loss of Communications | | | | — | — | X | X | X | X | X | X |
| B. One Engine Inoperative during Straight-and-Level Flight and Turns (Multiengine Airplane) | | | | — | — | X | X | X | X | X | X |
| C. One Engine Inoperative—Instrument Approach (Multiengine Airplane) | | | | — | — | — | — | X | X | X | X |
| D. Loss of Gyro Attitude and/or Heading Indicators | | | | — | — | X | X | X | X | X | X |
| **Postflight Procedures** | | | | | | | | | | | |
| A. Checking Instruments and Equipment | | | | — | A | X | X | X | X | X | X |

\* Aircraft required for those items that cannot be checked using a flight training device or flight simulator

## Appendix 2: Non-FSTD Device Credit

Deleted.

## Appendix 3: Judgment Assessment Matrix

| | | |
|---|---|---|
| **Acceptable Course of Action**<br>Action of the Applicant Is Acceptable Given the Dynamics of the Flight Environment | Judgment Based Upon the Following SRM Areas | Aeronautical Decision-Making |
| | | Risk Management |
| | | Task Management |
| | | Automation Management |
| | | Controlled Flight Into Terrain |
| | | Situational Awareness |
| **Unacceptable Course of Action**<br>Action of the Applicant Is Unacceptable Given the Dynamics of the Flight Environment | Judgment Based Upon the Following SRM Areas | Aeronautical Decision-Making |
| | | Risk Management |
| | | Task Management |
| | | Automation Management |
| | | Controlled Flight Into Terrain |
| | | Situational Awareness |

**Judgment Assessment Matrix**

**Flight Instructor Instrument** for Airplane and Helicopter

- I. Fundamentals of Instructing
- II. Technical Subject Areas
- III. Preflight Preparation
- IV. Preflight Lesson on a Maneuver
- V. Air Traffic Control Clearances
- VI. Flight by Reference to Instruments
- VII. Navigation Systems
- VIII. Instrument Approach Procedures
- IX. Emergency Operations
- X. Postflight Procedures

## Purpose of the Assessment

To measure the applicant's resource management and judgment skills during the Instrument Pilot practical test.

## Directions for Completion of the Assessment

1) For each Area of Operation in the Instrument PTS, the applicant can take either an unacceptable or acceptable course of action for the task being evaluated. The examiner should judge use of resource management for each of the resource management areas.

2) For each Area of Operation, mark the column for the course of action that best describes the applicant's decision during that phase of the evaluation. In order to pass, all decisions made by the applicant must be acceptable.

## Definitions of Resource Management Areas

*Aeronautical Decision Making (ADM)*—a systematic approach to the mental process of evaluating a given set of circumstances and determining the best course of action.

*Risk Management (RM)*—an aeronautical decision-making process designed to systematically identify hazards, assess the degree of risk, and determine the best course of action.

*Task Management (TM)*—the process pilots use to manage the many concurrent tasks involved in safely operating an aircraft.

*Automation Management (AM)*—the demonstrated ability to control and navigate an aircraft by correctly managing its automated systems. It includes understanding whether and when to use automated systems, including, but not limited, to the GPS or the autopilot.

*Controlled Flight Into Terrain Awareness (CFIT)*—the demonstrated awareness of relation to obstacles and terrain.

*Situational Awareness (SA)*—the use of the resource management elements listed above to develop and maintain an accurate perception and understanding of all factors and conditions related to pilot, aircraft, environment, and external pressures that affect safety before, during, and after the flight.

# AIRCRAFT INFORMATION

AIRPLANE MAKE/MODEL _____

## WEIGHT
- Gross: 2650
- Empty: 1656
- Pilot/Pasngrs: ____
- Baggage: ____
- Fuel (gal × 6): 48

## AIRSPEEDS
- $V_{SO}$: 56
- $V_{S1}$: ____
- $V_X$: 83
- $V_Y$: 87
- $V_A$: 114 (Full)  2100 (60)
- $V_{NO}$: 148
- $V_{NE}$: 186
- $V_{FE}$: 109
- $V_{LO}$: 130
- $V_R$: 110

## CENTER OF GRAVITY
- Fore Limit: ____
- Aft Limit: ____
- Current CG: ____

## FUEL
- Capacity: L 24 gal  R 24 gal
- Current Estimate: L 18 gal  R 18 gal
- Endurance (Hr.): 3.5
- Fuel-Flow -- Cruise (GPH): 10

### Instrument Panel
ASI | AI | ALT
TC | HI | VSI

### PRIMARY vs. SECONDARY INSTRUMENTS
(IFR maneuvers) -- instruments:
AI, ASI, ALT, TC, HI, VSI, RPM and/or MP
(most relevant to instrument instruction)

| | PITCH | BANK | POWER |
|---|---|---|---|
| ENTRY primary | ALT | AI/TC | ASI |
| supporting | VSI | HI | TACH |
| ESTABLISHED primary | ALT | AI HI | ASI |
| supporting | VSI/AI | TC/AI | TACH/MP |

## PERFORMANCE DATA

| | Airspeed | MP | RPM |
|---|---|---|---|
| Takeoff Rotation | 56 | MAX | 2700 |
| Climbout | 87 | MAX | 2700 |
| Cruise Climb | 96 | 25 | 2500 |
| Cruise Level | 125 | 22 | 2400 |
| Cruise Descent | 125 | 22 | 2400 |
| Approach** | 90 | 18 | 2500 |
| Approach to Land (Visual) | | | |
| Landing Flare | | | |

\* If you do not have a constant-speed propeller, ignore manifold pressure (MP).
\*\*Approach speed is for holding and performing instrument approaches.

## AIRCRAFT MAINTENANCE RECORDS

Date of Most Recent Annual Inspection [91.409(a)] _____

Date of Most Recent 100-Hour Inspection [91.409(b)] _____

Tachometer Time at Most Recent 100-Hour Inspection _____

Current Tachometer Time _____  Date _____

Date of Most Recent ATC Transponder Tests and Inspections (91.413) _____

Date of Most Recent ELT Inspection [91.207(d)] _____

© Gleim Publications, Inc., 1995-2017. Permission granted to reproduce for personal use.

# FAA INSTRUMENT RATING ORAL EXAM GUIDE

## Aircraft Information

The previous page has a blank form for you to write in information pertaining to the aircraft you will specifically use during the practical test. This page helps you (1) put this information into your long-term memory and (2) get organized and know if your aircraft is airworthy.

## Sample Evaluator Questions

The following sections contain questions that may be asked by your evaluator during the oral exam portion of your instrument rating practical test.

Part I covers Single-Pilot Resource Management. Because determining an applicant's ability to make sound decisions, even though (s)he is fully capable of flying an airplane, can be difficult, evaluators will emphasize this topic during your practical test through oral questioning. Evaluators must ensure that pilots are capable of managing risks according to specific scenario-based examples. Since it is impossible to cover every possible scenario, this section emphasizes processes you should be able to apply to a variety of situations. Below is a listing of the airplane tasks and the pages on which the related questions start.

| Part I: Single-Pilot Resource Management (SRM) | Page |
|---|---|
| 1. Aeronautical Decision Making | 94 |
| 2. Risk Management | 97 |
| 3. Task Management | 101 |
| 4. Situational Awareness | 101 |
| 5. Controlled Flight into Terrain Awareness | 103 |
| 6. Automation Management | 104 |

Part II covers the Airman Certification Standards (ACS) Tasks. We present the related questions in the order in which their associated subjects are listed in the ACS. However, your evaluator may ask these questions (or questions that are very similar) in any order (s)he wishes. Below is a listing of the airplane tasks and the pages on which the related questions start. Questions specific to flight instructor-instrument only are in a separate section following this one.

### Part II: Airman Certification Standards (ACS) Tasks

| | Page |
|---|---|
| I. PREFLIGHT PREPARATION | |
|    A. Pilot Qualifications | 105 |
|    B. Weather Information | 107 |
|    C. Cross-Country Flight Planning | 112 |
| II. PREFLIGHT PROCEDURES | |
|    A. Aircraft Systems Related to IFR Operations | 116 |
|    B. Aircraft Flight Instruments and Navigation Equipment | 118 |
|    C. Instrument Flight Deck Check | 128 |
| III. AIR TRAFFIC CONTROL CLEARANCES AND PROCEDURES | |
|    A. Compliance with Air Traffic Control Clearances | 129 |
|    B. Holding Procedures | 132 |
| IV. FLIGHT BY REFERENCE TO INSTRUMENTS | |
|    A. Instrument Flight | 134 |
|    B. Recovery from Unusual Flight Attitudes | 136 |
| V. NAVIGATION SYSTEMS | |
|    A. Intercepting and Tracking Navigational Systems and Arcs | 136 |
|    B. Departure, En route and Arrival Operations | 138 |
| VI. INSTRUMENT APPROACH PROCEDURES | |
|    A. Nonprecision Approach | 143 |
|    B. Precision Approach | 144 |
|    C. Missed Approach | 145 |
|    D. Circling Approach | 146 |
|    E. Landing from an Instrument Approach | 146 |
| VII. EMERGENCY OPERATIONS | |
|    A. Loss of Communications | 147 |
|    B. One Engine Inoperative during Straight-and-Level Flight and Turns (AMEL, AMES) | 148 |
|    C. Instrument Approach and Landing with an Inoperative Engine (Simulated) (AMEL, AMES) | 149 |
|    D. Approach with Loss of Primary Flight Instrument Indicators | 150 |
| VIII. POSTFLIGHT PROCEDURES | |
|    A. Checking Instruments and Equipment | 151 |

The questions contained in this oral exam guide cover primarily the oral tasks listed in the ACS. Be confident; you will do fine. You can never be totally prepared. If you have studied this book, you will pass with confidence. This book contains the answer to virtually every question, issue, and requirement that is possible on the oral exam portion of the instrument rating practical test. Good luck!

## Part I: SINGLE-PILOT RESOURCE MANAGEMENT (SRM)

### 1. Aeronautical Decision Making

| | | |
|---|---|---|
| 1. | What are the components of the 3P model used in Aeronautical Decision Making? | Perceive, process, and perform are the three components of the 3P model. |
| 2. | How would the 3P model come into play if you suspected an instrument failure in flight? | Perceive; I would recognize if a conflict existed between supporting instruments that suggested a potential failure. Process; I would determine how significant an effect this potential failure would have on flight safety. For instance, if the failure is in the VSI, it would be a minor issue, but if the failure is of the altimeter, that would be significantly more important. Perform; I would verify the failure and implement the best possible course of action to either continue the flight safely or terminate the flight early in the interest of safety. |
| 3. | The 3P model is associated with another acronym, PAVE. What does PAVE indicate? | PAVE is a reminder that makes it possible for the pilot to evaluate the various aspects that make up a successful flight. PAVE is a means of evaluating the Pilot, Aircraft, enVironment, and External Pressures associated with the flight in an organized manner. |
| 4. | In respect to PAVE, what is the question we want to ask ourselves as it pertains to each point? | For each element of PAVE, the pilot should ask, "What could hurt me, my passengers, or my aircraft?" PAVE is a defensive tool. |
| 5. | What is the rule of thumb when working with the processing phase of the 3P model? | If you find yourself thinking that you'll probably be okay on a given flight, that is a good indication that you really need to take time out for a reality check. "Probably" being okay is not a good starting point for any flight, nor is it an effective approach to risk management. |
| 6. | Is there a reminder associated with the Perform element of the 3P model? | Yes, it's ME. That stands for Mitigate (or eliminate) the risk, then Evaluate the outcome of your actions. |
| 7. | How would you describe the DECIDE model of aeronautical decision making? | The DECIDE model is a six-step process that allows the pilot to use a logical progression when involved in aeronautical decision making. |
| 8. | What are the six elements of the DECIDE model? | Detect, Estimate, Choose, Identify, Do, and Evaluate. |
| 9. | Does the DECIDE model scenario end with Evaluate? | No, DECIDE is a looping process of thoughts and actions that repeats. After completing the Evaluate element, the PIC would typically run through the process again, starting with Detect each time a change is recognized. |

| | | |
|---|---|---|
| 10. | Can you explain the function of each element of the DECIDE model? | Detect recognizes that the pilot in command has detected that a change has occurred. Estimate acknowledges the PIC's need to react to the change. Choose suggests the PIC should select a desirable outcome for the flight. Identify deals with the PIC identifying the steps necessary to successfully deal with the change. Do is the action step, where the PIC actually performs the steps necessary for the situation. And Evaluate is the point where the PIC will evaluate the result of his or her actions. |
| 11. | How many recognized hazardous attitudes do pilots need to concern themselves with? | There are five hazardous attitudes that have been identified. They are anti-authority, impulsivity, invulnerability, macho, and resignation. |
| 12. | What is resignation? | That is a passive hazardous attitude. If the pilot takes the attitude, "What's the use?," (s)he will not deal with problems effectively or in a timely manner. |
| 13. | Explain the macho attitude. | The catch phrase is, "I can do it." This is the belief that above all odds, regardless of how significant the issue, I can rise above the problem and save the day. This attitude is dangerous because the pilot assumes (s)he is better than any other pilot, which may lead to taking unnecessary risks. |
| 14. | Are female pilots immune from the macho attitude? | No, the term "macho" is not literal; it merely describes a thought process. Women are equally susceptible to the dangers of the macho attitude. |
| 15. | Why is impulsivity dangerous to a pilot? | The tendency to deal with problems quickly can be taken too far. If the goal is to do something, anything, as quickly as possible, the chances of doing the wrong thing due to a lack of consideration before taking action increases. Impulsivity can lead to accidents that could have been prevented if more time and care had been taken when making decisions. |
| 16. | What is the danger involved in the anti-authority attitude? | Anti-authority runs counter to the concept of cockpit resource management. Rather than availing himself or herself of all the information and assistance available to him or her, the anti-authority pilot shuts out all outside information and aid in order to handle the situation entirely on his or her own. This self-imposed isolation is not conducive to safe flight. |
| 17. | If a pilot was taxiing out to the runway with frost on the wings and shrugged off any suggestions to clear the airplane's surfaces first, what attitude might that indicate? | That would suggest Invulnerability. The pilot knows that frost can be dangerous but has convinced himself or herself that, "It won't happen to me." In truth, frost is an equal opportunity enemy of lift. The pilot should recognize the error of his or her ways, stop, and clean the wings before attempting a departure. |

| 18. | At the halfway point of a cross-country flight, you recognize that headwinds have caused a significantly slower groundspeed than anticipated. Your arrival time will now be 1 hour and 10 minutes later than planned. What concern might you have with that realization? | If my flight time will be extended for 1 hour and 10 minutes, I have to consider my fuel reserves. If I have enough fuel to reach my destination, I very likely would not have enough to meet my reserve needs. My best course of action would be to identify an airport along my route where I could stop for fuel, then make plans to divert to that airport.<br><br>It is better to be late on arrival with sufficient fuel than to be on time with empty tanks. |
|---|---|---|
| 19. | While flying a C-172 in IMC, you notice your RPMs are dropping. Your fuel gauges show more than half tanks available. Oil pressure and temperature are in the green. It is 55°F. What might you do? | With a temperature of 55°F while flying in visible moisture, I would suspect carburetor ice. I would apply carburetor heat in an effort to regain normal power. But while I was waiting for the carb heat to take effect, I would identify the nearest field to divert to should that become necessary. If the carb heat worked, I would apply it periodically to prevent carb ice buildup en route. If it did not work, I would plan a diversion to the airport I had previously identified. |
| 20. | Given the previous scenario, but with a temperature of 30°F, would your decisions change? | Yes, the lower temperature would make me susceptible to not only carburetor icing, but structural icing. I would request an altitude that would put me above or below the cloud layer (if possible), and if any indication of ice was apparent on the wings, I would ask for an immediate diversion for landing before the ice could build up enough to seriously effect the safety of the flight. |
| 21. | Where should you plan to touch down when landing behind a large aircraft that has just landed on the same runway? | Stay above the preceding aircraft's flight path. Observe where the large aircraft's nose touches down and plan to touch down well beyond that point. |
| 22. | When landing behind a large aircraft that has just taken off on the same runway? | Take note of the location of the large aircraft's rotation point and plan to land well before that point. |
| 23. | Is controlled flight into terrain (CFIT) as much of a danger for IFR operations as it is for VFR operations? | It could be argued that CFIT is a greater danger for IFR operations. It is the risk of CFIT that makes it imperative that instrument rated pilots maintain an awareness of risk elements like minimum en route altitudes, missed approach procedures, and rising terrain in the vicinity of their destination airports. Without the ability to see-and-avoid, adherence to established information and practices is imperative. |
| 24. | How can a risk management assessment benefit you as a pilot? | The PAVE checklist is appropriate for every flight operation. Pilot, Aircraft, enVironment, and External Pressures all come into play when planning, conducting, and concluding a flight. Because my workload is known to rise during the approach and landing phase of flight, it is important that I use a tool that will help assure the balance of safety remains on my side throughout the flight. |

| 25. | How is situational awareness important to the instrument pilot when being vectored to final approach? | Not only does it help the instrument pilot to be able to create a mental image of where (s)he is in relation to the airport throughout the approach, it is also beneficial to have a sense of where the other air traffic in the area is, too. This information encourages the pilot to maintain altitudes that assure obstacle clearance throughout the approach, as well as knowledge of how their flight might be affected by the maneuvers or position of aircraft in the air around them. This is especially true when flying in the vicinity of large aircraft that may produce wingtip vortices or turbulence that the unaware pilot would not be prepared to avoid in advance. |
|---|---|---|

## 2. Risk Management

| 26. | What are the four fundamental risk elements associated with any flight? | The pilot, the aircraft, the environment, and the type of operation. |
|---|---|---|
| 27. | What concerns might you have about yourself, the pilot? | I have to be on guard to evaluate my competency to safely conduct the flight. This includes my health, the level of physical and mental stress I am experiencing, my fatigue level, and even my emotional state. Each of these factors has to be considered when I make my go/no-go decisions. |
| 28. | What concerns might we have about the aircraft? | It is my responsibility to consider the limitations of the aircraft, including inoperative components that may be present. I have to be confident that the aircraft's performance capabilities exceed what will be asked of it during the flight, and that it complies with airworthiness requirements. |
| 29. | When we think of the environment, are we considering weather alone? | Not at all. Weather is a significant factor when we consider the environment, but we also have other considerations. The term environment is all encompassing. We consider every aspect of the environment, from weather, to terrain, to ATC services available to us during the flight. |
| 30. | Why are external pressures of significance to our planning processes? | Because external pressures can cause a pilot to make decisions based on factors that can degrade the safety margin of the flight. Meeting deadlines, pleasing people, and accomplishing secondary tasks can push a pilot to take risks that were unnecessary and may be to the detriment of the safety of the flight. |
| 31. | A flight is scheduled for 6:00 a.m. Among the factors to consider is the fact that the pilot completed his or her previous flight at 1:30 a.m. after a full day of flying. | The Pilot element of PAVE encourages us to examine pilot fitness to fly. This pilot has not had adequate rest to safely conduct the flight. Consequently, this flight should be postponed until the pilot has had sufficient rest. |

| | | |
|---|---|---|
| 32. | A flight is scheduled for 6:00 a.m. The aircraft has been tied down on the ramp overnight. It rained until past midnight, the temperature has dropped throughout the night, and it is currently 28°F. | The Aircraft element of PAVE encourages us to consider the airworthiness and condition of the aircraft. In this case, moisture on the airframe may have frozen in areas that are difficult to see but may affect aircraft performance. The aircraft should be moved to a heated hangar where the ice can thaw and flow out of the aircraft, or the flight should be postponed until the ambient temperatures allow the ice to thaw. Trapped ice that could inhibit free movement of flaps, ailerons, rudder, or elevator could affect the safety of flight. |
| 33. | The same flight as described in the previous question is scheduled to depart at 6:00 a.m. Light freezing rain has begun to fall. The aircraft has no deice or anti-ice capabilities. | The enVironment element of PAVE encourages us to consider all aspects of the environment that aircraft will be operating in. With no means of deicing wings or propellers, and freezing rain falling, the flight would violate regulations that prohibit flight into known icing by aircraft that are unequipped to deal with those conditions. The safety of this flight would be compromised. The flight should be postponed until more reasonable weather conditions exist. |
| 34. | After explaining that the flight will be delayed because of freezing rain, your passenger insists that he must leave promptly, or an important business deal will fall through. He offers to pay you a considerable amount of money for making the flight. | External pressures can cause a pilot to make poor decisions that may affect the safety of the flight. In this case, neither the importance of the business deal or the money for making the flight negate the fact that freezing rain is falling and your aircraft is not capable of flying in known icing conditions. Regardless of the incentives, the flight must be postponed until conditions improve. Further, private pilots cannot legally accept compensation for performing a flight. |
| 35. | How can a tool like the I'M SAFE checklist help pilots maintain a high level of safety? | Using the I'M SAFE checklist gives pilots a standardized approach to evaluating their fitness for flight, which provides for a more thorough self-examination of our condition. |
| 36. | What are the elements of the I'M SAFE checklist? | Illness, Medication, Stress, Alcohol, Fatigue, and Eating or Emotion. |
| 37. | If you have had an upsetting argument with your spouse just before leaving home for the airport, what element of I'M SAFE would that fall under? | The emotion element. An upsetting argument with your spouse could cause you to be distracted, or agitated. Neither is a desirable condition for a pilot who is preparing to initiate a flight. |
| 38. | Why is Eating an issue? | In addition to being healthy and well rested, it is equally important for pilots to be adequately nourished so that their thought processes can function normally and their motor skills are well maintained. |
| 39. | What weather phenomenon is suggested by the approach of a fast-moving cold front? | Squall lines can lead fast-moving cold fronts by a significant margin. Although the current weather may be excellent, the squall line can bring violent weather to the area quickly. |

| | | |
|---|---|---|
| 40. | When can you expect to encounter hazardous wind shear? | Hazardous wind shear is commonly encountered near the ground during periods of strong temperature inversion and near thunderstorms. |
| 41. | What is a microburst? | Microbursts are small-scale intense downdrafts that, on reaching the surface, spread outward in all directions from the downdraft center. |
| 42. | What effect does encountering a microburst have on an airplane which traverses it? | First the aircraft could see an increase in indicated airspeed (performance gained) from the headwind. Then the wind will switch to a tailwind (performance lost), which could cause contact with terrain. |
| 43. | Under what conditions are microbursts likely? | Microbursts commonly occur within the heavy rain portion of thunderstorms, but also in much weaker, benign-appearing convective cells that have little or no precipitation reaching the ground. |
| 44. | How long do microbursts normally last? | Microbursts seldom last longer than 15 min. from the time they strike the ground. |
| 45. | If the winds are light and the temperature and dew point are 5° or less apart, and closing at your destination airport, what weather phenomenon might this indicate is possible? | When temperature and dew point are within 5° and winds are light, fog and low clouds may form. |
| 46. | Why is fog particularly dangerous to pilots? | Because it hugs the ground, fog may give the appearance of being very thin and easy to see through when viewed from above. On an approach, fog may reduce visibility to near zero, however. |
| 47. | What are the two conditions that can cause fog to form? | Cooling air until the temperature equals the dew point or adding moisture to an air mass. |
| 48. | What is the risk of flying in IMC at temperatures below freezing? | Moisture in the clouds can transfer to the airframe as ice. |
| 49. | How can a thunderstorm be identified in flight? | Lightning flashes are an excellent indicator of a thunderstorm. However, if the thunderstorms are embedded it may be impossible to determine where the thunderstorm is specifically located. |
| 50. | What is one way of avoiding thunderstorms when they are embedded? | The best course of action is not to fly in those conditions. Embedded thunderstorms are an extreme hazard to aircraft and should be avoided at all times. |
| 51. | When flying in IMC, what resource will provide the most accurate indication of turbulence along your route? | Pilot reports are the most accurate indication of turbulence in flight. |
| 52. | If a pilot report suggests a similar aircraft cruising at the same altitude reported moderate turbulence along your route, how might you potentially avoid that turbulence? | Turbulence can sometimes be avoided or lessened by changing altitude. If pilot reports indicate moderate turbulence at the altitude I am cruising at, I can request information about the ride at higher and lower altitudes, and request a climb or descent as appropriate. |

| | | |
|---|---|---|
| 53. | What might be your first indication of icing while in flight? | Ice building on the leading edge of the wing may be my first indication of being in icing conditions. When flying in IMC at night, it is a good idea to have a flashlight available in order to check the condition of the leading edges periodically when flying in IMC with an OAT that is close to freezing. |
| 54. | If you see ice building on your wing's leading edge, and your airplane has no deice or anti-ice equipment available, what options are available to you? | If ice is building on the airframe and I have no deice or anti-ice equipment installed I need to make getting out of those icing conditions a priority. With clearance from ATC I can descend to an altitude that is warmer, where the ice will no longer form, I can climb to an altitude that will put me above the visible moisture, provided I can get there quickly so excessive ice doesn't form during the climb, or I can request a turn to get me out of the visible moisture. |
| 55. | What is the 5P model? | The 5P model is a method of systematically assessing risk in five specific areas that are pertinent to flight. |
| 56. | What are the five areas associated with the 5P model? | Plan, Plane, Pilot, Passengers, and Programming. |
| 57. | How does Plan relate to the 5P model? | Plan relates to the planning of the flight. It is a reminder to take care and gather all pertinent information for the flight as it relates to the route, fuel requirements, the weather, NOTAMs, etc. |
| 58. | How does Plane figure into the 5P model? | The airworthiness of the aircraft is critical to safety, so the Plane heading reminds pilots to verify the aircraft's mechanical fitness for flight, be familiar with its systems and their operation, and ensure that all required paperwork is in order. |
| 59. | Other than being present, how is the Pilot aspect of the 5P model important? | Showing up for the flight is important, but the pilot also has to realistically self-evaluate his or her health, fatigue and stress levels, and any medications (s)he may have taken. The I'M SAFE checklist can be a great aid to the pilot in making these determinations. |
| 60. | How does Passengers relate to safety in terms of the 5P model? | Passengers come in all types. Some are experienced pilots who may be able to help in an emergency. Others are noticeably uncomfortable with the idea of flying and may need to be reassured in turbulence or if an unexpected occurrence should rattle them. Knowing what sort of passengers you have on board, and recognizing how to deal with them in various flight situations can positively affect the safety of flight. |
| 61. | The last P in the 5P model is Programming. What does Programming have to do with the flight? | As cockpits transition to glass panels, automated systems become more common, and GPS navigation becomes a primary navigation tool, the importance of verifying the integrity and currency of databases and software is increased. The Programming line item in the 5P model literally refers to the programming that runs so many of the tools that a pilot may make use of today, and the importance of verifying that it is accurate and appropriate for the flight. |

## 3. Task Management

| 62. | Give me an example of where the ability to prioritize tasks might be important in flight. | If I had been cleared by ATC to proceed to a visual checkpoint, for instance, and had a map light go out while I was nearing the checkpoint. The priority would be to proceed as instructed, then deal with the map light issue. If I attempted to deal with the light first, I might miss the checkpoint and cause a safety issue to other aircraft, and increase the workload for ATC. |
|---|---|---|
| 63. | Are there situations before the flight departs when prioritization might be important? | Yes, when acting as PIC, it is always important to recognize the need to prioritize. Even before leaving the ground, it is possible that a passenger might want to ask questions while ATC is passing along instructions. It would be my responsibility to recognize that the ATC communication is the priority task. I would indicate to the passenger that I needed to focus my attention on ATC momentarily and would be free to answer questions afterward. |
| 64. | What about a situation in which there are no apparent problems, such as when entering the airport traffic pattern? Is there any need to prioritize your planning or your actions then? | Yes. Although everything is going according to plan, my priority is to set myself and the aircraft up for the next phase of the flight, prior to reaching that point. For pattern entry, I want to have reviewed the airport diagram and have become familiar with the airport area well in advance of arrival. I would have my radio set up for the airport early. By prioritizing the need to prepare, my flight will be less stressful and safety will be enhanced. |

## 4. Situational Awareness

| 65. | What is situational awareness? | Situational awareness refers to the pilot's accurate perception of the operational and environmental factors that affect the flight. It is about being aware. That awareness includes everything from the position of the aircraft in relation to other aircraft, its position in relation to a fix or a given runway, recognition of the terrain the aircraft is flying over, current weather conditions, resources available to the pilot, and even the type and use of the instrumentation available in the cockpit. |
|---|---|---|
| 66. | Why is good situational awareness so important? | A pilot who has a high level of situational awareness can make better decisions than one who is less aware. Situational awareness allows the pilot to make better decisions, earlier, than the pilot who is struggling to see how the flight, and the available resources, fit into any given scenario. |

| | | |
|---|---|---|
| 67. | Can you give me an example of when situational awareness is beneficial to a pilot? | When entering the airport traffic pattern, a good sense of situational awareness will allow the pilot to have a sense of where (s)he is in relation to the runway and airport. That situational awareness will prevent him or her from being surprised or caught off guard when unforeseen circumstances occur. The pilot will also be more confident in his or her awareness if familiar with the physical environment (s)he is flying in, with knowledge of the current weather, obstacle heights, and the location and intention of other traffic. |
| 68. | Can you give me an example where a lack of situational awareness could be a problem while in flight? | Perhaps the most obvious example would be the pilot who enters the approach and landing phase of flight without adequate preparation and planning. Poor situational awareness might cause him or her to violate airspace, cause a collision hazard, or result in forgotten or skipped steps that could lead to an accident. This lack of basic situational awareness can lead to tragic results. |
| 69. | What is fixation? | Fixation is the tendency to focus on one instrument, or a single issue, to the exclusion of everything else. |
| 70. | Why is fixation such a serious issue in instrument or visual flight? | Fixation is a potential problem for any pilot, but it is especially important for visual pilots to guard against because we need to incorporate all the information available to us in order to maintain flight safety. As an example, if I was to focus on just the altimeter, my heading would tend to wander. If I was to focus on just the GPS ground track, my altitude might vary enough to create a problem. All the while my focus would be inside the cockpit rather than outside, itself a serious hazard to flight safety. |
| 71. | Can you give me a real world example of how serious fixation can be? | Perhaps the best known example was Eastern Airlines Flight 401. The entire crew became fixated on a burned out gear indicator light, which prevented them from noticing that the aircraft was descending over terrain with no lights. By the time they recognized the problem, there was no time left to correct it. More than 100 passengers and crew were killed in that case, in large part due to the fixation of the crew. |

## 5. Controlled Flight into Terrain Awareness

| 72. | What does the acronym TAWS stand for? | TAWS is an abbreviation of Terrain Awareness and Warning System. |
|---|---|---|
| 73. | What does the abbreviation GPWS stand for? | GPWS refers to the Ground Proximity Warning System. |
| 74. | Do all aircraft have TAWS or GPWS installed? | No, but it is the pilot's responsibility to understand the specific system if it is installed and be able to use it correctly in order to enhance safety. |
| 75. | Are there similarities between the TAWS and the GPWS? | Yes, both systems are designed to give the pilot warnings meant to prevent accidents due to an excessive sink rate or flight into terrain. |
| 76. | Can a TAWS or GPWS always prevent controlled flight into terrain (CFIT) accidents? | No, there are limitations to aircraft performance that must be understood and planned for when flying in mountainous or other potentially hostile environments. Good planning and a high level of situational awareness are necessary to ensure safe flight, regardless of instrumentation and equipment available on board. |
| 77. | Can you give me an example of a CFIT accident scenario that could be prevented through good planning and maintaining situational awareness? | The classic example may be the poor decision to fly into a box canyon. With insufficient room to turn around, and insufficient performance to climb above the walls of the canyon, the accident becomes unavoidable as soon as the pilot enters the canyon, regardless of how long or far (s)he can fly before running out of clear airspace. |
| 78. | Are there other circumstances where CFIT accidents can be prevented? | Yes, the Steve Fossett crash is a good example of a good pilot who suffered a serious accident due to performance issues. The NTSB found that Fossett's Bellanca was forced into the ground by winds that exceeded his airplane's ability to overcome them. His crash is a good reminder that wind and weather can cause a CFIT accident. It is for that exact reason that it is so important that pilots maintain a sense of situational awareness and plan flights in such a way that the performance of their aircraft can deal with the situations that may arise during any given flight. |

## 6. Automation Management

| | | |
|---|---|---|
| 79. | How can you verify the mode of operation your autopilot is in? | The specific method differs from unit to unit, based on manufacturer, but in general there is an enunciation on the display that reads out the mode. |
| 80. | If you were tracking a VOR with the autopilot, what mode would you be using? | NAV mode would be the appropriate choice when tracking a VOR radial. |
| 81. | Can I fly all the way down the approach in NAV mode? | It would be a better choice to use the Approach mode. The Approach mode will maintain a higher degree of accuracy at tracking the localizer as the aircraft approaches the touchdown zone. |
| 82. | How can I manually transition from one mode to another? | The specific process varies by manufacturer and model, but in general you can manually transition from one mode to another by using a selector button located on the panel. Mode buttons are typically labeled HDG, NAV, and APR, although there may also be additional modes for reverse course and/or altitude. |
| 83. | Can you give me an example of a situation that might surprise a pilot with an unanticipated mode change on the autopilot? | Unanticipated mode changes can catch a pilot by surprise and are often self-induced. Input errors, or misunderstanding how the autopilot works in various modes, can result in the pilot issuing a command to do something other than that which (s)he intended. |
| 84. | How can a lack of understanding of the system lead to problems? | A good example might be the Garmin G1000, which will automatically switch the navigation source from GPS to the localizer when shooting an ILS approach. But it does not automatically switch the navigation source back again when a missed approach is initiated. The pilot who is unaware of this feature will find him or herself with navigation questions and an increasing workload during the missed approach because (s)he did not realize the need to manually make the switch back to GPS navigation. |
| 85. | How would the Garmin G1000 indicate that it was using the GPS or localizer information for navigation? | The HSI needle is magenta when the unit is using GPS information. It switches to green when it is tracking the localizer. |

## PART II: AIRMAN CERTIFICATION STANDARDS (ACS) TASKS

### AREA OF OPERATION I: PREFLIGHT PREPARATION

#### Task A: Pilot Qualifications

| | | |
|---|---|---|
| 1. | When is an instrument rating required? | An instrument rating is required when operating in Class A airspace, when operating under instrument flight rules, and when operating under special VFR within Class B, C, D, and E airspace between sunset and sunrise. An instrument rating is also required when operating in weather conditions that are below VFR minimums. |
| 2. | What limitations are imposed on commercial pilot operations performed by commercial pilots who do not possess an instrument rating? | A commercial pilot who does not possess an instrument rating will have the following limitation placed on his or her certificate: The carriage of passengers for hire in airplanes on cross-country flights in excess of 50 NM or at night is prohibited. |
| 3. | What are the required instruments and equipment for IFR flight? | To operate an aircraft under IFR, it must have all instruments and equipment required for day and/or night VFR flight installed and operable. It must also have the following additional items indicated by the acronym **GRABCARD**: <br> **G**enerator or alternator <br> **R**adios <br> **A**ltimeter <br> **B**all (inclinometer) <br> **C**lock (with a second hand) <br> **A**ttitude indicator <br> **R**ate of turn indicator (turn coordinator) <br> **D**irectional gyro (heading indicator) |
| 4. | Who is responsible for determining if the aircraft is in an airworthy condition? | The pilot in command is ultimately responsible for determining the airworthiness of an aircraft. |
| 5. | What recent flight experience is required if you are to act as pilot in command of an aircraft under IFR? Within what time frame must this experience be accumulated? | In order to act as pilot in command under IFR, one must have logged instrument time (actual or simulated) within the preceding 6 months in either the same category of aircraft to be used or in an airplane flight simulator or flight training device and must have performed the following procedures: <br> 1. At least six instrument approaches <br> 2. Holding procedures <br> 3. Intercepting and tracking courses through the use of navigation systems |
| 6. | May you operate under VFR in Class A airspace? | Unless otherwise authorized by ATC, no person may operate an aircraft in Class A airspace without an IFR clearance. |
| 7. | When flying VFR-on-top clearance, what altitude is appropriate? | A VFR-on-top clearance allows the pilot to operate in VFR weather at an altitude or flight level of his or her choice, subject to any ATC restrictions. |

| | | |
|---|---|---|
| 8. | With what information must the pilot in command familiarize him or herself with before beginning a flight under IFR? | Each pilot in command shall, before beginning a flight, familiarize him or herself with all available information concerning the flight. For a flight under IFR or a flight not in the vicinity of an airport, this information should include weather reports and forecasts, fuel requirements, alternatives available if the planned flight cannot be completed, and any known traffic delays of which (s)he has been advised by ATC. For any flight, the preflight information should include runway lengths at airports of intended use and landing distance data. |
| 9. | If a pilot does not log the appropriate experience within the required time frame, what must be done to regain instrument currency? | An instrument pilot who does not meet the experience requirements during the prescribed time or 6 months thereafter must then pass an instrument proficiency check (IPC). This check may be conducted by an FAA inspector, an FAA-designated examiner, or a certified instrument flight instructor. |
| 10. | Can a pilot take an IPC in any type of aircraft? | As long as the aircraft is of the appropriate category, there is no limitation on the make or model. |
| 11. | Can a flight simulator or flight training device be used when taking an instrument proficiency check? | Yes, a flight simulator or flight training device that is representative of the aircraft category is allowed. |
| 12. | What tasks are required when taking an instrument proficiency check (IPC)? | The IPC must include a representative number of tasks required by the instrument rating practical test. In effect, the Instrument Rating ACS is the guidebook for the evaluator providing the check. |
| 13. | Are you legally allowed to perform instrument holds or approaches if you have not completed the required minimum flight time and tasks within the 6 month time frame? | A pilot is still legally allowed to practice instrument holds and instrument approaches, although they can only be performed in VFR conditions. The pilot cannot file and fly an IFR flight plan until an instrument proficiency check has been successfully completed. |
| 14. | How can you determine if the required aircraft, systems, and equipment inspections have been performed? | Each inspection is entered in the aircraft maintenance logbooks and signed off by the person who completed the inspection. |
| 15. | When may you log instrument flight time? | According to 14 CFR 61.51, instrument time may be logged for that time when you operate the airplane solely by reference to instruments, whether under actual or simulated conditions. |
| 16. | Can flight time that simulates instrument flight be counted as instrument flight time in your logbook? | The flight time that includes simulation of instrument conditions can be logged as instrument flight time. However, not the entire flight time can be logged as instrument time. Taxi, takeoff, and landing must be performed visually, so those segments of the flight and any other time when the pilot could see outside the cockpit cannot be logged as instrument flight time. |
| 17. | When logging instrument flight experience to remain current, what must you include in your logbook record? | You will need to include the location and the type of each instrument approach you perform, and the name of the safety pilot if one is required for that flight. |

| 18. | Can time in a flight simulator or flight training device be recorded in your logbook and counted towards your instrument proficiency? | If an authorized instructor is present during the time when the flight simulator or flight training device is being used, the time can be logged and counted toward instrument proficiency. |
|---|---|---|
| 19. | Can you log instrument time in your logbook based on simulator flight time you obtained when acting alone? | No, an authorized instructor must be present in order to log flight simulator time or flight training device time as instrument time. |
| 20. | How can it be determined which simulator or flight training device time was performed with an authorized instructor present? | The instructor is responsible for noting his or her CFI number and expiration date, as well as a description of the training, the length of the lesson, and his or her signature. That notation qualifies simulator or flight training device time as instrument time in your logbook. |
| 21. | When are you required to log instrument flight time? | Only when using that time to qualify for a rating or to establish proficiency. |

## Task B: Weather Information

| 22. | What is a a standard weather briefing? | A standard briefing should be requested anytime you are planning a flight and have not received a previous briefing. |
|---|---|---|
| 23. | When is it appropriate to request an abbreviated briefing? | An abbreviated briefing should be requested when you need information to supplement mass disseminated data (e.g., TIBS, DUATS), to update a previous briefing, or when you need only one or two specific items. |
| 24. | When is it appropriate to request an outlook briefing? | An outlook briefing should be requested whenever your proposed time of departure is 6 hr. or more from the time of the briefing. |
| 25. | From which sources can you obtain weather information while en route? | FSS is available on 122.2 MHz and on assigned discrete frequencies. |
| 26. | What is a Center Weather Advisory? | A Center Weather Advisory (CWA) is issued by ATC to help aircrews anticipate and avoid adverse weather conditions in the en route and terminal environments. |
| 27. | From which weather reports can you obtain the only reliable information about observed icing conditions and cloud tops? | The only reliable information about observed icing conditions and cloud tops is obtained from pilot reports (PIREPs). |
| 28. | What useful information is presented by radar weather maps? | Weather radar data includes the type, intensity, location, and echo top of the precipitation. |
| 29. | What is the most accurate and reliable means of evaluating turbulence before making a flight? | PIREPs are the only direct means of observing turbulence and are often the most accurate description of the conditions that exist. |
| 30. | What is one great benefit of PIREPs while en route? | PIREPs are valuable because they can provide worthwhile indications of weather conditions between reporting stations where pilots would otherwise have to make assumptions about the conditions. |

| 31. | What is one way you can help maintain PIREPs as accurate reports of current conditions? | By making PIREPs when the opportunity warrants and by making them accurately. |
|---|---|---|
| 32. | What are the required elements found in a PIREP? | PIREPs include the type of report, the location, time, flight level, type of aircraft making the report, and at least one weather element that was encountered. |
| 33. | How are altitudes expressed in PIREPs? | Altitudes are expressed as MSL unless otherwise noted. |
| 34. | Is visibility expressed in statute or nautical miles in a PIREP? | Visibility is expressed in statute miles in PIREPs, but all other distances are nautical. |
| 35. | Are times in PIREPs expressed in local or Zulu time? | PIREPs show time as Zulu, or UTC, time. |
| 36. | When making a PIREP to report turbulence, what terminology might you use? | It is important that standard terminology is used when making a PIREP to avoid misinterpretation of the report. Turbulence should be reported with terms like "light," "moderate," or "severe" in order to accurately describe the conditions. |
| 37. | What is an urgent PIREP? | Extreme weather phenomenon like tornadoes, severe turbulence, or severe icing would qualify as urgent PIREP information. These are conditions that present a real risk to safety and should be disseminated to all pilots who might find themselves in the area. |
| 38. | Do local television news weather reports have any value to a pilot? | Yes, the radar information has value, and although the reports are not aviation specific, the trends, fronts, and pressure systems depicted can be helpful in general planning and decision making. |
| 39. | What is the purpose of using airborne weather avoidance radar? | It allows the pilot to navigate around weather. It is not intended to help a pilot penetrate thunderstorms or severe weather. |
| 40. | Does avoiding thunderstorms by using radar assure you of remaining clear of IMC? | No, the radar indicates precipitation, not clouds or obscuration such as fog or smoke. |
| 41. | What is the difference between radar and a stormscope? | Radar detects precipitation, while the stormscope indicates electrical discharges (lightning). |
| 42. | How can we tell when a given surface analysis chart was issued and be sure it is the most current version? | There is a date-time group printed in the lower left-hand corner of the chart that tells us when it was issued. If that date is current and the time is less than 6 hours old, it is the most current version. |
| 43. | What information is included in a surface analysis chart? | Surface analysis charts include pressure systems, fronts, and sea level pressure, as well as an indication of outflow boundaries and convergence lines. |
| 44. | How is pressure described in surface analysis charts? | Pressure is referred to in MSL, while all other elements are presented as they occurred at the surface point of observation. |

| | | |
|---|---|---|
| 45. | Is the surface analysis chart a forecast or an observation? | Surface analysis charts are a collection of observations presented as a combined report. |
| 46. | How can pilots use a surface analysis chart? | The surface analysis chart is a good tool to use when trying to establish a big-picture view of the weather over a large area. |
| 47. | How often does the National Weather Service issue surface analysis charts? | The NWS issues surface analysis charts every 6 hours. |
| 48. | How is sky condition depicted on surface analysis charts? | Sky conditions are indicated by circles that are empty, partially, or fully filled in to indicate clear, scattered clouds, mostly cloudy, or overcast conditions. |
| 49. | Significant weather charts are broken into low, medium, and high altitude versions. What altitudes are these charts valid for? | Low-level significant weather charts forecast aviation weather hazards for the contiguous 48 states, from 24,000 ft. MSL and below. The mid-level chart forecasts weather over a wider area, for flight levels from 10,000 ft. MSL to FL450. High-level significant weather charts forecast significant en route weather phenomenon for flight levels ranging from FL250 to FL630, as well as related surface weather features. |
| 50. | How are significant weather charts generally used? | The information they forecast is part of the decision-making process during flight planning and preflight briefings. |
| 51. | Of the three significant weather charts available, which would be most appropriate to our flight today? | The low-level significant weather chart would be our best choice because it provides a forecast of aviation weather hazards for the continental U.S., for the altitudes we will be flying in. |
| 52. | Is icing included in the significant weather charts? | Not specifically, but the possibility of icing can be inferred by noting the freezing level and the likelihood of visible moisture. |
| 53. | How are areas of IFR conditions indicated on the significant weather chart? | Areas of IFR weather conditions are indicated by a solid red line that outlines the area. |
| 54. | How are MVFR conditions indicated on the significant weather chart? | A scalloped line surrounds areas of forecast MVFR conditions. |
| 55. | How are VFR weather conditions indicated on the significant weather chart? | VFR conditions are not noted on the significant weather chart. |
| 56. | How are freezing levels depicted on the significant weather chart? | Freezing levels at the surface are depicted by a blue, saw-toothed symbol. Freezing levels above the surface are depicted by a fine, green, dashed line labeled in hundreds of feet MSL. This line begins at 4,000 feet, and uses 4,000-foot intervals. |
| 57. | Do significant weather charts indicate the current weather? | No, they depict a forecast of what the weather is expected to be 12 and 24 hours into the future. |
| 58. | How often are these charts issued? | They are issued four times a day, with both 12- and 24-hour prognostic charts available with each issuance. |

| | | |
|---|---|---|
| 59. | Are winds and temperatures aloft a report or a forecast? | Wind and Temperature Aloft is a forecast, identified by the abbreviation FB. |
| 60. | Is wind and temperature aloft information provided for every altitude? | It is provided at specific intervals, starting at 3,000 ft. To get the specific numbers for any given altitude, other than those specified, it is necessary to interpolate. |
| 61. | How are temperatures expressed in the Wind and Temperature Aloft Forecast? | Temperatures are given as a two-digit number in Celsius. |
| 62. | How are winds expressed in Wind and Temperature Aloft Forecasts? | Winds are shown as a four-digit number. The first two digits indicate the direction, and the second two digits indicate the velocity. |
| 63. | Are the winds given in relation to magnetic or true north on a Wind and Temperature Aloft Forecast? | Winds are given in relation to true north on the Wind and Temperature Aloft Forecast. |
| 64. | How often are Wind and Temperature Aloft Forecasts issued? | Wind and Temperature Aloft Forecasts are issued twice a day, at 0000Z and 1200Z. |
| 65. | What does it suggest when a Wind and Temperature Aloft Forecast lists 9900 at a particular altitude? | The code 9900 indicates the winds are light and variable. |
| 66. | How does the Wind and Temperature Aloft Forecast indicate wind speeds of more than 99 knots? | A wind speed of more than 99 knots is indicated by adding 50 to the wind direction number and subtracting 100 from the velocity number. It is decoded by using the opposite operation. For example, 1505 would indicate the wind is from 100° at 105 knots. |
| 67. | Is the freezing level chart a report or a forecast? | Freezing level charts are a forecast that provide an initial analysis, and provide expectations for the freezing level 3, 6, 9, and 12 hours into the future. |
| 68. | How is the freezing level indicated? | The chart is color coded to illustrate the freezing level at various altitudes, using 2,000-foot increments. |
| 69. | How often is the freezing level chart updated? | The initial analysis and the 3-hour forecast is updated hourly. The 6-, 9-, and 12-hour forecast is updated every 3 hours. |
| 70. | What is another term for a stability chart? | The lifted index chart is a common measure of atmospheric stability. |
| 71. | There are two pieces of information provided numerically on the lifted index chart. What do those two numbers represent? | The top number is the lifted index and the lower number is the K index. The chart includes a reminder of that arrangement of the numbers. |
| 72. | What does the lifted index measure? | The lifted index measures atmospheric stability. |
| 73. | What does it mean if the letter "M" is included in a lifted index chart? | The "M" indicates that data for that entry point is missing. |
| 74. | What does a positive number indicate in the lifted index? | The more positive the number, the more stable the air mass is. Conversely, a negative number indicates an unstable air mass. |

| | | |
|---|---|---|
| 75. | Is the K index of importance to pilots? | The K index is primarily of interest to meteorologists, not pilots. The K index suggests the temperature and moisture profile of the environment. It is not really a measure of stability. |
| 76. | How is severe weather information conveyed to pilots in chart form? | Radar summary charts include severe weather watch areas. |
| 77. | What types of weather phenomenon could trigger a severe weather warning? | There are two severe weather conditions that would result in a severe weather watch area being established. Tornado watches are abbreviated as WT. Severe thunderstorm watches are abbreviated as WS. |
| 78. | Is there a forecast of severe weather that pilots can look to for planning purposes? | Yes, the severe weather outlook chart, or convective outlook chart, is a forecast of severe weather over the contiguous 48 states. |
| 79. | What is a severe weather outlook chart? | The severe weather outlook chart, or convective outlook chart, is a graphic forecast for where convection or severe convection is expected in the coming 24-hour period. |
| 80. | How does a severe weather outlook chart indicate the likelihood of severe thunderstorm activity? | Abbreviations are used to indicate slight (SLGT), moderate (MDT), high (HIGH), or an approaching (APCHG) risk. |
| 81. | What is an AIRMET? | AIRMET is the acronym for Airmen's Meteorological Information. It is a concise description of the occurrence, or expected occurrence, of specific, significant weather phenomenon of importance to pilots. |
| 82. | Can you give me an example of the type of weather phenomenon that would qualify as an AIRMET? | Sustained surface winds in excess of 30 knots, widespread mountain obscuration, ceilings of visibility that have degraded to IFR conditions, moderate turbulence, and moderate icing all qualify as conditions that would warrant the issuance of an AIRMET. |
| 83. | How are altitudes given in AIRMETs? | All heights or altitudes are referenced to MSL in hundreds of feet. |
| 84. | What is a SIGMET? | SIGMET stands for Significant Meteorological Information, which is similar to an AIRMET, but indicates issues of greater intensity or higher potential risk to aircraft. |
| 85. | Can you give me an example or two of what sort of phenomenon a SIGMET might warn of? | Thunderstorms, hail, severe turbulence, severe icing, widespread sand storms, widespread dust storms, tropical cyclones, and volcanic ash are all phenomenon that a SIGMET could be issued for. |
| 86. | When a SIGMET is issued, does it automatically mean that these phenomenon are actively occurring? | No, a SIGMET can be issued for conditions that exist, or are expected to exist, that could have a significant effect on the safety of aircraft operations. |
| 87. | Would a severe thunderstorm be a good example of a weather condition that would warrant a SIGMET? | Actually, a thunderstorm would warrant a SIGMET, but a severe thunderstorm would cause the issuance of a Convective SIGMET. |

| 88. | Would a line of thunderstorms that stretched for 30 miles qualify as a Convective SIGMET? | Not necessarily. To reach the Convective SIGMET level, a line of thunderstorms would have to be at least 50 miles long, with thunderstorms affecting at least 40% of the length of that line. A squall line would qualify for a SIGMET, however. |
|---|---|---|
| 89. | What other phenomenon would qualify for a Convective SIGMET? | Embedded thunderstorms and obscured thunderstorms would qualify for a SIGMET. Tornadoes, hail of 3/4 in. or larger, and wind gusts of 50 knots or greater would qualify for a Special Convective SIGMET, which contains information that may not have been included in a previously issued SIGMET. |
| 90. | How often is the Automatic Terminal Information Service (ATIS) broadcast updated? | The ATIS is updated every hour, approximately on the hour. |
| 91. | Is the ATIS ever updated on other than an hourly basis? | The ATIS may be updated any time official weather is received or when a change is made in other pertinent data, such as a runway change. |
| 92. | What is the purpose of ATIS? | ATIS improves controller effectiveness and relieves frequency congestion by automating the repetitive transmissions dealing with weather and other non-control airport information. |
| 93. | How is each ATIS broadcast identified? | ATIS broadcasts are identified by a letter of the alphabet and progress in order. Broadcast Alpha is followed by broadcast Bravo, and so on. |

## Task C: Cross-Country Flight Planning

| 94. | What is an IFR preferred route? | IFR preferred routes are established between busier airports to increase system efficiency and capacity. When filing an IFR flight plan that could make use of an IFR preferred route, it is wise to plan the flight around the use of those routes. |
|---|---|---|
| 95. | Where can reference information for IFR preferred routes be found? | IFR preferred routes are listed in the Chart Supplement. |
| 96. | Under what circumstance would ATC be likely to route your cross-country flight without making use of IFR preferred routes? | If severe weather exists along the route, ATC may route your flight differently to avoid the risks associated with that weather. |
| 97. | Is a GPS unit required in order to obtain a direct routing clearance? | Not necessarily. If it is possible to navigate direct from one VOR to another, ATC may issue a direct route clearance, even if the aircraft is not equipped with a GPS receiver. |
| 98. | Are the forecasts and reports of winds at altitude provided in relation to true north or magnetic north? | Most weather products provide wind information in relation to true north. The exception to that rule-of-thumb is wind information transmitted to arriving pilots by ATC using radio transmission, or ATIS broadcast, which are both given relative to magnetic north. |

|  |  |  |
|---|---|---|
| 99. | What concern do you have when selecting a cruising altitude for an IFR cross-country that you did not have to consider when flying VFR? | When filing an IFR cross-country flight, I have to be familiar with the minimum en route altitude (MEA) and minimum obstruction clearance altitude (MOCA) for the route. |
| 100. | Can you operate below the MEA or MOCA when in cruise flight? | You cannot cruise below the MOCA; however, it is acceptable to fly below the MEA when within 22 NM of the VOR being used for navigation, provided you remain above the MOCA. |
| 101. | When cruising in Class G airspace on a magnetic course of 135°, are you at an odd thousand foot altitude or an even thousand foot altitude? | Below 18,000 ft. MSL, IFR flights cruising on a magnetic course from 0° to 179° can expect to be assigned an odd thousand foot altitude. |
| 102. | Is it permissible to penetrate a restricted area when en route on an IFR cross-country flight? | Yes, if cleared by ATC along a route, that clearance allows you to transition through restricted areas that lay along your route. |
| 103. | Is it permissible to penetrate a prohibited area when en route on an IFR cross-country flight? | No. The airspace within a prohibited area remains prohibited, even to aircraft operating on an IFR clearance. |
| 104. | What will determine the power settings you will use while en route? | Cruise power settings will be taken from the airplane's POH/AFM. |
| 105. | Which important aspects of performance are determined by your power setting and altitude? | True airspeed and fuel flow are both determined by the power setting and altitude chosen for the flight. |
| 106. | What variables would you consider when choosing an altitude for your flight? | The aircraft's performance and available equipment would be important factors in selecting an appropriate altitude. Wind speed and direction, freezing levels, turbulence, and the duration of the flight would also be variables that I would consider. |
| 107. | What would be the lowest altitude you would consider for your flight? | I would make sure my cruising altitude would be at or above the MEA throughout the cruise portion of the flight to ensure reception of navigation signals as well as obstacle clearance. |
| 108. | What performance factors are determined using forecast wind direction and speed? | With wind direction and speed information, we can predict our estimated time en route (ETE) and our fuel requirements with reasonable accuracy. |
| 109. | If we find that our groundspeed is different than we anticipated, what variable would we double-check for safety reasons? | Our ETE is dependent on our groundspeed. We would recalculate our fuel burn to verify that we would still have the necessary fuel reserves for the flight as planned. |
| 110. | What are the fuel requirements for an IFR flight when no alternate airport is required? | You need to be carrying enough fuel to fly to the airport of intended landing, then fly beyond that point for 45 minutes at normal cruise speed. |
| 111. | What are the fuel requirements for an IFR flight when an alternate airport is required? | You need to be carrying enough fuel to fly to the airport of intended landing, then fly beyond that point to the alternate airport, then fly beyond that point for 45 minutes at normal cruise speed. |

| 112. | Where would I find the regulations that pertain to minimum fuel requirements for IFR flight? | Minimum fuel requirements can be found in Part 91 of the Federal Aviation Regulations, General Operating and Flight Rules. The specific reference is 14 CFR 91.167. |
|---|---|---|
| 113. | Do weight and balance considerations for IFR flight differ from those you had when flying under VFR? | No, weight and balance remain critically important issues that must be calculated carefully and accurately for each flight, regardless of whether I fly IFR or VFR. |
| 114. | When using FAA charts, how can you verify that they are current? | FAA charts include an effective date. The charts are valid for 56 days. |
| 115. | How can you be sure Jeppesen charts are current? | Jeppesen provides NOTAMs to allow pilots to update the charts as necessary. |
| 116. | Why is it especially important to review your charts paying particular attention to your specific route of flight when flying IFR? | You need to be sure that you recognize not just the route, but also the appropriate altitudes for IFR flight and any navigational aids that may be available to you while in flight. |
| 117. | What is a STAR? | STAR stands for Standard Terminal Arrival Route. STARs are used at busier airports to simplify clearance delivery procedures. |
| 118. | If you are flying into an airport with a Standard Terminal Arrival Route, is it mandatory that you accept a STAR? | No, I can make a notation on my flight plan that says "No STARs," which will notify ATC that I am not able to accept Standard Terminal Arrival Routes. |
| 119. | What information must you have on hand in order to accept a STAR? | I have to be in possession of at least a textual description of the procedure. However, in actual practice it would be preferable to have a full printout of the STAR as a reference document. |
| 120. | When requesting a specific approach, what consideration is primary? | I must determine that my aircraft has the equipment required to shoot the approach. As an example, I should not request a VOR/DME approach if the airplane does not have DME equipment installed. |
| 121. | How is NOTAM information delivered to pilots? | NOTAMs are provided to pilots when they obtain their weather briefing, as well as being available in printed form in the Notices to Airmen Publication. |
| 122. | What does the keyword indicate when associated with a NOTAM (D)? | The keyword indicates what the nature of the NOTAM covers. For instance, if the keyword is "communications," it indicates that the NOTAM pertains to communications equipment or signals. The keyword "runway" indicates that the NOTAM has to do with a runway that may affect the pilot's decision-making process. |
| 123. | What is an FDC NOTAM? | An FDC NOTAM is regulatory in nature, as opposed to being strictly informational, as a NOTAM (D) would be. A change to a published approach procedure, or a Temporary Flight Restriction would be examples of issues that would prompt an FDC NOTAM. |

| | | |
|---|---|---|
| 124. | How often is the Notices to Airmen Publication issued? | The NTAP is issued every 28 days. |
| 125. | If a NOTAM is included in the Notices to Airmen Publication, how does that affect flight planning when getting your briefing? | Once a NOTAM is published in the NTAP, it is no longer provided as a part of the standard briefing unless the pilot specifically asks about it. |
| 126. | If you were flying IFR with an IFR approved GPS receiver, where could you obtain GPS NOTAMs and GPS RAIM aeronautical information? | I could obtain that information from the briefer when I call for my weather briefing, prior to my flight. |
| 127. | What is an example of a condition that you might fly into that would profoundly affect your aircraft's performance? | Icing is perhaps the best example of a condition that can be encountered in flight that will have a detrimental effect on the aircraft's performance. |
| 128. | How can you avoid or minimize the possibility of encountering adverse performance issues due to conditions of flight while en route? | It is imperative that I remain alert and aware at all times when flying IFR. By monitoring pilot reports, visually inspecting my own airframe to the extent possible, and watching the weather and temperature, I can reduce the likelihood that I might inadvertently find myself in conditions that may exceed the capability of my aircraft or myself. |
| 129. | When encountering icing, what should be your first course of action? | My first concern is to establish a plan for removing the aircraft from the situation where ice can form. I may be able to climb above the visible moisture or descend to warmer air or get below the cloud bases. Either of those options should prevent further ice formation. |
| 130. | Is it necessary to limit your time in icing conditions if your airplane is equipped with anti-ice or deice equipment? | Yes. There is no advantage to remaining in icing conditions if it is possible to remove the airplane from those conditions. Even an airplane that is equipped to deal with icing conditions is not designed to remain in icing conditions for extended periods of time unnecessarily. |
| 131. | What is the risk associated with icing that may be more pronounced at lower airspeeds than at cruise airspeed? | An unintentional stall at a higher than anticipated airspeed is one serious risk that comes with icing. The ice buildup on the leading edge of the wings may not appear detrimental at cruise speed, but when a higher angle of attack is adopted when slowing for an approach, the aircraft may unexpectedly stall due to the deformed leading edge of the wing. |
| 132. | Aside from the possibility of deforming the leading edge of the wing, what is another less than desirable aspect of icing? | The ice is adding weight to the airframe, which can not only affect the aerodynamics of the wing itself, but also the CG and total weight of the aircraft. |
| 133. | Can you give me an example of icing that can be encountered while still on the ground? | Frost is a common form of ice that is too often not taken seriously by pilots as the risk that it can present. Although it is not as heavy as clear ice, its rough texture can interrupt airflow significantly. Frost is a real danger and should be removed from the airframe before flight is attempted. |

## AREA OF OPERATION II: PREFLIGHT PROCEDURES

### Task A: Aircraft Systems Related to IFR Operations

| | | |
|---|---|---|
| 134. | What conditions are necessary for the formation of structural ice? | Two conditions are necessary for structural icing in flight: <br> 1. The aircraft must be flying through visible moisture, such as rain droplets or clouds. <br> 2. The temperature at the point where the moisture strikes the aircraft must be 0°C or colder. |
| 135. | Is the presence of frost on the aircraft's wings a significant operational consideration? | Yes; frost disrupts the smooth airflow over the wing and creates early airflow separation, making liftoff difficult. Frost on the leading edges and upper wing surfaces can reduce lift by 30% and increase drag by 40%. |
| 136. | What are the three types of structural icing? | Clear ice, rime ice, and mixed ice. |
| 137. | Under what conditions will structural ice accumulate at the greatest rate? | Encountering supercooled water increases the severity of icing and is essential to rapid accumulation. |
| 138. | What is the difference between anti-icing and deicing equipment? | Anti-icing equipment can be employed to prevent ice from forming on the structure of the aircraft. Deicing equipment is used to remove ice that is already present. |
| 139. | Is carburetor heat considered to be anti-icing equipment or deicing equipment? | It can meet either classification, depending on how it is used. In cruise flight, when carburetor icing is suspected, the application of carburetor heat would be a deicing tool. When preparing to land, but with no indication of carburetor icing, the application of carburetor heat would be considered an anti-icing tool. |
| 140. | Where is ice likely to form on the aircraft? | Predominantly on the areas that impact the relative wind directly, the leading edges of the wings, and empennage. Ice can also build up on or around control surfaces and on the leading edge of the propeller. |
| 141. | If your aircraft has no deicing systems installed, how much time can you safely spend in known icing conditions? | None. With no method of ridding the aircraft of ice buildup, it is a serious breach of safety and a violation of the Federal Aviation Regulations to fly into known icing conditions. |
| 142. | When ice builds up on the propeller, where is the heaviest concentration typically found? | Ice can build up on the leading edge, which can reduce thrust and potentially cause an imbalance of the propeller. The greatest buildup of ice is typically on the spinner and inner radius of the propeller. |
| 143. | What are some ways that ice can be removed from a propeller in flight? | Ice can be removed chemically by introducing alcohol or another substance onto the propeller blade to melt the ice away. It can also be removed by activating a heating system that will melt the ice and allow it to sling free of the propeller. |

| | | |
|---|---|---|
| 144. | How can you tell which method, if any, would be appropriate for your airplane? | The POH/AFM will include any systems that have been installed as standard equipment or retrofitted to the airplane. That manual will provide an explanation of the systems and instructions on their proper operation. |
| 145. | What is induction (carburetor) icing? | Induction icing occurs when ice forms in the air intake of an engine (impact icing due to freezing moisture) or in the carburetor (due to the drop in temperature that is caused by the pressure drop in the carburetor venturi and by evaporation of fuel), robbing the engine of air to support combustion. The downward moving piston or the compressor in a jet engine forms a partial vacuum in the carburetor intake. Adiabatic expansion in this partial vacuum cools the air. Ice forms when the temperature drops below freezing and there is sufficient moisture in the air for sublimation. |
| 146. | What can be done to prevent the formation of induction ice? | The use of carburetor heat will help prevent the formation of induction ice. Carburetor heat warms the air before it enters the induction system, thus limiting the chance of ice. |
| 147. | Is icing a problem with aircraft fuel? | Icing is not a problem with Avgas used in piston engines, although icing can be an issue in turbine aircraft because of the amount of water suspended in the fuel and the extremely cold environment turbines typically operate in. |
| 148. | How can ice be prevented in Jet A fuel systems? | Fuel additives can be used to prevent ice from forming. In some cases, the fuel also can be warmed within the system. |
| 149. | How would you use pitot heat in flight? | If I saw ice was forming on the airframe, I would turn on the pitot heat to prevent the ice from clogging the aperture, which would adversely effect the accurate operation of the airspeed indicator. |
| 150. | If your aircraft had no method of deicing the static port, how could you deal with the loss of static pressure should the port ice over? | Ideally, the airplane would have an alternate static source available that I could switch to. This would restore functionality of the pitot-static instrumentation even though accuracy would be affected slightly. |
| 151. | Why would the accuracy of your pitot-static instrumentation be affected by using the alternate static source? | The pressure inside the cabin, where the alternate static source is typically located, is lower than the actual static pressure outside the cabin. That small change in pressure would introduce a small error to my altimeter and airspeed indicator. |
| 152. | If no alternate static system was available and your static port froze over, what can you do to restore the operation of your pitot-static instruments? | If necessary, I could break the glass on the vertical speed indicator. That is not a mandatory instrument, and venting that instrument to the cabin would restore operation to my altimeter and airspeed indicator, which would be essential to continuing an IFR flight safely. |

## Task B: Aircraft Flight Instruments and Navigation Equipment

| 153. | Describe the pitot-static system in general terms. | The pitot-static system uses air pressure from two distinct sources. Ram air pressure is taken from the pitot tube, which is routed to the airspeed indicator. Static air pressure is taken from a vent or, more often, multiple vents on the aircraft and is made available to the altimeter, vertical speed indicator, and airspeed indicator. |
|---|---|---|
| 154. | Are the vents and inlets for the pitot-static system always located in different places on the airframe? | No. Typically the pitot tube is located somewhere along the wing or the wing strut, and the static port is on the fuselage. But they can be located wherever the design dictates them to be and are sometimes located together, with the static pressure port located on the pitot tube assembly. |
| 155. | What scientific instrument does an altimeter most closely equate to? | The altimeter is essentially a barometer that measures atmospheric pressure and displays the pressure in terms of feet (or meters) above a specific pressure level. |
| 156. | What is the purpose of the Kollsman window on an altimeter? | The value in the Kollsman window is variable. This allows the pilot to set a valid reference pressure to use as a base point throughout the flight. This increases the accuracy of the altimeter, as the airplane flies through an atmosphere with constantly changing pressure. |
| 157. | How often must an aircraft's altimeter and static system be inspected if it is to be flown under IFR? | The altimeter and static system must have been inspected within the preceding 24 calendar months. |
| 158. | If the static port were to become blocked, what indication would the altimeter give? | Because the pressure is trapped in a closed system, the altimeter would continue to show the altitude the airplane was at when the blockage occurred, regardless of the airplane's actual altitude. |
| 159. | If you selected the alternate static source, would the altimeter read higher than normal, lower than normal, or stay the same? | Because the alternate static source accesses a pressure that is lower than the actual static pressure outside the aircraft, the altimeter will read slightly higher than normal. |
| 160. | How does the airspeed indicator work? | By comparing ram air pressure to static pressure, the airspeed indicator can accurately display the speed of the aircraft through the air. It is essentially a differential pressure gauge. |
| 161. | If the pitot tube becomes blocked for any reason, what will the airspeed indicator read? | The blockage will create a fixed pressure in the reference pressure supplied by the pitot. That will cause the airspeed indicator to remain constant while the airplane remains at the altitude where the blockage occurred, even if the speed of the airplane changes. The indicated airspeed will rise as the airplane climbs and descend as the airplane descends because it will be acting as an altimeter does for as long as the pitot system is blocked. |

| | | |
|---|---|---|
| 162. | How would a blocked static port affect the airspeed indicator? | The error would be similar to but opposite from what would happen as a result of a blocked pitot tube. The airspeed indicator would show reduced airspeed as the airplane climbs and increased airspeed as the airplane descends. |
| 163. | What does the term "position error" mean when used to describe airspeed readings? | High pitch attitudes can lead to position errors, which cause a disturbed flow of air into the pitot tube and inaccurate airspeed indications. |
| 164. | How does the vertical speed indicator work? | The VSI measures the rate of change in pressure. A calibrated vent in the instrument's case causes the pressure to change inside the case slower than the pressure changes inside the aneroid installed in the instrument. As pressure changes due to a climb or descent, the VSI shows the rate of the change, which is calibrated into feet per minute. |
| 165. | What is the error built into the VSI? | Because of the nature of their design, VSIs have a lag time between when a trend starts or stops and when the instrument indicates that trend. Consequently, the VSI is a useful reference, but it is a support instrument, not a primary control instrument. |
| 166. | What power source is typically used with attitude indicators? | Most often they are powered by pneumatic pressure, provided by the vacuum system. The air pressure spins a wheel up to high speed, which acts as a gyroscope. |
| 167. | For those attitude indicators that are not powered by pneumatics, what is the next most common power source? | Electricity is used to drive a motor that spins the gyroscope. |
| 168. | What is a limitation of pneumatically powered attitude indicators that is of special interest to instrument pilots? | It takes time for the pneumatic system to spin the gyroscope up to a speed that allows it to be accurate and truly functional. If pilots rush through start-up, taxi, run-up, and takeoff, it is possible that they will be trying to orient themselves to an instrument that is not yet stable. This can have disastrous results. |
| 169. | How long does it take for an attitude indicator to come up to speed and erect itself? | It can take as long as 5 minutes, although they will typically become stable in 2 to 3 minutes. |
| 170. | What is the small error that an attitude indicator may exhibit during a rapid acceleration? | The attitude indicator may show a slight pitching up, due to an issue with the speed of response in the gyroscope's erection system. |
| 171. | What is a horizontal situation indicator? | The HSI is an instrument that combines a magnetic compass with navigational signals and a glideslope. Its value is that it can give the pilot an indication of the aircraft's location with respect to a chosen course. |
| 172. | What is the vertical line on the magnetic compass called? | The lubber line. |

| 173. | What is magnetic variation? | The term magnetic variation refers to the difference between true north and magnetic north. The degree of this error varies from one point to another on the globe. We compensate for this error by including a variable in our calculations that is shown by isogonic lines. We would subtract east variations and add west variations when planning our course. |
|---|---|---|
| 174. | What is deviation? | Deviation refers to the magnetic compass errors induced by magnetic fields in the aircraft. These can come from the use of the radio or any other electronic device. A compass correction card is mounted near the compass to alert the pilot to any deviation necessary to fly a given compass heading. |
| 175. | What does the dip error lead to when flying by the magnetic compass? | The dip error causes north and south turning errors when flying in the middle latitudes. It also causes acceleration and deceleration errors. |
| 176. | What is the northerly turning error? | When flying on an east or west heading in the middle latitudes, the compass will turn faster or slower than the airplane, depending on the direction of the turn. When turning from a westerly heading to the north, the compass card will accelerate faster than the actual turn, causing the pilot who rolls out on a heading of north to find that (s)he has overshot the heading significantly. |
| 177. | Is there a mnemonic device to help remember how to deal with dip errors when navigating by magnetic compass? | Yes, you can remember the mnemonic device, "See south, never north." That is a reminder to roll out from a turn from east or west to north before reaching the heading you are turning to. Conversely, you will roll out of a turn to the south after you have passed your heading on the compass card. |
| 178. | What is acceleration/deceleration error? | Acceleration/deceleration error is associated with the dip error too, but it appears when accelerating or decelerating on a heading of east or west. |
| 179. | Is there a mnemonic device for a(n) acceleration/deceleration error too? | Yes, we can remember ANDS, for Accelerate North, Decelerate South. When on an east or west heading, an acceleration will make the compass swing momentarily to the north. A deceleration will make the compass swing temporarily to the south. This compass swing is an error and does not indicate the airplane is actually turning. |
| 180. | When used as a supporting instrument, what axis of control can the magnetic compass indicate? | When used as a supporting instrument in conjunction with the heading indicator, the magnetic compass can indicate roll by showing a turn is occurring. |
| 181. | Is the magnetic compass ever used as a primary flight instrument? | The magnetic compass is an important reference tool that is vital to safe flight. But it can suffer from so many errors, it is commonly used as a back-up or secondary instrument for control, even while it is a primary reference for heading information. Most commonly, it is used as a reference that provides information, which is used to set the gyroscopic heading indicator. |

| | | |
|---|---|---|
| 182. | What is the difference between a turn-and-slip indicator and a turn coordinator? | The turn coordinator can provide bank rate information as well as turn rate information. The turn-and-slip only provides information on the turn rate. |
| 183. | Why do turn-and-slip indicators and turn coordinators have a time indication on them, usually labeled "2 min. turn?" | If the indicator is lined up with the white mark on the indicator, it signifies a standard rate turn of 3° per second, or 2 minutes to complete a full 360° turn. |
| 184. | Why is it important to have an indicator in the cockpit that can provide information on what constitutes a standard rate turn? | Because the rate of an aircraft's turn changes with the speed the aircraft is moving. The turn-and-slip indicator and turn coordinator provide a standard rate of turn reference that is valid regardless of the speed of the airplane. |
| 185. | What powers the turn-and-slip indicator or the turn coordinator? | They are typically powered by electricity. This is a redundancy issue, since most other gyroscopic instruments have been traditionally powered by pneumatic pressure supplied by the vacuum system. By using two separate power sources, one system can act as a check on the other. |
| 186. | While the gyroscopic heading indicator has none of the errors associated with the magnetic compass, it has one major failing. What is that limitation? | The gyroscopic heading indicator has no sensing ability of its own. It will indicate any heading that it is set to, or it will display a random heading if it is not set properly. It is this limitation that makes it imperative that we periodically check our heading indicator against the magnetic compass and make adjustments as necessary. |
| 187. | What powers the heading indicator? | Almost all mechanical heading indicators are pneumatically powered, using air from the vacuum system. |
| 188. | How often is it recommended that you check your heading indicator against your magnetic compass for accuracy? | It is recommended that we cross check the two instruments every 15 minutes to verify accuracy. |
| 189. | Why is it important that you do not go long periods of time without checking and correcting the heading indicator? | The earth rotates at 15° per hour so, even if the heading indicator is flawless, it will show an error over time due to the natural rotation of the earth. By checking every 15 minutes, we can keep our errors down to 4° or less throughout our flights. |
| 190. | What is the error that gyroscopes suffer from? | Gyroscopic precession. As the airplane turns, banks, pitches, and encounters turbulence, precession can lead to inaccuracies in the orientation or indications given by a gyroscope. Gyroscopic precession is another reason that we should verify our gyro information periodically. |

| | | |
|---|---|---|
| 191. | An airplane that is intended to fly IFR has a fairly complex electrical system, by design. How can we better understand the electrical system of our airplane before we get into the air with it? | By reading and studying the POH/AFM to the extent necessary. Each airplane will be slightly different. Instrumentation may be retrofitted to the airplane, as well as other equipment that may affect the electrical system. It is important in every case to become familiar with the specific aircraft we will be flying before leaving the ground. |
| 192. | Aside from nav/comm radios, what systems might be affected by an electrical failure? | Depending on the aircraft type and the severity of the failure, the pilot could lose the ability to deploy flaps, may have to extend retractable gear manually, and, in the case of an airplane with a glass panel, may lose the primary and multi-function flight displays. |
| 193. | In the event of an alternator failure, would all power to systems be lost immediately? | No, the battery should have sufficient electrical energy stored to allow some electrical power for a brief period of time. |
| 194. | If you suspect an alternator failure, what course of action would extend the available battery power? | If the alternator fails, it is important to shed as much electrical load as possible in order to preserve enough battery power to run radios and essential flight information until the aircraft can be safely landed. |
| 195. | How can pneumatic pressure be generated in order to run the gyroscopic instruments installed in an airplane? | There are two options. The older version that is still in use involves a venturi being mounted to the outside of the airplane, where the relative wind will pass through it. The newer and more common method uses a vacuum pump. |
| 196. | What is the limitation of vacuum systems powered by a venturi? | The venturi system does not produce significant vacuum pressure until the aircraft has gained significant speed. While on the ground and when departing the runway at takeoff, the venturi system has not yet generated pneumatic pressure of sufficient strength or for a sufficient amount of time for the pneumatically powered gyro instruments to be stable and reliable. |
| 197. | What is a needle valve? | The needle valve is installed in the vacuum system to decrease the suction for instruments that require less suction than the main system provides. |
| 198. | What is a suction relief valve? | The suction relief valve is a spring loaded device fitted into a vacuum pump system in order to regulate the amount of suction supplied to the instruments. |
| 199. | What is one advantage of electronic flight displays when viewed from the perspective of reliability? | Solid-state instruments have proven to have a failure rate far lower than the analog instruments they have replaced. |
| 200. | What is an advantage of electronic flight displays from the pilot's perspective? | The electronic flight display has simplified the instrument pilot's scan and provides a wealth of information to the pilot in a readily accessible format. |

|  |  |  |
|---|---|---|
| 201. | What is a potential negative aspect of the electronic flight display? | In the event of an electrical failure in IFR conditions, the pilot's workload would increase as (s)he adapts to the loss of the familiar electronic display and must work with less familiar analog back-up instrumentation, which makes the instrument scan more difficult than the scan made available by the electronic flight display. |
| 202. | What does a red X showing on the PFD indicate? | A red X showing on the primary flight display would indicate that the portion of information X'ed out is not reliable and should not be used. |
| 203. | What is a VHF Omnidirectional Range (VOR) station? | The VOR is a very high frequency (VHF) radio transmitting ground station that uses a paired rotating/pulsing signal to provide bearing information. |
| 204. | How often must a VOR accuracy check be performed if an aircraft is to be operated under IFR? What are the different kinds of accuracy checks, and what are their tolerances? | A VOR accuracy check must have been performed within the preceding 30 days if an aircraft is to be operated under IFR. The three types of VOR checks are ground check, airborne check, and dual systems check against one another. Ground check tolerances must be within ±4°, airborne check tolerances must be within ±6°, and dual systems check must be within 4°. A minimum of one type of VOR check must be performed and logged in the airplane logbook within the preceding 30 days for the VOR systems to be used for IFR flight regulations. |
| 205. | Explain the indications of a standard VOR indicator. | The VOR navigational instrument consists of:<br>1. An omnibearing selector (OBS), sometimes referred to as the course selector. By tuning the OBS, the desired course is selected and shown under the index.<br>2. A course deviation indicator (CDI), often referred to as the needle. It indicates the position of the selected course relative to your airplane.<br>3. A TO/FROM indicator. It shows whether the selected course will take your airplane to or from the station. When flying to the station, always fly the selected course with a TO indication. |
| 206. | Why does reverse sensing occur? | When flying from a station, always fly with a FROM indication shown. If this is not done, the CDI needle will indicate that the course lies on the opposite side of the aircraft (i.e., reverse), and you will have reverse sensing. |
| 207. | What is a Horizontal Situation Indicator (HSI)? | An HSI combines a heading indicator with a VOR/ILS indicator. The azimuth card rotates to show the heading under the index at the top. |
| 208. | Explain the indications seen on an HSI. | A VOR OBS/CDI type indicator is used to select course, provide CDI information, and create a picture of the aircraft's relationship to the selected course by rotating in relation to the aircraft's heading. Additional components include a TO/FROM indicator and a glide slope indicator. |

| | | |
|---|---|---|
| 209. | Explain how distance measuring equipment (DME) works. | Your airplane first transmits a signal (interrogation) to the ground station. The ground station (transponder) then transmits a signal back to your airplane. The equipment measures the time between the two signals and converts it into distance, groundspeed, and estimated time en route (ETE) information. |
| 210. | Under what conditions will the groundspeed and estimated time en route (ETE) information presented by a DME receiver be accurate? | Only when flying directly TO or FROM the station. |
| 211. | What is a DME arc? | A DME arc is a procedure in which an aircraft maintains a constant distance from a VOR/DME or a VORTAC station while flying a curved path around it. |
| 212. | What is the purpose of a DME arc? | DME arcs are used to help inbound aircraft become established on a final approach course or a segment of a DP or STAR. |
| 213. | How is a DME arc flown with a standard VOR indicator? | Orientation relative to the station is maintained by periodically rotating the OBS in order to select a radial that lies 10° ahead of the aircraft's position along the arc. As the aircraft approaches the radial, the CDI centers and the OBS is rotated another 10°. In order to maintain a constant DME distance from the station, the aircraft is turned to a heading that is roughly perpendicular to the selected radial. In order to correct for drift, the aircraft should be turned slightly toward the station if it drifts outside the arc and slightly away from the station if it drifts inside the arc. |
| 214. | How is a DME arc flown with an RMI? | The aircraft should be continually turned so as to keep the RMI needle pointed toward the wingtip reference mark corresponding to the inside of the arc. If the aircraft drifts outside of the arc, the RMI needle should be placed ahead of the wingtip; if it drifts inside of the arc, the RMI needle should be positioned behind the wingtip. |
| 215. | What is an ILS? | ILS stands for instrument landing system, a precision approach that provides both course and altitude guidance to a specific runway. |
| 216. | At a minimum, there are four components to an ILS. What are they? | The four basic components of an ILS are a localizer, a glide slope, marker beacons, and an approach light system. |
| 217. | As an active general aviation pilot with an instrument rating, what would be required to shoot a Category II ILS approach? | A general aviation pilot with an instrument rating can shoot a Category I ILS with an airplane that has the appropriate equipment. But to shoot Category II or Category III ILS approaches, I would need specific training on those operations, and the aircraft I fly would be required to have additional equipment certifications. |
| 218. | What is a typical ILS glide slope angle? | A typical ILS glide slope angle is 3°, although there may be some variation for individual approaches at specific runways. |

| 219. | When shooting an ILS approach, which marker beacons would you expect to encounter? | Typically I would expect to use the outer marker and middle marker. |
|---|---|---|
| 220. | What is the purpose of the marker system on an instrument approach? | The markers establish a specific point along the localizer during the approach. |
| 221. | What does the outer marker indicate? | The outer marker is generally located between 4 and 7 miles from the airport, and it indicates the position where the airplane should intercept the glide slope. |
| 222. | What indication do you have in the cockpit that you have reached the outer marker? | I will hear a low-pitched tone in the form of continuous dashes, and a blue marker beacon light on the panel will illuminate. |
| 223. | What does the middle marker indicate? | The middle marker is generally located at 3,500 feet from the landing threshold, on the centerline, at a position where the glide slope is roughly 200 feet above the touchdown zone elevation. |
| 224. | What indication will you get in the cockpit that suggests you have reached the middle marker? | I will hear a higher-pitched tone made up of dots and dashes, and an amber light will illuminate on the panel. |
| 225. | If there is an inner marker installed on the approach, what will indicate you have reached that point on the approach? | A high-pitched tone of dots will be generated, while a white indicator light will illuminate on the panel. |
| 226. | How often must an aircraft's transponder be inspected if it is to be used in visual and/or instrument meteorological conditions (VMC/IMC)? | The transponder must have been inspected within the preceding 24 calendar months, and a record must be kept in the aircraft's maintenance logbook. |
| 227. | Periodically you will see a light flicker on the face of your transponder. What does that light signify? | When the light flickers, it indicates the transponder has just been interrogated and has responded to a radar signal. |
| 228. | When ATC asks you to "ident," what does that mean, and what is the result of your actions? | When ATC asks me to "ident," they are asking me to press the ident button on my transponder. That action causes the icon that represents my aircraft to glow brighter on the controller's display, making it easier to locate me as I enter their airspace. |
| 229. | What action do you have to take as a pilot to ensure that your transponder is transmitting Mode C information to ATC? | I will need to verify that I have the transponder switched to the "ALT" position to generate pressure altitude information for the benefit of the controllers. If the transponder is merely switched to "ON," I will be transmitting my location but not my altitude information. |
| 230. | When must you set your transponder to "ALT?" | Mode C is required when operating in Class B and Class C airspace or within 30 miles of the primary airport in Class B airspace. It is not required, but it is a good idea to utilize Mode C at all times when in flight. |

| 231. | What is a non-directional beacon (NDB)? | An NDB ground station that transmits a non-directional signal operates on the frequency band of 190 to 535 kHz. Relative bearing to the station can be determined using airborne automatic direction finder (ADF) equipment. |
|---|---|---|
| 232. | Explain the indications of an automatic direction finder (ADF) indicator. | The ADF needle indicates the relative bearing TO or FROM the selected station. To determine the magnetic bearing to the station, use the following formula: Magnetic heading + Relative bearing = Magnetic bearing. If the resulting value is greater than 360°, subtract 360 from your result to find the magnetic bearing. |
| 233. | What is a radio magnetic indicator (RMI)? | An RMI is a heading indicator that is overlaid with one or two ADF-style needles that are capable of simultaneously providing relative bearing and magnetic bearing information about the selected VOR or NDB station(s). |
| 234. | Explain the indications seen on an RMI. | An RMI provides the same type of information as an ADF (i.e., the needle will always point to the station). The difference is that you can select whether the RMI will present information about a VOR or an NDB. Additionally, the RMI is tied to a compass slaving system that keeps the current heading under the top index. Thus, it automatically and simultaneously displays relative bearings and magnetic bearings. |
| 235. | What is receiver autonomous integrity monitoring (RAIM)? Why is it important? | RAIM is the method of verifying the accuracy of signals received from GPS satellites. RAIM allows the GPS receiver to verify that the signals sent by the GPS constellation are not corrupted. |
| 236. | Can GPS be used when flying a DME arc? | Yes, provided it is a GPS unit that is certified for IFR en route and terminal operations. |
| 237. | Can a handheld GPS be used to fly a WAAS approach? | No, handheld GPS units are not approved for flying instrument procedures as of yet. Panel-mounted models that are certified can be used, however. |
| 238. | Why would it be problematic to conduct an instrument flight using an ACME GPS unit in a rented airplane, if your GPS experience up to that point was conducted entirely with a Widget-manufactured GPS unit? | Unlike the navigational systems that preceded GPS, these systems are not all identical. GPS receivers manufactured by various companies have significant differences in basic operations, and the presentation of information can vary significantly from one unit to the next. Although no mandatory training is required to work with one GPS model or another, it is imperative that pilots fully understand how to use and effectively manage the equipment that they intend to use when they fly. |
| 239. | Does an up-to-date database absolve you of the need to check NOTAMs when navigating primarily by GPS? | No, a pilot should always check NOTAMs prior to a flight, regardless of what form of navigation (s)he is using. |

| | | |
|---|---|---|
| 240. | When using GPS as a primary navigation tool, how different is the process of planning an IFR flight? | It is virtually identical to planning a flight when other navigational tools are used. The main differences are the programming of the GPS and the method of retrieving information from the GPS unit. |
| 241. | What is a GPS overlay approach? | A GPS overlay approach is an existing approach, such as a VOR or NDB approach, which now includes the words "Or GPS" in the title. This means the approach is effectively unchanged from its original publication, but it can be flown either with the equipment originally stipulated or by using GPS. |
| 242. | Are all existing nonprecision approaches grandfathered in as GPS overlay approaches? | No, there are a number of approaches that for a variety of reasons cannot be coded for use with GPS and will not be published as overlay approaches. |
| 243. | Is a flight management system a navigation system? | No, although that is a common misconception. A flight management system (FMS) is an interface between the pilot or flight crew and the cockpit systems. The FMS is a means of automating the tasks required to operate the navigation systems or other onboard management systems. |
| 244. | What error is an inherent risk with working with flight management systems? | An input error on the part of the pilot. Any computerized system that requires inputs from the pilot presents the opportunity for error due to distraction, misunderstandings, or lack of familiarity with the equipment. |
| 245. | Is there a universal display system that all flight management systems make use of? | No, that is one of the challenges when using automated systems. Each system is unique, and pilots must gain a complete understanding of the system in order to use it safely and to the best advantage of the flight. |
| 246. | When flying an airplane with an electronic flight display, is it preferable to use the autopilot or not? | Indications are that flying an airplane with an EFD without using the autopilot increases pilot workload and decreases situational awareness. For that reason, it is preferable to utilize the autopilot when first learning to fly an aircraft equipped with these systems. |
| 247. | How do autopilots control the airplane in flight? | Each autopilot system is unique and must be studied and understood based on its design and installation. However, autopilot systems in general can control all three axes of flight and can use either hydraulic, electrical, or digital controls to accomplish that task. |
| 248. | How does the autopilot know which inputs to make in order to accomplish what the pilot expects of it? | Autopilot systems employ a series of gyroscopic sensors to base its control inputs on. The system functions as a position-based system, a rate-based system, or a system that combines the position- and rate-based systems into one in order to benefit from the best attributes of each. |

## Task C: Instrument Flight Deck Check

| 249. | What physical item would you inspect carefully during your preflight inspection that would affect nav/comm radio performance? | The various antennas on the aircraft. Even if the radios are in excellent condition, a loose or damaged antenna may prevent the radio from operating properly in flight. |
|---|---|---|
| 250. | How can you verify that each communications radio is working properly before flight? | By checking each with a test call, broadcasting "radio check." That allows me to verify that my transmission signal is readable and that the reception is acceptable prior to flight. |
| 251. | What could you look for that would indicate the airspeed indicator has been properly maintained? | The maintenance logbook should show that a pitot-static check has been successfully performed within the past 24 calendar months. |
| 252. | Is there any additional check you would perform that applies to the airspeed indicator specifically? | I would check the pitot heat to verify that it is working. |
| 253. | Is it necessary to check the vertical speed indicator prior to flight? | Yes, I would make a note of the indication being shown when the airplane is stable and not moving. For example, if the VSI shows a 50 fpm descent while sitting still on the ramp, I will remember to use that as my zero indication in flight. |
| 254. | How can you verify the altimeter is accurate during your preflight inspection? | By setting the correct pressure in the Kollsman window, I can record the indicated altitude and make a note of how that may differ from the known field elevation. I would add that discrepancy to my MDA or DA when shooting an approach to prevent myself from getting inadvertently low on an approach. |
| 255. | What is the maximum allowable error an altimeter can show and still be airworthy for IFR flight? | The maximum allowable error for an altimeter to be used in IFR conditions is plus or minus 75 feet. |
| 256. | Can the turn-and-slip indicator or turn coordinator be checked before flight? | Yes, while taxiing I will check that the ball moves to the outside of the turn freely in both directions. When taxiing straight, I want to verify that the miniature airplane stays level. |
| 257. | Can you test the attitude indicator immediately after starting your taxi in order to speed up your preflight checks? | Gyroscopes need a good 5 minutes to get up to speed and stabilize. I would not set my attitude indicator until then. |
| 258. | Once the gyro is up to speed, how would you check your attitude indicator? | I would set the alignment of the horizon bar and make sure that it remains steady. |
| 259. | How can you check your heading indicator during preflight? | After allowing the gyro to spin up and stabilize, I would set the attitude indicator and verify over the next few minutes that it agrees with the magnetic compass during our taxi operations. |
| 260. | Is there any check you can do for the magnetic compass? | Yes, I will verify that the compass is full of fluid and moving freely. I will also verify that it accurately reflects known headings while on the ground. |

| | | |
|---|---|---|
| 261. | How would you prepare and test a GPS unit for IFR flight? | I would verify that it is an IFR approved unit and that its database is current. Then I would follow the start-up and self-test procedures established by the manufacturer. |
| 262. | What is similar about testing both the ILS and ADF during preflight? | In both cases, I would tune to the appropriate frequency, identify if the appropriate unit is on the field, and verify a correct indication. |
| 263. | What is the mandated VOR accuracy check for IFR flight? | A VOR accuracy check must be performed and recorded within 30 days prior to the IFR flight. |
| 264. | What is the maximum allowable error when performing a VOR accuracy check? | Four degrees is the maximum allowable error for a VOR accuracy check when using a VOT, ground-based checkpoint or when comparing two VORs in the air. Six degrees is allowable for airborne checkpoints when checking a single VOR. |

## AREA OF OPERATION III: AIR TRAFFIC CONTROL CLEARANCES AND PROCEDURES

### Task A: Compliance with Air Traffic Control Clearances

| | | |
|---|---|---|
| 265. | What is a composite flight plan? | A composite flight plan is used when one portion of the flight will be conducted under instrument flight rules and another portion will be conducted under visual flight rules in VMC conditions. |
| 266. | On a flight with multiple planned altitudes, which altitude should be entered in block 7, cruising altitude, of an IFR flight plan? | The initial altitude requested should be entered into block 7 of an IFR flight plan. For flights with multiple planned altitudes, pilots should make subsequent requests directly to ATC. |
| 267. | On what portion of your flight should you base the time entered in block 10, time en-route, of an IFR flight plan? | Time en-route (block 10) should be based on the established arrival time at the point of first intended landing. |
| 268. | Based on which criteria would you select a cruising altitude for an IFR flight in Class G airspace? | When selecting a cruising altitude for an IFR flight in Class G airspace, the pilot should select an altitude based on published MOCA, MEA, and the magnetic course that will be flown to his or her destination. If the magnetic course is from 0° to 179°, the altitude must be odd thousands MSL (3,000, 5,000, etc.). If the magnetic course is from 180° to 359°, the altitude must be even thousands MSL (4,000, 6,000, etc.). |
| 269. | How can you determine how much fuel will be used for a given flight? | In order to determine the amount of fuel that will be used during a given flight, you must multiply the fuel consumption rate by the duration of the flight. |

| 270. | What are the minimum fuel requirements for flight under IFR? | If an alternate airport is not required, sufficient fuel must be carried to<br>1. Complete the flight to the first point of intended landing, and<br>2. Continue flight after that for 45 min. at normal cruise speed.<br>If an alternate is required, sufficient fuel must be carried to<br>1. Complete the flight to the first point of intended landing,<br>2. Continue flight from that airport to the alternate airport, and<br>3. Continue flight after that for 45 min. at normal cruise speed. |
|---|---|---|
| 271. | When is an IFR clearance required? | According to 14 CFR 91.173, no person may operate an aircraft in controlled airspace under IFR unless that person has filed an IFR flight plan and received an appropriate clearance. |
| 272. | What are the basic VFR visibility and cloud clearance minimums for Class B airspace? | 3 SM visibility, clear of clouds. |
| 273. | What are the basic VFR visibility and cloud clearance minimums for Class C airspace? | 3 SM visibility; 500 ft. below; 1,000 ft. above; 2,000 ft. horizontal. |
| 274. | What are the basic VFR visibility and cloud clearance minimums for Class D airspace? | 3 SM visibility; 500 ft. below; 1,000 ft. above; 2,000 ft. horizontal. |
| 275. | What are the basic VFR visibility and cloud clearance minimums for Class E airspace below 10,000 ft. MSL? | 3 SM visibility; 500 ft. below; 1,000 ft. above; 2,000 ft. horizontal. |
| 276. | What are the basic VFR visibility and cloud clearance minimums for Class E airspace at or above 10,000 ft. MSL? | 5 SM visibility; 1,000 ft. below; 1,000 ft. above; 1 SM horizontal. |
| 277. | What are the basic VFR visibility and cloud clearance minimums for Class G airspace at or below 1,200 ft. AGL? | Day: 1 SM visibility, Clear of clouds – Night: 3 SM visibility; 500 ft. below; 1,000 ft. above; 2,000 ft. horizontal. |
| 278. | What are the basic VFR visibility and cloud clearance minimums for Class G airspace above 1,200 ft. AGL but below 10,000 ft. MSL? | Day: 1 SM visibility; 500 ft. below; 1,000 ft. above; 2,000 ft. horizontal – Night: 3 SM visibility; 500 ft. below; 1,000 ft. above; 2,000 ft. horizontal. |
| 279. | What are the basic VFR visibility and cloud clearance minimums for Class G airspace at or above 10,000 ft. MSL? | 5 SM visibility; 1,000 ft. below; 1,000 ft. above; 1 SM horizontal. |

| 280. | What are the special VFR minimums? | Special VFR operations may be conducted only:<br>1. With an ATC clearance<br>2. Clear of clouds<br>3. With a flight visibility of at least 1 SM |
|---|---|---|
| 281. | May you operate under special VFR at night? | Operation under special VFR at night is prohibited unless the pilot is instrument rated and the aircraft is equipped for IFR flight. |
| 282. | What is the significance of a clearance void time? | When operating from an airport without an operating control tower, you may receive a clearance that contains a provision for your clearance to be void if you are not airborne by a certain time. If you depart at or after your clearance void time, you will not be afforded IFR separation and may be in violation of 14 CFR 91.173, which requires an ATC clearance prior to operating under IFR in controlled airspace. |
| 283. | When you transition from the VFR to the IFR portion of a composite flight plan, when must you cancel the VFR portion and obtain your IFR clearance? | When transitioning from the VFR to the IFR portion of a composite flight plan, you should contact the nearest FSS to close the VFR portion and request an IFR clearance either from the FSS or directly from ATC. |
| 284. | Under what conditions may you deviate from an ATC clearance? | Once given an ATC clearance, you may not deviate from it unless you obtain an amended clearance, an emergency exists, or the deviation is in response to a traffic alert and collision avoidance system (TCAS) resolution advisory. If you deviate from a clearance in an emergency or in response to a TCAS resolution advisory, you must notify ATC as soon as possible. If you are given priority by ATC in an emergency, you must submit a detailed report of the emergency within 48 hr. to the manager of that ATC facility if requested. |
| 285. | Is a VFR-on-top clearance a VFR clearance or an IFR clearance? | A VFR-on-top clearance is an IFR clearance in which the pilot is expected to maintain VFR while operating on an IFR flight plan. |
| 286. | When operating with a VFR-on-top clearance, do visual flight rules or instrument flight rules apply? | Both visual flight rules and instrument flight rules apply to a VFR-on-top clearance. |
| 287. | When operating with a VFR-on-top clearance, how should you select your cruising altitude? | You must comply with appropriate VFR cruising altitudes. |
| 288. | When flying VFR-on-top, can your altitude be below the minimum IFR altitude for your location? | No, your altitude must be at or above the minimum IFR altitude. |
| 289. | Are VFR-on-top operations allowed in Class A airspace? | VFR-on-top operations are prohibited in Class A airspace. |

## Task B: Holding Procedures

| 290. | Describe the components of a holding pattern. How is it typically flown? | Holding patterns are made up of the following components:<br>1. Holding fix–VOR, NDB, and Intersection/waypoint<br>2. Inbound leg<br>3. Outbound leg<br>4. Holding side (protected side)<br>5. Non-holding side<br>6. Fix end<br>7. Non-fix end<br><br>The holding pattern is a racetrack pattern (assuming no wind) in which a specified course is followed inbound to the holding fix followed by a 180° turn to fly a parallel course outbound. At the completion of the outbound leg, another 180° turn is made back to the inbound course to the holding fix. Each leg is typically 1 minute in length. |
|---|---|---|
| 291. | Which direction would the turns be made in when assigned to a standard holding pattern? | A standard holding pattern has all turns to the right. |
| 292. | Which direction would the turns be made in when assigned to a nonstandard holding pattern? | A nonstandard holding pattern has all turns to the left. |
| 293. | What are the three altitude blocks for which holding pattern speed limits have been established, and what are those speed limits? | The three altitude blocks and speeds are as follows:<br>1. From MHA through 6,000 ft.--200 kt.<br>2. From 6,001 ft. through 14,000 ft.--230 kt.<br>3. From 14,001 ft. and above--265 kt. |
| 294. | How many holding pattern entries are there? | There are three established holding pattern entries. |
| 295. | Describe the three types of holding pattern entries. | The three types of holding pattern entries are:<br>(1) Teardrop–Once you have crossed the holding fix, turn outbound to a heading (outbound heading minus 30E for a standard pattern or outbound heading plus 30E for a nonstandard pattern) for a 30E teardrop entry within the pattern (on the holding side) for a period of 1 min.; then turn in the direction of the holding pattern to intercept the inbound holding course. (2) Parallel– Once you have crossed the holding fix, turn to a heading to parallel the holding course outbound on the non-holding side for 1 min.; then turn opposite the direction of the holding pattern through more than 180E, and return to the holding fix or intercept the holding course inbound. (3) Direct–Once you have crossed the holding fix, turn to the outbound heading; at the completion of the specified leg length, turn to intercept the inbound course. |
| 296. | If a speed reduction is necessary when entering a holding pattern, when should the speed reduction take place? | Speed reductions should be initiated when 3 minutes or less from the holding fix. |

| | | |
|---|---|---|
| 297. | Is it mandatory that you enter a holding pattern with a specific hold entry? | No; as long as you do not leave the protected airspace, you can enter a holding pattern using any method you choose. But for safety and standardization, it is wise to use the appropriate hold entry when assigned a hold. |
| 298. | What is the most common hold entry to make? | Because it covers so many points on the compass, the direct entry is the most common. From 180° on the holding side of the fix, the direct entry makes the most sense. |
| 299. | What is the least common hold entry? | The teardrop entry is the preferred choice for a hold when approaching from only a 70° pie slice of sky. Because the teardrop is appropriate from such a small area, it is the least common. |
| 300. | How much wind correction should you apply on the outbound leg of a holding pattern if you had 5° of correction on the inbound leg? | Once you have determined the wind correction angle for the inbound leg, you should triple it when on the outbound leg in order to compensate for wind drift during the turns and on the straight legs. Thus, if you had a 5° wind correction angle during the inbound leg, you should have 15° of correction on the outbound leg. Note that wind correction should be made relative to the compass, not left or right (e.g., 5° and 15° west, not 5° and 15° left). |
| 301. | In order to obtain the desired performance on the inbound leg, how should you plan the timing of the outbound leg of the holding pattern? | You must adjust your outbound leg time to ensure that your inbound leg is 1 min. (at or below 14,000 ft. MSL) or 1.5 min. (above 14,000 ft. MSL).<br><br>1. One method to adjust your outbound leg timing is to double the inbound time deviation from the required time (e.g., 1 min.) and apply it to the outbound timing.<br>   a. If the inbound leg is 50 sec. (10 sec. short of the required 1 min.), double the deviation to 20 sec., and add it to the outbound time for a new time of 1 min. 20 sec.<br>   b. If the inbound leg is 1 min. 15 sec. (15 sec. more than the required 1 min.), double the deviation to 30 sec. and subtract it from the outbound time for a new time of 30 sec.<br>2. For excessive deviations from the required inbound time (e.g., 1 min.), other adjustments may be appropriate (e.g., equal to or half of the deviation added to outbound time).<br>   a. If the inbound leg is 2 min. (1 min. more than the required 1 min.), halve the 1-min. excess and subtract 30 sec. for a new outbound time of 30 sec.<br>3. Continue to make progressive adjustments until the correct outbound time is determined. |

| 302. | Under what conditions may timed approaches from a holding fix be conducted? | Timed approaches may be conducted only when the following conditions are met: 1. A control tower is in operation at the airport where the approach is to be conducted. 2. Communication is maintained between you and the center or approach controller until you are instructed to contact the tower. 3. If more than one missed approach procedure is available, none may require a course reversal. If only one missed approach procedure is available, the following conditions are met: a. Course reversal is not required. b. Reported ceiling and visibility are equal to or greater than the highest prescribed circling minimums for the IAP. |
|---|---|---|
| 303. | What is a minimum safe/sector altitude (MSA)? | An MSA is the altitude that guarantees obstacle clearance but not navigational coverage. |
| 304. | On what ground object is a minimum safe/sector altitude (MSA) normally based on? | The MSA is normally based on the primary facility on which the approach is predicated (VOR, NDB). |
| 305. | What are the normal dimensions of the area in which an MSA is applicable? | An MSA is normally applicable within a radius of 25 NM. |

## AREA OF OPERATION IV: FLIGHT BY REFERENCE TO INSTRUMENTS

### Task A: Instrument Flight

| 306. | When climbing, at what rate does ATC expect you to climb, unless otherwise authorized? | ATC expects all climbs and descents to be made at the optimum rate for the aircraft until it is within 1,000 ft. of the assigned altitude, at which point a rate of between 500 fpm and 1,500 fpm should be used. If at any time you are unable to climb or descend at a rate of at least 500 fpm, you must advise ATC. |
|---|---|---|
| 307. | When leveling off from a climb, what is the standard rule to determine by how many feet before the desired altitude you should lead the level-off? | Take 10% of your rate of climb and use that number as a lead factor to begin your level-off. Example: You are climbing at 500 fpm. You should begin your level-off 50 ft. before your desired altitude. |
| 308. | What does it mean when you are cleared to climb "at pilot's discretion?" | "Pilot's discretion" means ATC has offered you the option to begin climbing when you wish and to use any rate of climb desired. |
| 309. | What is the aircraft speed limit below 10,000 ft. MSL? | No person may operate an aircraft at an indicated airspeed that is greater than 250 kt. at an altitude below 10,000 ft. MSL. |
| 310. | What is the significance of primary vs. supporting instruments in attitude instrument flying? | For each phase of flight, primary and supporting instruments can be designated for the parameters of pitch, bank, and power. The concept of primary vs. supporting instruments in no way lessens the value of any instrument. Primary instruments are the ones that will show the greatest amount of useful information. |

| | | |
|---|---|---|
| 311. | When descending, at what rate does ATC expect you to descend, unless otherwise authorized? | ATC expects all climbs and descents to be made at the optimum rate for the aircraft until it is within 1,000 ft. of the assigned altitude, at which point a rate of between 500 fpm and 1,500 fpm should be used. If at any time you are unable to climb or descend at a rate of at least 500 fpm, you must advise ATC. |
| 312. | What does it mean when you are cleared to descend "at pilot's discretion?" | The term "pilot's discretion" means that ATC has offered you the option to begin descending when you wish and to use any rate of descent you desire. |
| 313. | When leveling off from a descent, what is the standard rule to determine by how many feet before the desired altitude you should lead the level-off? | Take 10% of your rate of descent and use that number as a lead factor to begin your level-off. Example: You are descending at 500 fpm. You should begin your level-off 50 ft. before your desired altitude. |
| 314. | What is a procedure turn? | A procedure turn (PT) is the maneuver prescribed when it is necessary to perform a course reversal in order to establish the aircraft inbound on an intermediate or final approach course. A typical procedure turn consists of two 45° turns in opposite directions, separated by a 180° turn. |
| 315. | What is the purpose of a procedure turn? | The purpose of a procedure turn is to establish the aircraft inbound on the approach course by means of a course reversal. |
| 316. | What is the significance of the symbol "NoPT" on an IAP chart? | The symbol "NoPT" on an IAP indicates that a procedure turn is neither required nor listed for that particular section of the IAP. |
| 317. | If you have been cleared for an approach and are established on a published segment of the approach, may you descend from your assigned altitude to the MEA of the segment of the published approach on which you are established, even if you are not specifically cleared to do so? | Yes; after being cleared for an approach, you should descend to the appropriate minimum altitude published on the IAP chart unless instructed by ATC to do otherwise. |
| 318. | What is the significance of the different aircraft approach categories? On what criterion is an aircraft's approach category based? | Different aircraft approach categories are established for fixed-wing aircraft based on final approach speeds, defined as 1.3 $V_{SO}$. As final approach speeds increase, TAP minimums also increase in order to allow sufficient room and/or time to safely complete a landing.<br><br>    Category A–90 kt. or less<br>    Category B–91 - 120 kt.<br>    Category C–121 - 140 kt.<br>    Category D–141 - 165 kt.<br>    Category E–Above 165 kt.<br><br>Aircraft approach speeds are based on an airspeed of 1.3 $V_{SO}$ (1.3 times the stalling speed of the aircraft in the landing configuration at maximum certificated gross landing weight). |

| 319. | How is an aircraft's approach speed determined? | Use the approach category that corresponds to the speed at which the approach will actually be flown (e.g., if 1.3 $V_{SO}$ is 80 kt. but the approach will be flown at 110 kt., use Category B). |
|---|---|---|
| 320. | If a Category A aircraft makes an approach at a Category B approach speed, which approach minimums (i.e., Category A or B) apply? | If you must fly an approach at a higher speed than normal, use the minimums for the approach category that correspond to your planned approach speed. |

*Task B: Recovery from Unusual Flight Attitudes*

| 321. | Can you give me a few examples of situations that might lead to an inadvertent unusual attitude in flight? | Turbulence, an instrument failure, or pilot disorientation could result in an unusual attitude. So could distraction, preoccupation with tasks other than airplane control, or a careless or casual attitude toward the task of flying the airplane. |
|---|---|---|
| 322. | In a nose-low attitude with a 30° bank, what are the first steps in the recovery procedure? | Reduce power to limit the buildup of speed, and level the wings before raising the nose to prevent excessive load factors and an inadvertent aggravated stall. |
| 323. | In a nose high unusual attitude, what are your first steps of recovery likely to be? | I would increase power and lower the nose to prevent a stall. Then I would level the wings and re-establish level flight. |
| 324. | How can proper trim techniques play a role in unusual attitudes? | Proper trim techniques can prevent the onset of unusual attitudes by lowering the pilot's workload and preventing unnecessarily large control inputs or loss of control due to fatigue. |
| 325. | When recovering from unusual attitudes by reference to instruments, what special concern do you have? | It is necessary to cross-check instrumentation to evaluate the situation before making control inputs. Initiating a recovery based on a single instrument may exacerbate the situation if the failure of that instrument was a link in the chain of events that led to the unusual attitude in the first place. |

# AREA OF OPERATION V: NAVIGATION SYSTEMS

*Task A: Intercepting and Tracking Navigational Systems and Arcs*

| 326. | What is a waypoint? | A waypoint is a geographical position determined by a radial and distance from a VOR/DME or a VORTAC station or in terms of latitude/longitude coordinates. |
|---|---|---|
| 327. | Explain how you would intercept a particular VOR radial. | In order to intercept a particular radial, twist the OBS until the radial appears under the top index (if tracking outbound) or the bottom index (if tracking inbound). Note the direction of needle deflection and turn to a heading that is no more then 90° to the left or right of the number under the top index, depending on where the needle is deflected (i.e., turn toward the needle). When the needle begins to move toward center, gradually turn back toward the heading shown under the top index. |

| | | |
|---|---|---|
| 328. | What is bracketing? | Bracketing is a method used to determine the correct heading to fly in order to track a course when a cross wind exists. This method is also referred to as a trial and error method. |
| 329. | Operationally, what is the difference between a VOR, a VOR/DME, and a VORTAC? | VORTACs and VOR/DME stations provide azimuth and range information, while VORs provide only azimuth information. |
| 330. | How do you determine on what radial you are located relative to a given VOR station using a standard VOR indicator or an HSI? | Using a VOR and HSI, center the CDI needle with a FROM indication and read the radial under the top index. |
| 331. | How do you determine on what radial you are located relative to a given VOR station using an RMI? | The magnetic bearing needle should be centered. Then, look at the heading to find out what radial you are on in correlation to the station. |
| 332. | How do you identify an intersection of two VOR radials? | It is best to use two VOR receivers when identifying two radials. Tune each receiver to a different station, each with the desired radial selected. When both needles center, you have reached the intersection. |
| 333. | How do you identify an intersection of a VOR radial and an NDB bearing? | When the CDI needle is centered on the desired radial, and the head of the ADF indicator is pointed to the appropriate bearing TO or FROM the station, you have reached the intersection. |
| 334. | What is the difference between homing and tracking? | Tracking involves flying a straight path to the desired station by correcting for wind drift. Homing involves flying to the station by keeping the nose of the airplane pointed at the station at all times, ignoring wind drift. The resultant path to the station is curved. |
| 335. | Explain how you would intercept a particular NDB bearing. | Begin by turning to the magnetic heading corresponding to the desired bearing. Note the bearing indicated by the needle; the station (and therefore, the desired bearing) lies toward the head of the needle. Establish an intercept angle that is no greater than 90°. When the desired magnetic bearing is indicated, turn inbound and track the bearing to the station. |
| 336. | How should you verify that the navigational facility you are using is the desired facility and that it is operational? | Each navigational aid has its own specific Morse code identifier. The correct Morse code is shown on each chart in the navigational aid information box. Monitor the identification feature of your navigation radios briefly in order to identify each station. |
| 337. | How do you identify station passage using a VOR? | Station passage of a VOR occurs when the TO/FROM flag changes its indication (e.g., TO changes to FROM). |
| 338. | How do you identify station passage using an ADF? | When station passage occurs, the ADF needle turns 180° to indicate the station is now behind you. |

## Task B: Departure, En route and Arrival Operations

| | | |
|---|---|---|
| 339. | What documents must be aboard an aircraft when it is being operated? | Use the acronym **ARROW**. You must have on board the<br><br>**A**irworthiness Certificate,<br>**R**adio Station license,<br>**R**egistration Certificate,<br>**O**perating limitations, and<br>**W**eight and balance data. |
| 340. | What information will be included in an IFR departure clearance? | An IFR clearance will always contain at least the following items, indicated by the acronym **CRAFT**:<br><br>**C**leared to?<br>**R**oute<br>**A**ltitude<br>**F**requency<br>**T**ransponder code<br><br>You may find it helpful to write CRAFT vertically on your notepad before requesting your clearance and then fill in the information as it comes. Note that some of these items may be contained in a departure procedure (DP). |
| 341. | How can you obtain your departure clearance at a controlled field? | At a controlled airfield in Class B or C airspace, departure clearances can be obtained on the clearance delivery frequency. In Class D airspace or in Class E or G airspace at an airport with an operating control tower, departure clearances are usually obtained on either the ground control or tower frequency. |
| 342. | How can you obtain a departure clearance at an uncontrolled field? | At an airport without an operating control tower, a departure clearance can be obtained by contacting the nearest FSS by telephone or radio before takeoff. These clearances may have a void time. |
| 343. | What does it mean when your departure clearance indicates that you are "cleared as filed?" | The phrase "cleared as filed" indicates that the route of flight that is listed on your flight plan can be issued with little or no revision. |
| 344. | Are you required to accept a departure procedure (DP) if one is assigned by ATC? | Pilots may refuse a DP when it is issued as part of a clearance. |
| 345. | How can you avoid being assigned a DP? | You can avoid a DP by including the notation "No DP" in the remarks section of your flight plan. |
| 346. | What is the purpose of DPs? | DPs are issued to simplify clearance delivery procedures when deemed appropriate by ATC. |
| 347. | What must you possess in order to accept a DP? | You must possess at least a textual description of the procedure in order to accept a DP. |
| 348. | What is the standard minimum climb gradient for a DP? | The standard minimum climb gradient for a DP is at least 200 feet per nautical mile unless the DP specifies a higher climb gradient or a crossing restriction has been issued by ATC. |

| | | |
|---|---|---|
| 349. | Are there takeoff minimums for operations under Part 91? | Except when nonstandard takeoff minimums apply as noted on the approach chart, there are none for 14 CFR Part 91. |
| 350. | What is a good self-imposed (i.e., non-regulatory) policy regarding the minimum conditions you should consider acceptable for takeoff? | Using the minimums for the illustrated approach at the airport from which you are departing provides safe conditions for returning to the departed airport in case of an emergency. |
| 351. | What is wake turbulence, and under what conditions is it strongest? | Wake turbulence is the violent disruption of the air as an object passes through it. It is worst when the aircraft is heavy, clean, and slow, such as just after takeoff. |
| 352. | Where should you plan to lift off when departing behind a large aircraft which has just landed on the same runway? | Plan to depart beyond the point where the nose wheel of the large aircraft touched down. |
| 353. | When departing behind a large aircraft that has just taken off on the same runway? | Plan to depart prior to the large aircraft's departure point and stay above its flight path. |
| 354. | What is an ILS critical area? | Aircraft that are on the ground in close proximity to localizer/glide slope transmitters can cause signal interference. The area in which interference is likely to occur is called the ILS critical area. |
| 355. | During ground operations, how can you be sure that you are not inside an ILS critical area? | A taxiway marking will indicate where to stop and wait if instructed, to avoid crossing into an ILS critical area. The marking includes parallel yellow lines that cross the taxiway. Short parallel bars connect the two longer lines. |
| 356. | Describe runway hold-short lines and signs. | Runway holding position markings indicate where an aircraft is supposed to stop. They consist of four yellow lines, two solid and two dashed, extending across the width of the taxiway or runway. The solid yellow lines are always on the side where the aircraft is to hold. In addition to markings painted on the taxiway, there are also runway holding position signs. These have a red background with white numbers identifying the runways. The numbers are arranged to reflect the direction of each runway's threshold. For example, a sign that shows 15-33 indicates that the threshold of Runway 15 is to the left, and the threshold of Runway 33 is to the right. |
| 357. | What color are runway lights? | Runway edge lights are white, except that on instrument runways yellow replaces white on the last 2,000 ft. or half the runway length, whichever is less. Runway centerline lights are white until the last 3,000 ft. of the runway. Then they alternate red and white until 1,000 ft. from the end of the runway. For the last 1,000 ft. of the runway, all lights are red. |
| 358. | What special signs are visible on the runway? | Runway distance remaining signs, which indicate the remaining runway distance in thousands of feet, are seen only on the runways. |

| | | |
|---|---|---|
| 359. | If you are climbing in VFR conditions, who is responsible for maintaining separation between your aircraft and other traffic? | You, as the pilot in command, are responsible to see and avoid other aircraft while in VFR conditions. |
| 360. | What is a minimum en route altitude (MEA)? | A minimum en route altitude (MEA) is the lowest published altitude between radio fixes that assures acceptable navigational signal coverage along the entire route segment and meets obstacle clearance requirements between those fixes. |
| 361. | What is a minimum obstruction clearance altitude (MOCA)? | A minimum obstruction clearance altitude (MOCA) is the lowest published altitude in effect between radio fixes on VOR airways, off-airways, or route segments that meets obstacle clearance requirements for the entire route segment and that assures acceptable navigational signal coverage only within 25 SM (22 NM) of a VOR. |
| 362. | What is a minimum reception altitude (MRA)? | A minimum reception altitude (MRA) is the lowest altitude at which an intersection can be determined. |
| 363. | What information is found on en route low altitude charts? | The following items are depicted on en route low altitude charts:<br>1. Airways<br>2. Limit of controlled airspace<br>3. VHF radio aids to navigation (frequency, identification, and geographic coordinates)<br>4. Airports that have an IAP or a minimum 3,000 ft. hard surface runway<br>5. Off-route obstruction clearance altitudes (OROCAs)<br>6. Reporting points<br>7. Special-use airspace<br>8. Military training routes (MTRs) |
| 364. | What is a changeover point? | A changeover point (COP) is a point along the route or airway segment between two adjacent navigation facilities or waypoints where changeover in navigation guidance should occur. The COP is usually located midway between the navigation facilities for straight route segments, or at the intersection of radials or courses forming a dogleg in the case of dogleg route segments. |
| 365. | How is a changeover point depicted on en route charts? | When a COP must be located at some other point due to terrain or other considerations, it is indicated by a roughly "S"-shaped symbol consisting of a long line that is perpendicular to the route segments with two shorter lines extending from either end, parallel to the route segment and in opposite directions. The distance from the COP to each facility is shown above and below the shorter lines, which point to each facility. |

| | | |
|---|---|---|
| 366. | If no MEA is published for your route of flight, what is the minimum prescribed altitude for operating an aircraft under IFR in non-mountainous areas? | For off-airways or direct routes in non-mountainous areas, you are required to maintain an altitude of at least 1,000 ft. above the highest obstacle within 4 NM of the centerline of your intended course. |
| 367. | If no MEA is published for your route of flight, what is the minimum prescribed altitude for operating an aircraft under IFR in mountainous areas? | For off-airways or direct routes in mountainous areas, you are required to maintain an altitude of at least 2,000 ft. above the highest obstacle within 4 NM of the centerline of your intended course. |
| 368. | May you operate below the published MEA prescribed for your route? If so, when? | Assuming proper ATC authorization, you may operate below the MEA only when there is also a MOCA prescribed for the route segment. In this circumstance, you may operate below the MEA down to the MOCA when you are within 22 NM of the VOR. |
| 369. | What is a cruise clearance? | A cruise clearance assigns the pilot a block of airspace from the minimum IFR altitude up to and including the prescribed altitude (e.g., cruise 6,000). |
| 370. | Are you required to accept a standard terminal arrival route (STAR) if one is assigned by ATC? | Pilots may refuse a STAR when it is issued as part of a clearance. |
| 371. | How can you avoid being assigned a STAR? | By including the notation "no STAR" in the remarks section of your flight plan, ATC will be notified that you do not wish to be assigned a STAR. |
| 372. | What is the purpose of a STAR? | STARs are issued to simplify clearance delivery procedures when deemed appropriate by ATC. |
| 373. | What must you possess to accept a STAR? | In order to accept a STAR, you must possess at least a textual description of the procedure. |
| 374. | What is the difference between a visual approach and a contact approach? | A visual approach can be assigned by ATC, while a contact approach must be requested by the pilot. |
| 375. | Can a contact approach be assigned by ATC? | No; a contact approach must be requested by the pilot. |
| 376. | What are the four segments of an instrument approach procedure (IAP)? | The four segments of an instrument approach are:<br>1. Initial approach segment<br>2. Intermediate approach segment<br>3. Final approach segment<br>4. Missed approach segment |
| 377. | What is a feeder route? | Feeder routes (also called transition routes), while not technically approach segments, may be depicted on an IAP chart to designate routes that may be used to proceed from the en route structure to the IAF. |
| 378. | What is an initial approach fix (IAF)? | An initial approach fix is a set point where a particular approach is to begin. There may be several IAFs for one approach. |

| 379. | What is a final approach fix (FAF)? | The FAF is the point of the approach where the aircraft should be configured to land. On a precision approach, the FAF is the glide slope intercept point. The final approach point is the point where the aircraft is established inbound on the final approach course after completion of the procedure turn and where descent to the MDA may be commenced. |
|---|---|---|
| 380. | What is the difference between a final approach fix (FAF) and a final approach point? | A final approach fix is a specific fix defined relative to a NAVAID or GPS waypoint at which descent to the MDA should be commenced. A final approach point is found on a VOR or NDB IAP with no depicted FAF (such as an on-airport VOR or NDB) and is designated only by completion of the procedure turn inbound. |
| 381. | What transponder code is appropriate for an aircraft that has lost radio communication? | Aircraft that experience a loss of radio communications should squawk 7600. |
| 382. | What report, if any, must be made to ATC in the event that a navigation or communication radio fails? | As soon as practicable, the pilot in command must report the following:<br>1. Aircraft I.D.<br>2. Equipment affected<br>3. Degree to which the capability of the pilot to operate under IFR in the ATC system is impaired<br>4. Nature and extent of assistance desired from ATC |
| 383. | What are the procedures for dealing with a loss of radio communications in IMC? | Loss of communications in IMC conditions.<br>1. Route (first that applies):<br>  a. By the route assigned in the last ATC clearance received;<br>  b. If being radar vectored, by the direct route from the point of radio failure to the fix, route, or airway specified in the vector clearance;<br>  c. In the absence of an assigned route, by the route that ATC has advised may be expected in a further clearance; or<br>  d. The route filed on the flight plan.<br>2. Altitude (highest of the following):<br>  a. The altitude of flight level assigned in the last clearance,<br>  b. Minimum IFR altitude, or<br>  c. Expected altitude. |
| 384. | What are the procedures for dealing with a loss of radio communications on an instrument flight plan in VMC? | Pilots experiencing a loss of radio communications in VMC or pilots encountering VMC following a loss of communications in IMC should continue the flight under VFR and land as soon as practicable to notify ATC of the situation. |

# AREA OF OPERATION VI: INSTRUMENT APPROACH PROCEDURES

## Task A: Nonprecision Approach

| 385. | What minimum weather conditions must be forecast at your selected alternate airport, which has a non precision approach, for it to be acceptable as an alternate? | Ceiling 800 ft. Visibility 2 SM. |
|---|---|---|
| 386. | What does the phrase, "minimum descent altitude (MDA)" mean? | A minimum descent altitude (MDA) is the lowest altitude to which descent is authorized on the final approach segment of a nonprecision approach without adequate visual reference for landing. |
| 387. | What is a visual descent point (VDP)? | A visual descent point is a defined point of the final approach course on a nonprecision, straight-in approach from which a normal descent from the MDA to the runway may begin, provided that the required visual reference is established. |
| 388. | Name and describe several types of nonprecision approaches. | VOR approach: An approach with the course guidance based on a specific radial and often requiring a course reversal (procedure turn or holding pattern). <br><br> NDB approach: An approach with the course guidance based on a specific bearing and often requiring a course reversal (procedure turn or holding pattern). <br><br> GPS approach: An approach based on courses flown between GPS waypoints. These approaches are designed to be flown as depicted, and it is unlikely that aircraft will be vectored onto the final approach course. <br><br> LOC approach: An approach with the course guidance provided by a localizer. This signal provides you with guidance along the runway centerline. |
| 389. | Explain the procedures for flying a typical nonprecision approach that incorporates a procedure turn. | Typical procedures for flying a nonprecision approach that incorporates a procedure turn involve proceeding to the initial approach fix (IAF), heading outbound from the IAF on the reciprocal of the inbound approach course, performing a procedure turn in order to re-intercept the approach course inbound, and descending to the appropriate intermediate and minimum descent altitudes as depicted on the IAP chart. |
| 390. | What are the differences between a simplified directional facility (SDF), a localizer-type directional aid (LDA), and a standard localizer (LOC)? | The differences between the three facilities are <br><br> SDF: Course width of 6° OR 12°. SDF does not have glide slope information. <br><br> LDA: Similar to an LOC, but NOT aligned with the runway. Also, LDA may have a glide slope. <br><br> LOC: Course width of 3° to 6° and aligned with the runway. ILS combines a LOC with glide slope information. |

| | | |
|---|---|---|
| 391. | What methods can be used to define/determine the missed approach point (MAP) for a nonprecision approach? | The MAP can be identified by an intersection, a DME fix, or the NAVAID (VOR or NDB) itself, or it may be determined by time from the FAF. |
| 392. | If you break out of the clouds at the minimum descent altitude (MDA) for a nonprecision approach to a runway with a visual approach slope indicator (VASI) system and you are below the glide slope, what should you do? | You should momentarily level off to intercept the proper glide path. |

### Task B: Precision Approach

| | | |
|---|---|---|
| 393. | What minimum weather conditions must be forecast at your selected alternate airport, which has a precision approach, for it to be acceptable as an alternate? | Ceiling 600 ft. Visibility 2 SM. |
| 394. | What does the term "decision altitude" mean? | A decision altitude (DA) is the height at which a decision must be made on an ILS or PAR approach regarding whether to continue the approach or execute a missed approach. |
| 395. | Explain the procedures for flying a typical precision approach that involves radar vectors to the final approach course. | Typical procedures for flying a precision approach involve being assisted or requesting "vectors to final," which will greatly reduce your workload. Set the inbound course for the approach under the index of a standard VOR indicator as a reminder or of an HSI to insure proper CDI sensing. The controller will provide vectors to enable you to intercept the inbound course with sufficient distance before the FAF to allow a stabilized approach. |
| 396. | Name and describe two types of precision approaches. | A precision approach radar (PAR) approach is one in which a controller provides you with highly accurate navigational guidance in azimuth (runway centerline) and elevation (glide slope). An ILS is a precision approach that uses paired localizer and glide slope transmitters to provide accurate lateral and descent path guidance. The pilot must keep the localizer and glide slope needles accurately centered. |
| 397. | Describe precision instrument runway markings. What is their purpose? | Precision instrument runway markings consist of all markings found on a nonprecision runway plus touchdown zone markings and fixed-distance markings. Touchdown zone markings provide aiming points for aircraft. They are spaced at 500 ft. intervals. The touchdown zone markings and fixed-distance markings inform the pilot of the amount of runway distance remaining. |

| 398. | If you find yourself two dots off the localizer as you approach DA, but the runway is still not in sight, what is your best course of action? | I would make a slight correction in the direction of the localizer and continue with my approach. I do not want to make a dramatic maneuver during an approach that might adversely affect safety or impede my ability to transition to a landing if I were to break out of the clouds. |

### Task C: Missed Approach

| 399. | What is a missed approach point (MAP)? | The missed approach point is the point at which the pilot must have the runway in sight or perform the prescribed missed approach procedures. |
| 400. | Where is the missed approach point on an instrument landing system (ILS) approach? | The MAP on an ILS approach is reached when the aircraft arrives at the decision height (DH) with the glide slope needle centered. |
| 401. | When would it be appropriate to familiarize yourself with the missed approach procedure and get set up for it? | Because the missed approach point or decision altitude is reached at a low altitude with no landing possible, it is imperative that I familiarize myself with the missed approach procedure before I initiate the approach and get set up to be ready to perform the missed approach procedure before I reach the missed approach point or decision altitude. |
| 402. | What would cause you to execute a missed approach? | One of two situations will result in a missed approach being necessary. Either I will shoot the approach properly but find the weather conditions do not allow for a safe landing, or I will need to go missed because I did not maintain the lateral or vertical limits during the approach. |
| 403. | Under what circumstances is obstacle clearance assured during a missed approach? | Only when the missed approach is commenced at the published missed approach point or above the DA. |
| 404. | Where is the entire missed approach procedure listed for a given approach? | The full textual description of the missed approach procedure is included in the pilot briefing section, at the top of the approach plate. |
| 405. | When initiating a missed approach, what information should you transmit to ATC? | I would make a radio call notifying ATC that I am going missed on the approach and give them the reason why. This might mean my call is "Cessna 12345 going missed, runway environment is not in sight." or "Cessna 12345 going missed after losing the localizer." |
| 406. | If you initiated a missed approach before reaching the MAP or DA, would it be permissible to initiate a turn right away? | I would continue to fly the approach course at or above MDA or DA until I reached the missed approach point, then I would initiate a turn if one was called for in the missed approach procedure. |
| 407. | Is there any circumstance that would cause you to ignore the missed approach procedure after going missed? | I would fly the missed approach procedure unless ATC instructed me to do otherwise. In that case, I would comply with ATC's instructions. |

## Task D: Circling Approach

| 408. | What is a circling approach? | A circling approach is an approach technique that allows an aircraft to maneuver to land on a runway that does not meet the criteria for a straight in approach. |
|---|---|---|
| 409. | Is there adequate obstacle clearance when performing a circling approach? | A minimum of 300 feet obstacle clearance is provided in the circling segment. However, there may be limitations on circling approaches because of the inability to provide sufficient obstacle clearance. In that case, a procedural note will be included on the approach plate specifying that circling approaches are not allowed in a particular area of the airport environment. |
| 410. | Is obstacle clearance guaranteed for all aircraft within the circling approach area? | Aircraft shooting the approach in higher speed categories may not be able to maneuver in such a way as to remain within the circling approach area throughout the approach. The PIC is responsible for verifying that the flight can remain within the approach area and ensuring obstacle clearance throughout the approach procedure. |
| 411. | When is it permissible to descend below the circling minimum altitude? | A pilot can descend below the circling minimum altitude only when the airplane is in a position where a normal descent to landing can be made to the intended runway. |

## Task E: Landing from an Instrument Approach

| 412. | What physical activity should be avoided during landing? | Sudden head movements can induce disorientation and should be avoided during the landing phase of the flight. |
|---|---|---|
| 413. | What illusion might you suffer from if you encountered haze on the final approach segment? | Haze can create the illusion of being higher over the runway or farther away than it might appear. This can lead to an inadvertently low approach. |
| 414. | How is resource management important during landing? | A pilot's workload is relatively high during landing. Good use of resource management skills can reduce that workload and the associated stress to make the process of transitioning from flight to landing safer. |
| 415. | In order to let down below your MDA or DA, you have to have something in sight. Can you tell me what that is? | Actually, you can descend below MDA or DA if at least one of several things is in sight. That would include the approach light system; the threshold, threshold markings, or threshold lights; the VASI or REILs; the touchdown zone lights or markings; or the runway lights or markings. |
| 416. | Are there any limitations on the position of the aircraft prior to a descent for landing? | Yes, the aircraft has to be continuously in a position that allows for a descent to landing on the intended runway using a normal descent rate and normal maneuvers. |
| 417. | Is there any other requirement in order to transition from the approach to a landing? | Yes, the flight visibility cannot be less than is prescribed for the approach being used. |

| 418. | Who or what is the ultimate authority on whether the flight visibility meets the minimums published for the approach? | The PIC is the one responsible for making the ultimate determination about flight visibility, although ATC may provide significant assistance in the form of the latest weather data available. |
|---|---|---|
| 419. | If shooting a circling approach, what concern do you have when you break out of the clouds and prepare to land? | It is necessary to remain clear of clouds and maintain a visual on the runway environment throughout a circling approach. If the runway is in sight, but the conditions may not allow me to keep it in sight throughout the landing phase of the approach, I need to execute a missed approach. |
| 420. | Given a ceiling at or near the DA on an ILS approach, if the airplane ahead of you reports the runway environment in sight and makes a landing, does that suggest you will have the same experience? | Not necessarily. The weather is constantly changing; it can even change to some degree over the course of a minute or two. With ceilings that low, I should shoot the approach with the possibility of a missed approach being necessary as part of my thought process. There is no guarantee that I will break out at the same altitude the pilot ahead of me did. |
| 421. | If shooting an approach into an uncontrolled airport, is the ATC clearance to shoot the approach also a clearance to land? | No, ATC is not authorizing a landing when they clear me for the approach. It is my responsibility to monitor the CTAF for the uncontrolled field, ascertain whether there is other traffic in the pattern, and perform adequate collision avoidance techniques as I transition into the airspace. |

## AREA OF OPERATION VII: EMERGENCY OPERATIONS

### Task A: Loss of Communications

| 422. | Where would I find information about what is expected if I were to lose radio communications while on an IFR flight plan? | 14 CFR 91.185 specifically pertains to two-way radio communication failure for IFR operations. |
|---|---|---|
| 423. | What route would you fly if you lost two-way radio communications en route while on an IFR flight plan? | I would fly the route that was assigned in my last ATC clearance. |
| 424. | If no route was assigned in the last ATC clearance, what route would you fly following two-way radio communications failure? | I would fly the route that was filed in my flight plan. |
| 425. | If ATC had cleared you to 6,000 feet, with an expected further clearance to 8,000 feet, what altitude would you fly for the route segment you were on in the event of communications failure? | The Federal Aviation Regulations tell me to fly the highest of the altitudes cleared, or expected to be cleared, for the segment I am on. With that in mind, I would climb and maintain 8,000 feet as ATC suggested would be my further clearance. |
| 426. | If radio failure occurs before arriving at a clearance limit where an approach can be initiated, when would you begin your approach? | I would begin my approach at the expect further clearance time, if one was given. If no EFC time was given, I would begin my approach based on my estimated time of arrival as filed or as amended en route. |

| 427. | If the clearance limit is not a fix where an approach can be initiated from, when would you depart the clearance limit in order to shoot an approach at your destination? | I would either leave at the expect further clearance time or, if an EFC time was not given, I would continue past the clearance limit in order to commence descent and make my approach as close to my filed or amended estimated time of arrival time as possible. |
|---|---|---|
| 428. | How would you indicate to ATC that you had a two-way communications failure? | Once I had verified that I had a failure and was unable to communicate with ATC, I would set my transponder code to 7600, in the hopes that they would receive that signal and recognize that I was unable to contact them by radio. |
| 429. | Is there any circumstance that would make a deviation from your IFR flight plan a reasonable choice? | Yes. If an emergency exists, or in the event of a collision avoidance alert, I am permitted to deviate from my clearance. I might also decide to deviate from my flight plan if the aircraft suffered a two-way communications failure and I encountered VFR conditions that would allow me to deviate and land safely at an airport other than my intended destination. |
| 430. | If you are flying on an IFR flight plan when you lose two-way communications, but encounter VFR conditions, should you continue on the IFR flight plan as filed or revert to VFR? | 14 CFR 91.185 specifies that, if I am in VFR conditions when the failure occurs or if I encounter VFR conditions after the failure occurs, I should continue the flight under VFR and land as soon as practicable. |
| 431. | If you were to complete the flight under VFR and land safely, what task do you need to perform as soon as possible after landing? | I need to contact ATC to close my IFR flight plan. Even if I squawk 1200 on my transponder for the VFR portion of the flight, ATC will maintain my IFR flight plan until I cancel it. |
| 432. | Are there regulations that provide specific guidance on the topic of deviating from a clearance? | 14 CFR 91.123 specifies that a pilot cannot deviate from a clearance unless an amended clearance is obtained, an emergency exists, or the deviation is in response to a traffic alert and collision avoidance system resolution advisory. |
| 433. | If you deviate from your flight plan, even if that deviation is in response to a two-way communications failure, what responsibility do you have in relation to ATC? | I am required to advise ATC as soon as possible. In the event I am able to navigate by VFR, I would need to land at the first opportunity in order to contact ATC by phone to cancel my IFR flight plan and acknowledge that I deviated from my clearance in response to the communication failure. |

## Task B: One Engine Inoperative during Straight-and-Level Flight and Turns (AMEL, AMES)

| 434. | When an engine fails in instrument conditions, how will you determine which engine failed? Will the engine instruments be used? | The only way to properly determine which engine has failed is to note the rudder pressure required to maintain straight-and-level flight. Remember, "dead leg, dead engine." The leg that is not applying rudder pressure represents the engine that has failed.<br><br>The engine instruments are misleading and cannot be relied on to accurately determine which engine has failed. |
|---|---|---|

| | | |
|---|---|---|
| 435. | Why is it important to feather the propeller on the engine that has failed? | The windmilling propeller produces large amounts of drag. Most light twins will not generate the performance required to climb with one engine inoperative unless the propeller on the failed engine is feathered. |
| 436. | Is there a need to verify the failed engine in instrument conditions? It may be best to feather the windmilling prop as quickly as possible if it has such a negative impact on performance. | Yes. I will always verify the failed engine prior to feathering any propellers. Feathering the wrong propeller would lead to a complete loss of performance and a certain accident. |
| 437. | How will you verify a failed engine? | I will advance both mixture levers to full rich. I will then advance both propeller levers to the full forward position. Next, I will advance both throttles to the full forward position. At that point, I will reduce the throttle on the engine that I believe has failed to idle. If performance is unaffected, I will know I have correctly identified the failed engine. I will bring the propeller lever for the failed engine to the feather detente and then bring the mixture setting on the failed engine to the idle cut-off position. At that point, I will complete any items recommended by the POH/AFM and complete the appropriate checklists. |
| 438. | Once one of the engines has failed, what airspeed will you attempt to establish? | I will attempt to establish $V_{YSE}$. |
| 439. | How will you determine $V_{YSE}$ for the type of aircraft you are flying today? | $V_{YSE}$ is depicted by a blue line on the airspeed indicator. I could also consult the POH/AFM to determine $V_{YSE}$. |
| 440. | Does the instrument ACS require a multi-engine pilot to determine the reason for the engine failure? | It does, but not at the expense of aircraft control. The airplane's altitude, heading, and speed must all stay within ACS standards. |

### Task C: Instrument Approach and Landing with an Inoperative Engine (Simulated) (AMEL, AMES)

| | | |
|---|---|---|
| 441. | What are the appropriate ACS for a one-engine-inoperative instrument approach? | I must maintain my specified altitude within ±100 feet; airspeed within ±10 knots; and, if within the aircraft's capability, the heading within ±10°. |
| 442. | The loss of an engine on approach sounds like a dangerous situation. Is it possible that the PIC can operate the aircraft contrary to the manufacturer's operating limitations to ensure the flight arrives safely on the ground? | No. The PIC must always observe the manufacturer's limitations. The ACS mandates that the PIC avoid a loss of aircraft control and flight contrary to the operating limitations of the aircraft during a single-engine approach. |
| 443. | What are the ACS for the final approach segment on a one-engine-inoperative instrument approach? | I will allow no more than 3/4 scale deflection of the localizer, glideslope, or GPS indications or within ±10° or 3/4 scale deflection of the nonprecision final approach course. |

| 444. | Is single-pilot resource management a consideration on a one-engine-inoperative instrument approach? | Not only is it a consideration, it is a requirement of the ACS. Single-pilot resource management and decision-making processes must always be taken into account regardless of the situation. My instructor has prepared me well for this eventuality by applying carefully selected and thought-provoking scenarios to my training that replicate engine failures and force me to use the 3P and DECIDE models in simulated real-world environments. |
|---|---|---|

### Task D: Approach with Loss of Primary Flight Instrument Indicators

| 445. | How can you verify that your flight instruments are working correctly during an approach? | I can verify that my instruments are working properly by consistently cross-checking primary and supporting instruments throughout my approach to be sure they provide valid information. |
|---|---|---|
| 446. | If you suspect or can verify that an instrument is failing, what must you do as soon as possible? | I am required by regulation to report the failure to ATC as soon as possible. |
| 447. | When reporting an instrument failure to ATC, what information are you required to provide? | I am required to identify the aircraft and equipment that is affected by the failure. I am also required to advise ATC about the degree of impact the failure has on my ability to operate under IFR and indicate the type of assistance I need from ATC in response to the failure. |
| 448. | How would you determine whether the heading indicator is accurate during an approach? | I can cross-check the heading indicator against the magnetic compass, the attitude indicator, and the turn coordinator. If one instrument shows a turn in progress but the others show no turn, I can isolate the malfunctioning instrument and disregard the erroneous information it is providing. |
| 449. | Why is it important to cross-check the heading indicator to multiple instruments rather than just with the attitude indicator? | Both the heading indicator and the attitude indicator are powered pneumatically by the vacuum system. It is possible that both would indicate a similar error, which might lead me to believe they were accurate when they weren't. By cross-checking a pneumatic system with an electrically driven gyro and the magnetic compass, I can more easily and accurately identify a failure should one occur. |
| 450. | How would you identify an airspeed indicator failure? | The airspeed indicator can be cross-checked with the power setting, the attitude indicator, and the VSI. By being familiar with power settings for cruise, climb, and descent, and knowing what the appropriate pitch attitude and anticipated performance should be, I can judge the accuracy of the airspeed indicator to a reasonable degree. |
| 451. | What instruments would you use to verify the accuracy of the attitude indicator? | The turn coordinator, heading indicator, and magnetic compass would cross-check the bank information, while the altimeter, airspeed, and VSI can support the pitch information. |

| | | |
|---|---|---|
| 452. | How can the airspeed indicator support the pitch information provided by the attitude indicator? | If the attitude indicator is improperly set or failing, the airspeed indicator will show either an increase or decrease in airspeed when the attitude indicator shows level flight. The VSI can support that information because the trend will become apparent if the aircraft is actually climbing or descending, even if only gradually. |
| 453. | What instrumentation can you use to verify power settings? | The tachometer, manifold pressure, fuel flow, and airspeed indicators all give an indication of power. If one of these instruments fails, the others can provide reasonably accurate information to the pilot. |
| 454. | Assuming you have a glass panel and the loss of that instrumentation, can you continue under IFR and shoot the approach at your destination? | Probably not. The majority of glass panel aircraft have redundancy in the form of analog versions of the airspeed indicator, attitude indicator, altimeter, and a magnetic compass. Those few instruments would make it possible to fly in IFR with guidance from ATC, but precise navigation during an approach would be extremely difficult. The better choice following a failure of the glass panel displays would be to request vectors to VMC in order to land at an alternate airport under VFR. |
| 455. | What pilot-induced error could cause a complete failure of your glass panel displays during an approach? | If I was to inadvertently switch off the avionics master switch, it would kill the glass panel displays immediately. A pilot must be aware of that potential and be on guard not to make that error as the workload rises during an approach. |
| 456. | If turning the avionics master switch off will kill your glass panel displays, won't turning it back on again restore them? | Yes and no. Turning the avionics master switch on again will restore power to the glass panel displays, but it will take 3 to 5 minutes for the system to fully boot up and become usable. |
| 457. | If a glass panel display failure should occur on the approach, what would you do? | I would execute a missed approach using the redundant back-up gauges and alert ATC to my need for vectors in order to maintain separation while my glass panels reboot and become functional again. |

## AREA OF OPERATION VIII: POSTFLIGHT PROCEDURES

### Task A: Checking Instruments and Equipment

| | | |
|---|---|---|
| 458. | What is the proper method of powering down the various communication and navigation equipment installed in the aircraft at the conclusion of a flight? | In some older aircraft with limited equipment, it may be necessary to power down each unit individually. Most aircraft equipped for instrument flight include an avionics master switch, however. We would follow the shut-down checklist and use the avionics master switch to power down all the communication and navigation equipment simultaneously. |
| 459. | What is the advantage of using an avionics master switch rather than working with each unit individually to power it up? | Simplicity leads to enhanced safety in this case. If each unit had to be powered up individually, it is possible that a pilot might forget to power up specific units, which could create a higher workload for the pilot when the discovery is made that a needed piece of equipment is not working. |

| | | |
|---|---|---|
| 460. | When we arrive at the tie-down spot, how will we conduct the shut-down process? | As with every other aspect of the flight, we will shut down using the appropriate checklist. By always using a checklist, we establish good practices that encourage safety and can prevent unintentionally damaging equipment by operating it improperly during the start-up or shut-down process. |
| 461. | Let's assume that after shutting down the aircraft and powering down the electronics, you hear a high pitched whine throughout the cabin. What is making that sound? | The high pitched whine is the sound of the various gyros spinning down. |
| 462. | Is there any need to listen to the whining sound of the gyros spinning down, or can that noise be ignored? | After shutdown is really the only time you can hear the gyros spinning at all. It takes some time for them to spin down, and there is a real advantage to being able to hear them. A constant whine that gets lower in tone and slower in speed indicates the gyros are in good condition. If a buzzing or rattling sound is heard, that might be an indication that at least one gyro is having issues and should potentially be monitored for signs of impending failure. If the buzzing or rattling is significant, it would be reasonable to report the observation to maintenance for further action. |
| 463. | If you discovered an instrument or piece of equipment was inoperative in flight, what action would you take after landing? | My specific actions would depend on whether I own or rent the aircraft, but the general objective is the same. I would make the owner or operator aware that the instrument or equipment was inoperative by submitting a written squawk list. It would then be the responsibility of the owner or operator to repair or replace the defective equipment. |
| 464. | If the inoperative equipment was the second communication radio, would the airplane still be airworthy to fly again? | The issue of the airworthiness of aircraft with inoperative equipment is covered in 14 CFR 91.213. That regulation would allow an airplane with an inoperative second radio to fly, provided the radio was deactivated and placarded as being inoperative. |
| 465. | If the fluid leaked out of the magnetic compass in flight, leaving the compass card unable to move freely, would the airplane remain airworthy? | No. The magnetic compass is one of the instruments required for VFR-day flight. All instruments and equipment that fall under that heading must be operational for the aircraft to be airworthy. The compass would have to be repaired prior to the next flight. |
| 466. | I noticed that you had to reset the heading indicator more than once during our flight; does that suggest that you should squawk that instrument for maintenance to look at? | Not necessarily. Because of gyroscopic precession and the continuous rotation of the earth causing small discrepancies between the heading indicator and the magnetic compass, it is normal to check and reset the heading indicator throughout the flight. I would report the issue to maintenance, however, if the heading indicator wandered or was unable to hold a setting for at least 10 minutes. |

# FAA FLIGHT INSTRUCTOR–INSTRUMENT ORAL EXAM GUIDE

**Sample Examiner Questions**

The following pages contain questions that may be asked by your designated examiner during the oral exam portion of your flight instructor–instrument practical test. We present these questions in the order their associated subjects are listed in the Flight Instructor–Instrument Practical Test Standards. However, your designated examiner may ask these questions (or questions that are very similar) in any order (s)he wishes. Below is a listing of the Tasks and the pages on which the related questions start. The only Tasks included are those not already covered in the Instrument Rating Oral Exam Guide.

| *From PTS Areas of Operation:* | Page* |
|---|---|
| **I. Fundamentals of Instructing** | |
|     A. Learning Process - Oral | 154 |
|     B. Human Behavior and Effective Communication - Oral | 155 |
|     C. Teaching Process - Oral | 157 |
|     D. Teaching Methods - Oral | 158 |
|     E. Critique and Evaluation - Oral | 161 |
|     F. Flight Instructor Characteristics and Responsibilities - Oral | 162 |
|     G. Planning Instructional Activity - Oral | 164 |
| **II. Technical Subject Areas** | |
|     B. Aeromedical Factors - Oral | 166 |
|     D. Logbook Entries Related to Instrument Instruction - Oral | 170 |
| **IV. Preflight Lesson on a Maneuver to Be Performed in Flight** | |
|     A. Maneuver Lesson - Oral | 170 |
| **VI. Flight by Reference to Instruments** | |
|     A. Straight-and-Level Flight - Flight | 171 |
|     B. Turns - Flight | 172 |
|     C. Change of Airspeed in Straight-and-Level and Turning Flight - Flight | 172 |
|     D. Constant Airspeed Climbs and Descents - Flight | 173 |
|     E. Constant Rate Climbs and Descents - Flight | 173 |
|     F. Timed Turns to Magnetic Compass Headings - Flight | 174 |
|     G. Steep Turns - Flight | 174 |

*Page number on which questions for Task begin.

The questions contained in this oral exam guide cover primarily the oral tasks listed in the PTS. Be confident; you will do fine. You can never be totally prepared. If you have studied this book, you will pass with confidence. This book contains the answer to virtually every question, issue, and requirement that is possible on the oral exam portion of the practical test. GOOD LUCK!

## AREA OF OPERATION I: FUNDAMENTALS OF INSTRUCTING

### Task A: Learning Process

| 1. | Briefly define learning. | Learning can be defined as a change in behavior as a result of experience. |
|---|---|---|
| 2. | Can learning have a physical effect? | Yes. Through learning, a student can perform maneuvers more consistently and with better control. |
| 3. | Can you give me an example of how learning might affect a student psychologically? | A student can benefit from a better attitude or a better decision making process due to lessons learned. |
| 4. | What are the characteristics of learning? | Learning is purposeful, comes through experience, is multifaceted, and is an active process. |
| 5. | What is the law of readiness? | Individuals learn best when they are ready and eager to learn. Students with a strong purpose, a clear objective, and a well-fixed reason for learning tend to progress better than those who lack motivation. |
| 6. | What is the law of exercise? | Things most often repeated are best remembered. This is the basis for practice and drill. |
| 7. | What is the law of effect? | Learning is strengthened when accompanied by a pleasant or satisfying feeling. Whatever the learning situation, it should contain elements that affect students positively. |
| 8. | What is the law of primacy? | Things learned first often create a strong, almost unshakable impression. Therefore, it is better to teach the right way, the first time. |
| 9. | What is the law of intensity? | A student will learn more from the real thing than from a substitute. |
| 10. | What is the law of recency? | Things most recently learned are best remembered. Instructors should repeat important matters at the end of a lesson to make sure the student remembers them. |
| 11. | What are the various levels of learning? | Rote, understanding, application, and correlation. |
| 12. | What are the three domains of learning? | Cognitive (knowledge), affective (attitudes, beliefs, and values), and psychomotor (physical skills). |
| 13. | What is the most effective way for an instructor to teach a new maneuver? | With a clear, step-by-step example. The instructor provides a demonstration, emphasizing the steps and techniques, to provide the student with a clear impression of what to do. |
| 14. | Why is it important that the student perform a maneuver, or apply a skill, correctly the first time? | That first experience will be the image (s)he maintains as a reference to the maneuver or skill. As an instructor, I have to be sure that I can lead the student to a successful completion of the task so that (s)he can picture that process and improve on the correctly executed performance in the future through practice. |

| 15. | What does the learning curve demonstrate? How is it useful? | The learning curve provides the instructor with a pattern of the student's progression and informs the instructor when to expect a plateau, followed by further learning. |
|---|---|---|
| 16. | Why is the length of a lesson important? | A lesson that is too long may result in increased errors and decreased motivation. |
| 17. | What are the three processes of memory? | The sensory register, working or short-term memory, and long-term memory. |
| 18. | What are the three theories of forgetting? | The theories of disuse, interference, and repression. |
| 19. | How can an instructor decrease the amount of knowledge forgotten? | An instructor can decrease the amount of knowledge forgotten by providing positive feedback and meaningful repetition, promoting favorable attitudes toward learning, emphasizing associations between bits of information or actions, and facilitating the use of all the student's senses in the learning process. |
| 20. | What is a positive transfer of learning? What is a negative transfer of learning? | Positive transfer occurs when the learning of one skill aids in the learning of another skill. Negative transfer occurs when a previously learned skill interferes with the learning of a new skill. |
| 21. | How can an instructor facilitate the transfer of learning? | An instructor can facilitate the transfer of learning by planning for learning transfer, making sure the student understands the material, maintaining high-order learning standards, and providing meaningful learning experiences. |

## Task B: Human Behavior and Effective Communication

| 22. | How should the instructor control the behavior of his or her student? | In a way that encourages a goal and puts the instructor in a position of authority. |
|---|---|---|
| 23. | What is the ultimate goal of the instructor controlling student behavior? | The instructor creates an environment that will enable students to ultimately help themselves. |
| 24. | Can you recite the list of human needs in the order they are fulfilled? | The list of human needs includes physiological, safety and security, love and belonging, esteem, cognitive and aesthetic, and self-actualization. Human needs are fulfilled in ascending order. A higher need cannot be fulfilled unless the lower needs already have been fulfilled. |
| 25. | Is it reasonable for the instructor to attempt to help a student satisfy their self-actualization needs before satisfying their safety and security needs? | No. The safety and security needs of the student must be fulfilled in order to be truly successful. If the student feels unsafe, (s)he will not be capable of focusing sufficient attention on attaining self-actualization needs. |
| 26. | Why do humans use defense mechanisms? | Humans use defense mechanisms to soften feelings of failure, alleviate feelings of guilt, and protect feelings of worth. |

| | | |
|---|---|---|
| 27. | What are some of the common defense mechanisms? | Some common defense mechanisms are repression, denial, compensation, projection, rationalization, reaction formation, fantasy, and displacement. |
| 28. | What happens to effective pilot decision making when a defense mechanism is involved? | Effective pilot decision making is decreased because defense mechanisms create a distortion of reality. |
| 29. | Do defense mechanisms affect the student's ability to learn? | Yes. A student's defense mechanisms will often be detrimental to the process of learning new material. That is why it is so important that the instructor be familiar with these mechanisms. By recognizing them when the student employs a defense mechanism, the instructor can help the student avoid a counter-productive mental detour and refocus them on the task at hand. |
| 30. | Why is it important that an instructor react to the student in positive ways? | Students experience a number of different emotions, not all of which are productive to the process of learning. The instructor has to remain positive and supporting in order to support and encourage the student's progress. |
| 31. | Is it important to communicate each of your expectations with your students? | Yes. By keeping my students informed and aware of what is expected of them, I can help them avoid developing a sense of insecurity and maintain focus on the maneuvers or concepts we are working on. |
| 32. | What is the difference between criticism and constructive criticism? | Criticism is nothing more than telling the student that (s)he has performed a maneuver or task improperly. Constructive criticism points out the improper performance but provides positive input on how the maneuver might be done better or praises the student for doing a portion of the maneuver correctly then points out how the remainder of the performance can be improved to meet the completion standards for the lesson. |
| 33. | If you commit an error during an instructional flight, what is your best course of action? | I would assure my student that instructors are people too and let him or her know that we can make mistakes from time to time, too. By admitting my mistake, I can show my student that there is no benefit to attempting to cover up an error and raise his or her confidence that it is acceptable to make a mistake, provided you notice it, admit it, and correct for it. |
| 34. | How would you define effective communication? | If the message I intended to transmit is substantially similar to the message the student receives, we have established effective communication. |
| 35. | What are the three basic elements of communication? | The three basic elements of communication are the source, symbols, and the receiver. |
| 36. | If you are the source and your student is the receiver, what are the symbols? | The symbols of communication can include a wide assortment of options. They could be words or images, facial expressions, and even gestures. |

| 37. | Is communication a one-way transmittal of ideas or is it a two-way process? | Communication is a two-way transmittal of ideas. The source and the receiver change roles throughout the course of the process. |
|---|---|---|
| 38. | How can the receiver's personal experience affect the quality of communication? | A good example would be a receiver who is not familiar with the terminology the sender is using. If I speak using standard pilot jargon to a student who has no frame of reference for the terms I'm using, much of the clarity of my message will be lost. |
| 39. | What is the greatest barrier to effective communication? | It is a lack of common experience between the sender and receiver. The receiver has to be able to understand and relate to the message in order to process the information and make use of it in the future. |
| 40. | Can you give me an example of how a student might suffer from confusion between the symbol and the symbolized object during a lesson? | When discussing primary flight controls, I might use the term aileron without actually showing the student what an aileron is. The student might think the flaps are the ailerons based on a poor explanation that only specified that the ailerons are on the wings. When the student actually gets to the airplane, (s)he would find the operation and movement of the ailerons to be confusing because (s)he is thinking of an entirely different component of the aircraft. |
| 41. | How can abstractions adversely affect a student? | If I were to use the term "empennage" repeatedly in a lesson without specifically explaining to the student that I was talking about the tail group as a whole, (s)he would suffer from the detrimental effects of an abstraction. The student has no sense of what the empennage is, so much of the value of the lesson would be lost. |
| 42. | How can an outside source cause a barrier to good communication? | A student who is distracted because (s)he isn't feeling well during the lesson, is excessively tired, or is concerned about an external issue, such as an approaching weather system, can suffer from the interference of that distraction. |
| 43. | How can you learn to improve your communication skills over time? | The task of instructing is a good method of developing improved communication skills. I can also do role playing exercises with fellow instructors to work out lessons that can be transmitted clearly, and I can learn more about communication techniques by seeking out additional instruction myself. |

## Task C: Teaching Process

| 44. | How should a flight instructor prepare for a productive flight lesson? | An instructor should determine the material to be covered, the objectives of the lesson, and the goals to be attained. |
|---|---|---|
| 45. | What is a lesson plan? | A lesson plan is an organized outline for a single instructional period. Lesson plans should be prepared in writing for each instructional period, regardless of the instructor's experience or the student's skill level. |

| 46. | What are performance-based objectives? | Performance based objectives are lesson plans that set measurable, reasonable standards that describe the desired performance of the student. |
|---|---|---|
| 47. | Why is it so important to write down performance-based objectives when preparing a lesson? | If the objectives are not written down, they can become subject to fallibility of recall, interpretation, or loss of specificity over time. |
| 48. | How would you progress through the development of a particularly complex lesson? | There are several options, which all depend on a logical approach. I could move from the past to the present, from the simple to the complex, or from the known to the unknown. As long as the system follows a logical progression that the student can follow, successful communication should take place and the student should benefit from the lesson. |
| 49. | When should the lecture method of presentation be used? | The lecture method should be used primarily to introduce students to new material. |
| 50. | When should the demonstration-performance method be used? | The Demonstration-performance method is used extensively for flight training. It is a very good method to use when introducing new maneuvers to a student in flight. |
| 51. | What is the instructor's responsibility regarding the PTS? | The instructor should teach the Practical Test Standards so students will be prepared when they are tested on them. |
| 52. | Why should an instructor always conduct reviews and evaluations after student demonstrations? | Reviews and evaluations make students aware of their progress and prepare them for future lessons. |
| 53. | Why is it important for students to be aware of their progress? | A lack of awareness may form a barrier between the student and instructor. Also, the student rarely has the opportunity to gauge his or her progress against that of another student. It is the instructor's responsibility to keep the student apprised of his or her progress by evaluating performance with both praise and constructive criticism when it is appropriate. |

### Task D: Teaching Methods

| 54. | Is the lecture method a good means of evaluating student performance? | No. The lecture method is a poor method of evaluating student performance. Its primary purpose is to present new material, not evaluate progress. |
|---|---|---|
| 55. | Are all lectures formal? | No. Lectures can be formal or informal. |
| 56. | What is the advantage of an informal lecture? | An informal lecture provides the students with more opportunities for participation by asking questions of the instructor during the presentation. |
| 57. | What is the computer-assisted learning (CAL) method? | CAL can be anything from a simple electronic presentation to a complete course of training. Such tools are incredibly useful in helping students pace themselves and study at the level they desire. |

| | | |
|---|---|---|
| 58. | What is the main advantage to the computer-assisted learning (CAL) method? | Students can work and progress at their own pace. |
| 59. | Can the student or the instructor rely on computer-assisted learning exclusively? | Computer-assisted learning is a tool, much like a textbook or video might be. As a part of a larger instructional plan, it can be useful. If relied on to the exclusion of other methods, the student's progress would suffer. For that reason, it would be unwise to rely exclusively on computer-assisted learning or any other single training tool. |
| 60. | Does the instructor have any role in a student's computer-assisted learning program? | The instructor always has a role in evaluating the progress of a student and guiding him or her through subject matter the student may find difficult to grasp or master. |
| 61. | What is the effect of the skillful use of questions in the guided discussion method? | Skillful use of questions brings about discussion and develops an understanding. |
| 62. | When asking questions in a guided discussion, what kind of questions would you ask? | The questions have to be open ended to be most useful. Open ended questions require the students to answer in a way that indicates their level of understanding of the topic under discussion. If the questions can be answered by a simple yes or no, they have minimal value. |
| 63. | How does the guided discussion method differ from the lecture method? | In the lecture method the instructor is telling the student(s) what (s)he knows. In the guided discussion the instructor is drawing out responses from the student to better understand what the student knows. |
| 64. | Why is the guided discussion such a useful teaching method? | The guided discussion encourages the student to move past simple rote learning to a higher level of learning by challenging them to explain concepts and procedures rather than just repeat the component parts from memory. |
| 65. | Why is a summary important in the guided discussion method? | It is important that the instructor summarize the accomplishments of the lesson in order to provide clarity and promote a positive motivation for the students. The summary emphasizes what students have learned and points out aspects they may have missed. |
| 66. | Is it reasonable to include pre-solo students in a guided discussion of cross-country flight planning with more advanced students? | No. The guided discussion is most useful when the students can participate by using knowledge they have already attained. To include a student who has no background knowledge of the subject matter would be a poor choice. It would be of little value to the newer student and potentially be counter-productive to the lesson as a whole. |

| | | |
|---|---|---|
| 67. | If you were teaching cross-country flight planning, which method of instruction would you use? | I would consider combining two methods over the course of the lesson. I would begin with the lecture method so that I could introduce the concepts that are necessary to begin performing cross-country flight planning. Then I would gradually employ the guided discussion method to identify weak areas that the student may need additional work in. |
| 68. | What are the steps used in the demonstration-performance method? | There are four steps: (1) instructor tells, instructor does; (2) student tells, instructor does; (3) student tells, student does; and (4) instructor supervises and evaluates. |
| 69. | If you were teaching a student how to perform a power-off stall in the airplane, which method of instruction would be the most appropriate? | The Demonstration-performance method would be best because it gives the student a physical demonstration of the maneuver, the ability to perform the maneuver himself or herself, and an evaluation and critique of his or her performance. |
| 70. | How should instructors address their own mistakes made during demonstrations as a part of the demonstration-performance method? | Instructors should point out their own mistakes and correct them as necessary. Any attempt to downplay or ignore mistakes would create confusion for the student and send a mixed message that could create interference to the learning process. |
| 71. | Is there any advantage to bringing one of your mistakes to the student's attention when using the Demonstration-performance method of instruction? | Yes. By pointing out your error and showing the student how to correct it, the student's confidence in the instructor is enhanced. It also sends the message that small mistakes can be a normal part of the flight that can be corrected safely by applying the lessons being taught in the cockpit. The combination of these messages can combine to make the student more confident and motivated to learn. |
| 72. | What does it mean when we talk about the Integrated Flight Instruction method? | The Integrated Flight Instruction method is recommended by the FAA as a means of teaching flight maneuvers. In essence, the object is to teach the maneuver using outside visual references, initially, then transition to performing the maneuver by reference to instruments. |
| 73. | What is the goal of using the Integrated Flight Instruction method? | The goal is to teach my students how to develop good habits by monitoring the flight and engine instrumentation while performing maneuvers visually, using outside references. |
| 74. | What tasks would you expect a student to be able to master while using the Integrated Flight Instruction method? | I would expect my students to be able to maintain altitude, heading, and airspeeds while using the Integrated method. |

## Task E: Critique and Evaluation

| 75. | When your student first attempts to perform a new maneuver, would you quietly allow them to complete the full maneuver, or would you provide guidance throughout the maneuver to correct the student's errors? | I would provide guidance throughout the maneuver. Using the demonstration-performance method, I would make comments if necessary while the student was performing the maneuver. That direction would help the student be aware of the various parameters required to perform the maneuver correctly and prevent him or her from establishing bad habits right from the start. |
|---|---|---|
| 76. | What form does the review and evaluation of a student's performance take? | It can be informal and presented orally during a discussion or it can be a written record that illustrates the student's progress in the course. |
| 77. | How often should you provide your students with an evaluation of their performance? | Each lesson should include a review and an evaluation of things previously learned. This allows the instructor to help the student correct deficiencies and provides an opportunity to praise the student for making progress, which keeps the student motivated and engaged in the learning process. |
| 78. | What are an instructor's evaluations based on? | Student performance evaluations are based on the objectives and goals established in the instructor's lesson plan. |
| 79. | What are the characteristics of an effective oral question? | An effective oral question has only one correct answer; applies to the subject being taught; is brief, concise, and clear; centers on one idea; and presents a challenge. |
| 80. | What types of oral questions should be avoided? | Trick, irrelevant, or too general questions should be avoided. |
| 81. | Does the length of a question have any bearing on its value? | Questions should be concise, specific, brief, and to the point. |
| 82. | What is the disadvantage of asking questions that your students will find to be very simple to answer? | Easy questions don't stimulate learning very well. It is better to ask your students questions that present a challenge. |
| 83. | What are the attributes of a good test question? | A good test question is reliable, valid, usable, comprehensive, and discriminating. |
| 84. | How should the instructor respond to a question to which (s)he does not know the answer? | (S)he should admit to not knowing the answer and volunteer to help the student find the answer. |
| 85. | Why does a critique have to be thoughtful? | Because the instructor needs to be sure (s)he is critiquing the student's performance and nothing else. The instructor cannot let his or her own frustration or emotional experience affect the critique since that is not within the student's control and cannot help him or her improve performance. |

| 86. | Why does a critique have to be specific? | It is important that the instructor not only let the student know what (s)he did wrong or outside of the anticipated completion standards, but (s)he also needs to explain how the student can improve his or her performance in specific terms that the student can apply to the next attempts at the maneuver or task. If the student cannot use the critique to improve performance, the critique is of no benefit. |
|---|---|---|
| 87. | How much material should a critique cover? | The critique should be of specific tasks, maneuvers, and decisions the student made. The instructor should be sure the student will be able to focus on each element of a critique and grasp the full consequence of it. A critique that is too broad or covers too many topics will be less effective as the student becomes overwhelmed with input. |
| 88. | Are absolute statements desirable, or should they be avoided in critiques? | Absolute statements should be avoided. Using terms such as never, always, all, or none tend to send a message that is not altogether true, which can confuse a student and adversely effect the student/instructor relationship. |
| 89. | Are critiques always given orally? | Not necessarily. There are times when it can be beneficial to provide a written critique, but it is important to be sure the written critique agrees with any oral critique the instructor may offer. |

### Task F: Flight Instructor Characteristics and Responsibilities

| 90. | Why should instructors approach students as individuals? | Instructors who limit their thinking to an entire group are generalizing and cannot give particular students the individual attention they need. |
|---|---|---|
| 91. | Is there any reason that instructors should or should not be personally interested in the progress of their students? | No. Having a genuine interest in the positive outcome of their students' training can lend a positive aspect to the effectiveness of the instructors. |
| 92. | Why is it important to establish standards of performance? | Students will rise to the standard you set for them. If you set your expectations low, your students will perform to those standards. However, if you establish standards of performance that challenge your students, they will strive to meet those standards and become better pilots in the process. |
| 93. | Why is it important for instructors to praise and give constructive criticism? | Praise and constructive criticism deflect study frustration and make students feel that they are accomplishing something. |
| 94. | What can you do as an instructor to encourage your student to feel comfortable? | By emphasizing the positive aspects of flight training, I can help make my students feel more comfortable, which creates a better learning environment for them to work in. |

| | | |
|---|---|---|
| 95. | Why should you provide an evaluation on a continuing basis with your students? | It is important that the students have a clear understanding of their performance level. By sharing evaluations on a regular basis, the student will be able to progress with knowledge of his or her current abilities and a clear vision of what the ultimate completion standards are. |
| 96. | Who is ultimately responsible for the safety of a student pilot? | The flight instructor is responsible for the safety of the student, even when the student is on a solo flight. |
| 97. | Why should a flight instructor not give a student a solo endorsement if the student is not ready to solo? | It is a breach of faith between the instructor and student and, more importantly, it is unsafe for everyone involved. |
| 98. | Who is accountable when a student is found to be deficient in an area of operation on a practical test? | The instructor is accountable. The endorsement provided by the instructor suggest that (s)he considers the applicant to be capable of passing the practical test. |
| 99. | How long must you keep a record of endorsements you have given students? | For 3 years. |
| 100. | What records must you keep regarding endorsements you have given to students? | The record of all endorsements has to include the student's name, the date, and the type of endorsement, as well as a record of all written and practical test endorsements. |
| 101. | Where can you get official information regarding endorsement requirements? | AC 61-98, Currency and Additional Qualification Requirements for Certificated Pilots, includes information about endorsements. |
| 102. | What is the flight instructor's responsibility regarding the flight review? | CFIs should not sign off anyone who has not satisfactorily completed the flight review. Instead, the training should only appear as dual in the logbook. |
| 103. | What is the standard of completion for a flight review? | Flight reviews should be conducted using current regulations and the practical test standards established for the level of pilot certificate the applicant holds. |
| 104. | What are some qualities of a flight instructor who seeks to be a professional? | Sincerity, a good personal appearance, a professional image, the exercise of safe and good judgment, and the desire to better oneself through learning. |
| 105. | Why is an instructor's demeanor important? | The instructor has to be positive, professional, and consistent when dealing with students. Anything less will erode the sense of confidence the student needs in order to succeed with their instructor. |
| 106. | How is language pertinent to flight instruction? | Instructors must use appropriate language when dealing with students. There is a considerable amount of aviation specific jargon for students to learn, as well as a need for them to learn to speak correctly and clearly when making radio calls. They will emulate the language and demeanor of their instructor, so it is important that a solid, professional example be set and maintained throughout the students flight training experience. |

| 107. | Should all students be treated exactly the same? | No. All students should be treated as unique individuals with unique motivations and unique problems to overcome. By treating students as individuals, the instructor can help them in a more meaningful way to achieve their goals. |
|---|---|---|
| 108. | Why is it so important that instructors criticize constructively? | Criticism is a negative interaction while constructive criticism is a positive interaction between the student and the instructor. |

### Task G: Planning Instructional Activity

| 109. | What is the first step in planning a lesson? | The first step is to determine the objectives and completion standards for the lesson. |
|---|---|---|
| 110. | What are the contents of a training syllabus? | A training syllabus is an abstract or digest with blocks of learning organized in an efficient order. A syllabus should be flexible to allow an instructor to change it to the most effective training possible. |
| 111. | Is each block of learning in a syllabus arranged in a particular way? | Yes. The blocks of learning included in a syllabus should be arranged so that the most basic information is covered first. The student will move through material from the known to the unknown, and the blocks will become smaller and more concise as the complexity of the material increases. |
| 112. | What is the purpose of a lesson plan? | A lesson plan should provide the best instruction possible within the given period and make sure the instructor keeps a constant check on his or her own activity. |
| 113. | How should a lesson plan be developed? | The lesson plan should be developed to show specific knowledge and/or skills to be taught. The lesson plan is a guide for the instructor in that it tells him what to do, in what order to do it, and what procedure to use in teaching the material. |
| 114. | What are the characteristics of a well-planned lesson? | A well-planned lesson has unity, good content, scope, practicality, instructional steps, and flexibility. |
| 115. | Can a lesson plan be a mental outline? | No. To be effective, the lesson plan must be in writing. Another instructor should be able to take the lesson plan and carry out the activity. |
| 116. | How should the lesson plan be used? | The lesson plan should be used as a guide, but not as a substitute to thinking. |
| 117. | Why should a new lesson be made for every student and every instructional period? | Not every student and training environment is the same. Failure to create a new lesson plan can result in an ineffective lesson. |
| 118. | What are the elements of a lesson plan? | The elements of a lesson plan are: objective, elements involved, schedule, equipment, instructor's actions, student's actions, and completion standards. |

| 119. | What is the purpose of the "elements involved" section of the lesson plan? | The "elements involved" section is a statement of the elements of knowledge and skill necessary for the fulfillment of the lesson objective. It can include new or previously learned material. |
|---|---|---|
| 120. | Is the lesson plan designed to be of value to the instructor or the student? | Both. The lesson plan helps the instructor by providing a useful framework for teaching each skill or maneuver, and it benefits the student by making sure that any instructor can teach useful information that is pertinent to the student's current status. |
| 121. | At what point does an instructor have enough experience to discontinue the use of a lesson plan? | Never. Even a highly experienced instructor can benefit from the use of a written lesson plan. In fact, it is fair to say that the use of a printed lesson plan is a sign of professionalism. |
| 122. | What might you hope to accomplish in the introduction of a lesson? | I would hope to capture the attention of the student(s), describe what would be covered in the lesson, and establish an understanding of the benefits the student(s) could expect from learning the material. |
| 123. | What is one purpose of the conclusion of a lesson? | The conclusion can relate the important elements of the lesson to the objective. |
| 124. | What should you avoid doing in the conclusion to a lesson? | It would be inappropriate and potentially counter-productive to introduce new material in the conclusion. With no introduction of ability to expand on the material, any new material thrown in at the conclusion of the lesson could potentially confuse or distract the student. |
| 125. | As an instructor, what concerns do you have about equipment when planning a lesson? | I have to verify that all the equipment necessary to demonstrate and perform the lesson's tasks is available and in good operating condition. |
| 126. | How should an effective lesson be organized? | Every lesson should be organized into three phases: introduction, development, and conclusion. |
| 127. | Why is a detailed written plan necessary for a lesson to be truly effective? | Any given task, maneuver, or knowledge area includes a wide selection of information. In order to be sure that I cover each of the necessary components of any given lesson, I have to create a written lesson plan that allows me to track each component of the lesson and verify that it has been addressed to the extent necessary to provide the student with a sufficient understanding of the material. |

## AREA OF OPERATION II: TECHNICAL SUBJECT AREAS

### Task B: Aeromedical Factors

| 128. | What is a good rule for flying if taking medication? | DO NOT fly if you are taking medication unless the medication is approved by the FAA or you are certain that the medicine will NOT impair your abilities. |
|---|---|---|
| 129. | What if the medication is a common, over-the-counter drug? | The same rule applies. Pilots should not fly when taking medication unless the medication is approved by the FAA or they are absolutely certain that the medicine will not impair their judgment or abilities. |
| 130. | How long must one wait after consuming alcohol before acting as a required crewmember on a civil airplane? | You must wait 8 hours after consuming alcohol before acting as a required crewmember on a civil airplane. |
| 131. | What is hypoxia? | Hypoxia is an insufficient supply of oxygen in the body. |
| 132. | What are the signs of hypoxia? | Impairment of night vision, judgment, alertness, coordination, and the ability to make calculations. Headache, drowsiness, dizziness, and a possible sense of euphoria or belligerence may occur. Unconsciousness may be the end result of prolonged hypoxia. |
| 133. | How can hypoxia be prevented or treated? | Hypoxia can be prevented or treated by flying at a lower altitude or by using supplemental oxygen. |
| 134. | Once an individual becomes hypoxic, how long after beginning treatment will it take for him or her to regain his or her faculties? | Recovery from hypoxia is almost immediate. The person suffering from hypoxia will regain his or her faculties very quickly after sufficient oxygen is made available. |
| 135. | What is hyperventilation? | Hyperventilation is a condition that describes insufficient supply of carbon dioxide in the blood. |
| 136. | What are some indications of hyperventilation? | Dizziness, rapid heart rate, tingling in the fingers and toes, and ultimately unconsciousness. |
| 137. | How can hyperventilation be treated? | Hyperventilation can be treated by taking slow, deep breaths or by breathing into a bag. |
| 138. | Why is it important that pilots not fly when they have a cold or allergic condition that causes congestion? | Pressure differences during climb or descent can cause severe pain and hearing loss due to ear blockage. Congestion can block the Eustachian tube and prevent the pressure equalization necessary to avoid this sort of aeromedical issue. |
| 139. | Does the problem of pressure equalization only pertain to ear and hearing problems? | No. Blocked passages in the sinuses can cause pain and possibly the discharge of bloody mucus from the nasal passages. |
| 140. | If you were scheduled to fly but had a cold, would it be advisable to take an over-the-counter decongestant to avoid ear or sinus issues? | No. Pilots should not fly when taking medication unless the medication is approved by the FAA or they are absolutely certain that the medicine will not impair their judgment or abilities. Decongestants can have side effects that can significantly impair pilot performance. |

| | | |
|---|---|---|
| 141. | What is spatial disorientation? | Spatial disorientation is a state of temporary spatial confusion that results from misleading information being sent to the brain from various sensory organs. |
| 142. | Can you give me an example of how spatial disorientation might occur in flight? | When visibility is limited, the brain will rely on other input for orientation information. The ear may not be reliable because of fluid movement that does not correspond with the movement of the aircraft. This could cause the pilot to feel as if (s)he is in a steep turn when the aircraft is actually flying straight-and-level. It could also cause the pilot to feel as if (s)he is flying straight-and-level when (s)he is actually in a steep turn. That is why spatial disorientation can be a dangerous condition. |
| 143. | What is the graveyard spiral? | If descending during a coordinated constant-rate turn that has ceased stimulating, the motion-sensing system can create the illusion of being in a descent with the wings level. A disoriented pilot will pull back on the controls, tightening the spiral and increasing the loss of altitude. |
| 144. | On what sense does your brain rely primarily when it receives conflicting information from the senses? | When given conflicting information, the brain tends to favor the information provided visually. |
| 145. | What are some illusions that lead to landing error? | Illusions that can lead to landing error include runway width, runway terrain, featureless terrain, and atmospheric illusions. |
| 146. | What are some illusions that lead to spatial disorientation? | Some illusions that lead to spatial disorientation are the leans, Coriolis illusion, graveyard spiral and spin, somatogravic illusion, inversion illusion, elevator illusion, false horizon, autokinesis, and size-distance illusion. |
| 147. | How can you recover from spatial disorientation? | The best way to recover from spatial disorientation is to focus on the flight instruments and rely on their indications. |
| 148. | Does motion sickness come on rapidly? | Not usually. Motion sickness is often an incremental progression of symptoms. |
| 149. | How can you identify impending motion sickness in yourself or a passenger? | First, the subject loses his or her appetite. Heavy perspiration might follow with a tendency to salivate. Nausea, disorientation, and headaches may also occur. |
| 150. | How can you combat or prevent motion sickness? | By opening the air vents and getting air circulating in the cockpit. I would encourage passengers to loosen their clothing and avoid unnecessary head movements. I would also advise them to focus their eyes on a distant point near the horizon. While doing all this, I would be either returning to land at my home airport if it was close by or diverting to a nearby airport to land. |

| | | |
|---|---|---|
| 151. | What is carbon monoxide poisoning? | Carbon monoxide poisoning occurs when carbon monoxide enters the blood, thereby causing hypoxia. Carbon monoxide poisoning is of particular concern to pilots because this colorless, odorless gas can cause incapacitation. |
| 152. | What is the primary source of carbon monoxide in aircraft cockpits? | The most common source of carbon monoxide in aircraft cockpits is exhaust fumes leaking from a defective heater or other source. |
| 153. | Why is the recognition of carbon monoxide poisoning so important to pilots? | Loss of consciousness and death are very real possibilities if the exposure to carbon monoxide continues. |
| 154. | If you suspect carbon monoxide poisoning is occurring, what would be a reasonable course of action? | Ventilate the cabin to the extent possible and land at the first opportunity to seek first aid, if necessary. After dealing with the human element, I would make sure the aircraft was inspected and the leak found and repaired before it was flown again. |
| 155. | What other aeromedical condition can carbon monoxide poisoning mimic? | The effects of carbon monoxide poisoning are very similar to the effects of hypoxia. |
| 156. | Can carbon monoxide poisoning be treated with oxygen, like hypoxia, resulting in a quick recovery? | No. Oxygen may be beneficial to the person suffering from carbon monoxide poisoning, but the carbon monoxide must be removed from the individual's bloodstream, which is a process that takes time. It cannot be remedied as rapidly as hypoxia. |
| 157. | How can stress affect your flying? | Stress degrades decision-making ability and slows your reactions. |
| 158. | When we talk about stress and flying, what kind of stress are we talking about? | Everyday stress that comes from personal interactions, job stress, family responsibilities, busy schedules in our lives. Stress can be subtle, but cumulative, building to the point that it adversely affects the individual's ability to perform normal functions reliably. |
| 159. | How can stress affect you as a pilot? | It can cause distraction that affects my decision-making abilities and might cause my judgment to erode to the point that I take unnecessary risks. |
| 160. | What is acute fatigue? | Acute fatigue refers to the everyday tiredness felt after a long period of physical or mental activity that leaves the individual feeling drained. |
| 161. | How can acute fatigue be remedied? | By getting sufficient rest, sleep, exercise, and nutrition. |
| 162. | What is chronic fatigue? | Chronic fatigue occurs when there is insufficient recovery time between bouts of acute fatigue. Performance and judgment continue to degrade. Because it is a deeper form of fatigue, the recovery period requires a prolonged period of rest. |

| | | |
|---|---|---|
| 163. | What is dehydration? | Dehydration occurs when the body is deprived of fluids. Dehydration can occur on flights of long duration in which the pilot fails to drink adequate amounts of water, or it can be a pre-existing condition that started prior to the flight. |
| 164. | How can dehydration affect you as a pilot? | Dehydration acts as a stressor and can degrade your decision-making ability. |
| 165. | How does flying affect dehydration for pilots and passengers? | At altitude, the atmosphere is thinner and contains less moisture. This leads to more body fluids being lost. |
| 166. | How can you combat dehydration? | Ensure an adequate intake of fluids before and, if necessary, during flight. |
| 167. | What is hypothermia? | Hypothermia occurs when your body is unable to maintain its normal temperature. An internal temperature of 96°F or lower signals hypothermia. |
| 168. | What are some signs that a person is suffering from hypothermia? | Extreme shivering; stiffness of the arms or legs; confusion or sleepiness; slow, slurred speech; and poor control over body movements all suggest the possibility of hypothermia. |
| 169. | Does it have to be extremely cold for a pilot or passenger to succumb to hypothermia? | No. A drafty cockpit and especially an open cockpit aircraft can cause a poorly prepared pilot or passenger to experience hypothermia in temperatures that might seem moderate when standing on the ground with no wind. |
| 170. | How can hypothermia be prevented? | By dressing appropriately. Pilots and passengers should be aware that the temperature at altitude is usually lower than the temperature on the ground, and the wind blowing through the cockpit will cause our bodies more difficulty at maintaining a normal body temperature. |
| 171. | What is the maximum allowable blood alcohol content while acting as a required crewmember on a civil airplane? | You may not act as a required crewmember on a civil aircraft while having .04% or more blood alcohol content by weight. |
| 172. | How long should pilots and passengers wait to fly after scuba diving? | If a controlled ascent was required during the dive, wait 24 hr. before flying. If a controlled ascent was not required, wait 12 hr. before flying up to 8,000 ft. and 24 hr. for any altitude above 8,000 ft. |
| 173. | Why is it important to wait before flying after scuba diving? | Just as the pressure decrease while ascending in the water can cause nitrogen gas trapped in the tissues to escape rapidly, a condition known as the bends, the same can occur when the ambient pressure decreases during an airplane's ascent. To avoid that possibility, individuals should wait before flying after scuba diving, to give the nitrogen gas time to leave the body. |

### Task D: Logbook Entries Related to Instrument Instruction

| 174. | Please present the two endorsements CFIIs are expected to give. | The FAA recommends instructors use the endorsements listed in the current version of AC 61-65. |
|---|---|---|
| | | **Prerequisites for instrument practical test: 14 CFR § 61.39(a)(6)**<br>I certify that (First name, MI, Last name) has received and logged the required flight time/training of § 61.39 (a) in preparation for the practical test within 2 calendar-months preceding the date of the test and has satisfactory knowledge of the subject areas in which he/she was shown to be deficient by the FAA airman knowledge test report. I have determined he/she is prepared for the Instrument—airplane practical test.<br><br>Signed  Date  Name  CFI Number  Expiration Date<br><br>**Flight proficiency/practical test: § 61.65(a)(6)**<br>I certify that (First name, MI, Last name) has received the required training of § 61.65(c) and 61.65(d). I have determined he/she is prepared for the Instrument—airplane practical test.<br><br>Signed  Date  Name  CFI Number  Expiration Date |

## AREA OF OPERATION IV: PREFLIGHT LESSON ON A MANEUVER TO BE PERFORMED IN FLIGHT

### Task A: Maneuver Lesson

| 175. | What method of instruction is required during the teaching of a maneuver? | The Demonstration-performance method of instructing. |
|---|---|---|
| 176. | What are the elements of the Demonstration-performance method of instructing? | Instructor explanation, instructor demonstration, student performance with instructor supervision, and instructor evaluation. |
| 177. | Discuss the three "instructor explanation" requirements. | Discuss proper setup procedures. Have the student fill out a flight maneuver analysis sheet (FMAS) or review one you have already constructed. |
| | | Detail the steps of the maneuver and illustrate the maneuver either with a reference book or other form of visual aid. Have the student fill in this information on the FMAS worksheet. |
| | | Explain proper recovery and maneuver termination procedures. Emphasize completion standards per the appropriate PTS or instructor expectations. |

| 178. | Discuss the three "instructor demonstration" requirements. | Configure aircraft.

Perform the maneuver while explaining the steps. Watch for common errors that you might make and be ready to discuss them with your student after the demonstration. Even instructors make mistakes sometimes. Some students may request additional demonstrations. Do not refuse them. Always ensure understanding before asking the student to perform a maneuver.

Recover from the maneuver and discuss completion standards – Demonstrate proper recovery techniques and ask the student whether or not the completion standards were met. Have the student critique your demonstration. |
|---|---|---|
| 179. | Discuss the three "student performance with instructor supervision" requirements. | Student configures aircraft – Instructor watches for proper checklist usage and setup procedures.

Student performs maneuver – The instructor should try not to interfere with the student's performance, allowing him or her to make mistakes as long as safety is not jeopardized. These mistakes will be a central part of the critique you offer later.

Student recovers from maneuver and gives a self-critique – The instructor has the student critique his or her own performance to keep the student involved in the learning process. |
| 180. | Discuss the three "instructor evaluation" requirements. | Instructor critiques student performance with both positive and negative comments.

Student practices maneuver as needed to reach or exceed completion standards, the instructor should allow the student several chances to repeat the maneuver to ensure understanding. The student must meet or exceed the completion standards in order to progress to the next element or lesson.

Once student reaches satisfactory skill level, incorporate realistic distractions. I will simulate the real world environment by incorporating distractions into the lesson plan. |

## AREA OF OPERATION VI: FLIGHT BY REFERENCE TO INSTRUMENTS

### Task A: Straight-and-Level Flight

| 181. | What are the conditions that determine the pitch attitude required to maintain level flight? | Conditions that determine the pitch attitude required to maintain level flight are airspeed, air density, wing design, and angle of attack. At a constant angle of attack, any change in airspeed will vary the lift. Lift varies directly with changes in air density. An airplane's wing has lift characteristics that are suited to its intended uses. Lift increases with any increase in the angle of attack (up to the critical angle). |
|---|---|---|

| 182. | Which instruments should be used to make a pitch correction when you have deviated from your assigned altitude? | The pitch instruments are the attitude indicator, the altimeter, the vertical speed indicator, and the airspeed indicator. The attitude indicator gives you a direct indication of changes in pitch attitude when correcting for altitude variations. The rate and direction of the altimeter and vertical speed indicator confirm the correct pitch adjustment was made, and the altimeter is used to determine when you have reached your assigned altitude. |
|---|---|---|
| 183. | As a rule of thumb, altitude corrections of less than 100 feet should be corrected by using? | As a general rule, altitude corrections of less than 100 ft. should be corrected by using a half-bar-width (i.e., less than a full-bar-width) correction on the attitude indicator. |
| 184. | What are the three fundamental skills involved in attitude instrument flying? | The three fundamental skills involved in all instrument flight maneuvers are instrument cross-check, instrument interpretation, and aircraft control. Cross-checking is the continuous and logical observation of the instruments for attitude and performance information. Instrument interpretation requires you to understand each instrument's construction, operating principle, and relationship to the performance of your airplane. Aircraft control requires you to substitute instruments for outside references. |

## Task B: Turns

| 185. | What force causes an airplane to turn? | An airplane, like any object, requires a sideward force to make it turn. This force is supplied by banking the airplane so that lift is separated into two components at right angles to each other. The lift acting upward and opposing weight is the vertical lift component, and the lift acting horizontally and opposing centrifugal force is the horizontal lift component. The horizontal lift component is the sideward force that causes an airplane to turn. |
|---|---|---|
| 186. | What is the relationship between centrifugal force and the horizontal lift component in a coordinated turn? | When a turn is coordinated, horizontal lift equals centrifugal force. This is indicated when the ball on the turn coordinator or turn-and-slip indicator is centered. |
| 187. | Why must the angle of attack be increased to maintain a constant altitude during a coordinated turn? | In comparison to level flight, a bank results in the division of lift between vertical and horizontal components. To provide a vertical component of lift sufficient to maintain altitude in a level turn, an increase in the angle of attack is required. |

## Task C: Change of Airspeed in Straight-and-Level and Turning Flight

| 188. | When airspeed is increased in a turn, what must be done to maintain a constant altitude? | To compensate for added lift, which would result if airspeed were increased during a turn, the angle of attack must be decreased and the angle of bank increased if a constant altitude is to be maintained. |
|---|---|---|

| 189. | When airspeed is decreased in a turn, what must be done to maintain level flight? | To compensate for the decreased lift resulting from decreased airspeed during a turn, the angle of bank must be decreased and/or the angle of attack increased. |

### Task D: Constant Airspeed Climbs and Descents

| 190. | To enter a constant-airspeed descent from level-cruising flight and maintain cruising airspeed, what should the pilot do? | To enter a constant-airspeed descent from level cruising flight and maintain cruising airspeed, you should simultaneously reduce the power smoothly to the desired setting and reduce the pitch attitude slightly by using the attitude indicator as a reference to maintain the cruising airspeed. |
| --- | --- | --- |
| 191. | To level off at an airspeed higher than the descent speed, the addition of power should be made, assuming a 500 FPM rate of descent, at approximately what height? | To level off from a descent at an airspeed higher than the descent speed, it is necessary to start the level-off before reaching the desired altitude. At 500 FPM, an effective practice is to lead the desired altitude by approximately 100 to 150 ft. above the desired altitude. At this point, add power to the appropriate level flight cruise setting. |
| 192. | While cruising at 160 knots, you wish to establish a climb at 130 knots. When entering the climb, it is proper to make the initial pitch change by increasing back elevator pressure until what point? | To enter a constant-airspeed climb from cruising airspeed, raise the miniature aircraft in the attitude indicator to the approximate nose-high indication appropriate to the predetermined climb speed. The attitude will vary according to the type of airplane you are flying. Apply light elevator back pressure to initiate and maintain the climb attitude. The amount of back pressure will increase as the airplane decelerates. |
| 193. | What instruments are considered supporting bank instruments during a straight, stabilized climb at a constant airspeed? | During a straight, stabilized climb at a constant airspeed, the heading indicator is the primary instrument for bank. The supporting bank instruments are the turn coordinator and the attitude indicator. |

### Task E: Constant Rate Climbs and Descents

| 194. | During a constant rate climb or descent, which instrument will serve as the primary instrument for pitch? | The vertical speed indicator. |
| --- | --- | --- |
| 195. | What instruments are primary for pitch, bank, and power, respectively, when transitioning into a constant rate climb from straight-and-level flight? | When you are entering a constant rate climb, the attitude indicator is the primary pitch instrument, the heading indicator is the primary bank instrument, and the tachometer or manifold pressure gauge is the primary power instrument. Once established in the climb, the VSI will replace the attitude indicator as the primary pitch instrument. |
| 196. | In a constant rate climb or descent, which control will allow you to adjust the rate? | The throttle. |

### Task F: Timed Turns to Magnetic Compass Headings

| 197. | On what headings will the magnetic compass read most accurately during a level 360° turn with a bank of approximately 15°? | In a turn through north or south, the compass indication will usually be incorrect. But in a turn through east or west, the compass indication is usually accurate. Therefore, the compass should be indicating properly when passing through 90° and 270°. This holds true for only medium to shallow bank turns, e.g., 15-30°. |
|---|---|---|
| 198. | If using the magnetic compass to turn right from a heading of 090° to a heading of 180°, how long will the turn take assuming a standard rate turn? | 30 seconds. |
| 199. | If turning left from a heading of 360° to a heading of 210°, how long will the turn take assuming a standard rate turn? | 50 seconds. |
| 200. | How long does it take for an airplane to complete a 360° turn while turning at a standard rate? | 2 minutes. |
| 201. | During a standard rate turn, how many degrees of heading change will be observed per second? | 3° per second. |

### Task G: Steep Turns

| 202. | What are the parameters you will be concentrating on when performing a steep turn? | I want to be sure I roll into the maneuver and maintain a 45° bank angle throughout a full 360° turn. My goal is to maintain my altitude plus or minus 100 feet and roll out of the maneuver within 10° of the heading I rolled into it on. |
|---|---|---|
| 203. | How would you correct for a loss of altitude during a steep turn? | I would reduce the bank slightly, increase back pressure on the elevator control, and increase power slightly until I reached my target altitude. Then, I would increase bank angle to my target bank angle, ease off the back pressure on the elevator, and evaluate whether I should maintain the higher power setting or retard it slightly. |
| 204. | How would you correct for a gain in altitude while performing a steep turn? | I would increase the bank angle if possible, reduce some of the back pressure on the elevator, and perhaps reduce power slightly if that was warranted. |

# APPENDIX A
# SOURCES

The sources we used for the questions and answers in this book include those below. These publications can be obtained from the FAA (www.faa.gov) and aviation bookstores.

| | |
|---|---|
| 14 CFR Part 61 | Certification: Pilots, Flight Instructors, and Ground Instructors |
| 14 CFR Part 68 | Requirements for Operating Certain Small Aircraft Without a Medical Certificate |
| 14 CFR Part 91 | General Operating and Flight Rules |
| AC 00-6 | *Aviation Weather* |
| AC 00-45 | *Aviation Weather Services* |
| AC 60-28 | *FAA English Language Standard for an FAA Certificate Issued Under 14 CFR Parts 61, 63, 65, and 107* |
| AC 91-74 | *Pilot Guide: Flight in Icing Conditions* |
| AC 91.21-1 | *Use of Portable Electronic Devices Aboard Aircraft* |
| ACL | Aeronautical Chart Legend |
| *AIM* | *Aeronautical Information Manual* |
| ASF | Air Safety Foundation |
| FAA-H-8083-2 | *Risk Management Handbook* |
| FAA-H-8083-3 | *Airplane Flying Handbook* |
| FAA-H-8083-6 | *Advanced Avionics Handbook* |
| FAA-H-8083-15 | *Instrument Flying Handbook* |
| FAA-H-8083-16 | *Instrument Procedures Handbook* |
| FAA-H-8083-25 | *Pilot's Handbook of Aeronautical Knowledge* |
| FAA-P-8740-50 | *On Landings, Part III* |
| IAP | Instrument Approach Procedures |
| NTSB | National Transportation Safety Board regulations |
| P/C Glossary | Pilot/Controller Glossary *(AIM)* |
| POH/AFM | Pilot's Operating Handbook/FAA-Approved Airplane Flight Manual |

Other:
  Chart Supplements
  Navigation Charts
  NOTAMs

NOTE: Users should reference the current edition of the reference documents listed above. The current edition of all FAA publications can be found at www.faa.gov.

# APPENDIX B
## ABBREVIATIONS AND ACRONYMS
## USED BY INSTRUMENT PILOTS

| | | | | |
|---|---|---|---|---|
| 14 CFR | Title 14 of the Code of Federal Regulations | | EFD | electronic flight display |
| A&P | certified mechanic | | EFIS | electronic flight information system |
| AATD | advanced aviation training device | | EGPWS | Enhanced Ground Proximity Warning System |
| AC | advisory circular or convective outlook bulletin | | ELSA | experimental light-sport aircraft |
| ACS | Airman Certification Standards | | ELT | emergency locator transmitter |
| AD | airworthiness directive | | ETA | estimated time of arrival |
| ADC | air data computer | | ETE | estimated time en route |
| ADF | Automatic Direction Finder | | FAA | Federal Aviation Administration |
| ADIZ | Air Defense Identification Zone | | FADEC | full authority digital engine control |
| ADM | aeronautical decision making | | FAF | final approach fix |
| AFM | Airplane Flight Manual | | FAR | Federal Aviation Regulations |
| AFS | Flight Standards Service | | FB | winds and temperatures aloft forecast |
| AGL | above ground level | | FBO | fixed-base operator |
| AHRS | attitude and heading reference system | | FDC | Flight Data Center |
| AI | attitude indicator | | FFS | full flight simulator |
| *AIM* | *Aeronautical Information Manual* | | FIP | forecast icing potential |
| AIRMET | Airmen's Meteorological Information | | FITS | FAA-Industry Training Standards |
| ALD | available landing distance | | FL | flight level |
| ALT | altimeter | | FMS | flight management system |
| AM | Automation Management | | fpm | feet per minute |
| AME | aviation medical examiner | | FRZ | flight restricted zone |
| AMEL | Airplane – Multiengine Land | | FSDO | Flight Standards District Office |
| AMES | Airplane – Multiengine Sea | | FSS | flight service station |
| AOA | angle of attack | | FSTD | flight simulation training device |
| AOO | Area of Operation | | FTD | flight training device |
| APV | approach with vertical guidance | | GA | general aviation |
| ASEL | Airplane – Single-Engine Land | | GAJSC | general aviation joint steering committee |
| ASES | Airplane – Single-Engine Sea | | GBAS | Ground Based Augmentation System |
| ASI | airspeed indicator | | GBAS GLS | Ground Based Augmentation Landing System |
| ASOS | automated surface observing system | | GLS | GNSS Landing System |
| ATC | air traffic control | | GMT | Greenwich Mean Time |
| ATD | aviation training device | | GNSS | Global Navigation Satellite System |
| ATIS | Automatic Terminal Information System | | GPH | gallons per hour |
| ATP | airline transport pilot | | GPS | global positioning system |
| ATS | Air Traffic Service | | GPWS | Ground Proximity Warning System |
| AWC | aviation weather center | | HAT | height above touchdown |
| AWOS | automated weather observing system | | HI | heading indicator |
| AWSS | automated weather sensor system | | HIWAS | hazardous inflight weather advisory service |
| AWW | severe weather forecast alert | | HSI | horizontal situation indicator |
| BATD | Basic Aviation Training Devices | | IA | inspection authorization |
| BECMG | becoming | | IAF | initial approach fix |
| CAS | calibrated airspeed | | IAP | instrument approach procedure |
| CAT | clear air turbulence | | IAS | indicated airspeed |
| CDI | course deviation indicator | | ICAO | International Civil Aviation Organization |
| CFI | certificated flight instructor | | IFR | instrument flight rules |
| CFII | instrument flight instructor | | ILS | instrument landing system |
| CFIT | controlled flight into terrain | | IMC | instrument meteorological conditions |
| CG | center of gravity | | IPC | instrument proficiency check |
| COP | changeover point | | IR | Instrument Rating |
| CP | completion phase | | IRA | Instrument Rating Airplane |
| CRM | crew resource management | | KOEL | kinds of operation equipment list |
| CTAF | Common Traffic Advisory Frequency | | LAA | local airport advisory |
| CWA | center weather advisory | | LAHSO | land and hold short operations |
| DA | decision altitude | | LDA | localizer type directional aid |
| DH | decision height | | $L/D_{MAX}$ | best lift/drag |
| DME | distance measuring equipment | | LED | light-emitting diode |
| DOD | department of defense | | LLWAS | low-level wind shear alert system |
| DP | departure procedure | | LNAV | lateral navigation |
| DPE | designated pilot examiner | | LOC | ILS localizer |
| DUATS | Direct User Access Terminal System | | LP | localizer performance |
| EFC | expect further clearance | | LPV | localizer performance with vertical guidance |

Appendix B: Abbreviations and Acronyms Used by Instrument Pilots

| | | | |
|---|---|---|---|
| LRU | line replaceable unit | SRM | single-pilot resource management |
| MAP | missed approach point | SSR | secondary surveillance radar |
| MC | magnetic course | STAR | standard terminal arrival |
| MDA | minimum descent altitude | STC | supplemental type certificate |
| MEA | minimum en route altitude | STOL | short takeoff and landing |
| MEF | maximum elevation figure | SUA | special use airspace |
| MEL | minimum equipment list | T&SI | turn-and-slip indicator |
| METAR | aviation routine weather report | TAA | terminal arrival area |
| MFD | multi-function display | TAC | terminal area chart |
| MH | magnetic heading | TACAN | tactical air navigation |
| MLS | microwave landing system | TAF | terminal aerodrome forecast |
| MOA | military operations areas | TAS | true airspeed |
| MOCA | minimum obstruction clearance altitude | TAWS | Terrain Awareness and Warning System |
| MP | manifold pressure | TC | turn coordinator or true course |
| MRA | minimum reception altitude | TCAS | traffic alert and collision avoidance system |
| MSA | minimum safe altitude | TCH | threshold crossing height |
| MSL | mean sea level | TDWR | terminal Doppler weather radar |
| MTR | military training routes | TEM | threat and error management |
| MVFR | marginal VFR | TFR | temporary flight restriction |
| NAS | National Airspace System | TIS | traffic information system |
| NAVAID | navigational aid | TM | task management |
| NDB | nondirectional beacon | TRSA | terminal radar service areas |
| NEXRAD | next generation radar | TSA | Transportation Security Administration |
| NM | nautical miles | TSOC | transportation security operations center |
| NOTAM | notice to airmen | UTC | universal coordinated time |
| NPA | nonprecision approach | $V_A$ | design maneuvering speed |
| NSA | national security areas | VASI | visual approach slope indicator |
| NSP | National Simulator Program | $V_{Best\ Glide}$ | best glide speed |
| NTSB | National Transportation Safety Board | VDP | visual descent point |
| NWS | National Weather Service | $V_{FE}$ | maximum flap extended speed |
| OAT | outside air temperature | VFR | visual flight rules |
| OBS | omnibearing selector | VHF | very high frequency |
| OCS | obstacle clearance surface | VHF/DF | VHF direction finder |
| OEA | obstacle evaluation area | $V_{LE}$ | maximum landing gear extended speed |
| PA | precision approach or Private Airplane | $V_{LO}$ | maximum landing gear operating speed |
| PAPI | precision approach path indicator | VMC | visual meteorological conditions |
| PAR | Private Pilot Airplane or precision approach radar | $V_{MC}$ | minimum control speed with the critical engine inoperative |
| PAT | Private Pilot Airplane/Recreational Pilot - Transition | | |
| PC | proficiency check | $V_{ME}$ | maximum endurance speed |
| PFD | primary flight display | VNAV | vertical navigation |
| PIC | pilot in command | $V_{NE}$ | never-exceed speed |
| PIM | Pilot's Information Manual | $V_{NO}$ | maximum structural cruising speed |
| PIREP | pilot weather report | VNR | VFR flight not recommended |
| POA | plan of action | VOR | VHF omnidirectional range |
| POH | Pilot's Operating Handbook | VOR/LOC | VOR/localizer |
| PROG | short-range surface prognostic | VORTAC | co-located VOR and TACAN |
| PSK | personal survival kit | $V_R$ | rotation speed |
| RAIM | receiver autonomous integrity monitoring | $V_S$ | stall speed |
| RM | risk management | $V_{S1}$ | stalling speed in a specified configuration |
| RMI | radio magnetic indicator | VSI | vertical speed indicator |
| RMP | risk management process | $V_{SO}$ | stalling speed in the landing configuration |
| RNAV | area navigation | $V_{SSE}$ | safe, intentional one-engine-inoperative speed (originally known as safe singe-engine speed) |
| RNP | required navigation performance | | |
| ROT | rate of turn | VV | vertical visibility |
| RVR | runway visual range | $V_X$ | best angle of climb speed |
| SAAAR | Special Aircraft and Aircrew Authorization Required | $V_{XSE}$ | best angle of climb speed with one engine inoperative |
| SAS | Stability Augmentation System | $V_Y$ | best rate of climb speed |
| S.B. | service bulletin | $V_{YSE}$ | best rate of climb speed with one engine inoperative |
| SDF | Simplified Directional Facility | | |
| SFRA | special flight rules area | WA | AIRMET |
| SIAP | standard instrument approach procedure | WAAS | Wide Area Augmentation System |
| SIGMET | Significant Meteorological Information | WCA | wind correction angle |
| SIGWX | significant weather | WS | severe thunderstorm watch or SIGMET |
| SM | statute miles | WSP | weather system processor |
| SMS | Safety Management System | WST | convective SIGMET |
| SODA | statement of demonstrated ability | WT | tornado watch |
| SOP | standard operating procedures | | |

178  Notes

# INDEX

3P model. . . . . . . . . . . . . . . . . . . . . . . . . . . . 94
    One engine inoperative. . . . . . . . . . . . . . . . 150

5P model. . . . . . . . . . . . . . . . . . . . . . . . . . . . 100

Abbreviated briefing. . . . . . . . . . . . . . . . . . . . 107
Abbreviations and acronyms. . . . . . . . . . . . . . 176
    ACS. . . . . . . . . . . . . . . . . . . . . . . . . . . . . . 47
Abstractions. . . . . . . . . . . . . . . . . . . . . . . . . . 157
Acceleration error. . . . . . . . . . . . . . . . . . . . . . 120
ACS, instrument rating. . . . . . . . . . . . . . . . . . . 2
Acute fatigue. . . . . . . . . . . . . . . . . . . . . . . . . 168
ADF. . . . . . . . . . . . . . . . . . . . . . 126, 129, 137
ADM. . . . . . . . . . . . . . . . . . . . . . . . . . . . . . . 94
    PTS. . . . . . . . . . . . . . . . . . . . . . . . . . . . . . 60
Aeromedical factors. . . . . . . . . . . . . . . . . . . . 166
    PTS. . . . . . . . . . . . . . . . . . . . . . . . . . . . . . 71
Aeronautical decision making. . . . . . . . . . . . . 94
    PTS. . . . . . . . . . . . . . . . . . . . . . . . . . . . . . 60
Air traffic control clearances. . . . . . . . . . . . . 131
    And procedures. . . . . . . . . . . . . . . . . . . . 129
        ACS. . . . . . . . . . . . . . . . . . . . . . . . . . . . 10
        PTS. . . . . . . . . . . . . . . . . . . . . . . . . . . . 74
Airborne weather avoidance radar. . . . . . . . . 108
Aircraft
    Flight instruments and navigation equipment. . . 118
        ACS. . . . . . . . . . . . . . . . . . . . . . . . . . . . . 8
        PTS. . . . . . . . . . . . . . . . . . . . . . . . . . . . 70
    Maintenance logbooks. . . . . . . . . . . . . . . . 106
    Requirements and limitations ACS. . . . . . . . 40
    Systems related to IFR operations. . . . . . . 116
        ACS. . . . . . . . . . . . . . . . . . . . . . . . . . . . . 7
Airman
    Certification Standards, instrument rating. . . . . . 2
    Knowledge test report. . . . . . . . . . . . . . . . . 31
Airmen's Meteorological Information. . . . . . . . 111
AIRMET. . . . . . . . . . . . . . . . . . . . . . . . . . . . 111
Airspeed
    After engine failure. . . . . . . . . . . . . . . . . . 149
    Indicator. . . . . . . . . . . . . . . . . . . . . 118, 151
        Blocked static port. . . . . . . . . . . . . . . . . 119
        Failure. . . . . . . . . . . . . . . . . . . . . . . . . 150
        Maintaining. . . . . . . . . . . . . . . . . . . . . . 128
        VYSE. . . . . . . . . . . . . . . . . . . . . . . . . . 149
Alcohol. . . . . . . . . . . . . . . . . . . . . . . . 166, 169
Alternate
    Airport. . . . . . . . . . . . . . . . 113, 130, 143, 144
    Static source. . . . . . . . . . . . . . . . . . . 117, 118
Alternator. . . . . . . . . . . . . . . . . . . . . . . . . . . 122
Altimeter. . . . . . . . . . . . . . . . . . . . . . . . 118, 128
Altitude. . . . . . . . . . . . . . . . . . . . . . . . . 113, 172
Amended clearance. . . . . . . . . . . . . . . . 131, 148
ANDS, Accelerate North, Decelerate South. . . . . . 120
Antennas. . . . . . . . . . . . . . . . . . . . . . . . . . . 128
Anti-
    Authority, hazardous attitude. . . . . . . . . . . . 95
    Icing. . . . . . . . . . . . . . . . . . . 98, 100, 115, 116

Approach. . . . . . . . . . . . . . . 114, 135, 146, 147
    Category. . . . . . . . . . . . . . . . . . . . . . 135, 136
    Light system. . . . . . . . . . . . . . . . . . . 124, 146
    Mode. . . . . . . . . . . . . . . . . . . . . . . . . . . . 104
    Plate. . . . . . . . . . . . . . . . . . . . . . . . . 145, 146
    Speeds. . . . . . . . . . . . . . . . . . . . . . . 135, 136
    With loss of primary flight instrument indicators. 150
        ACS. . . . . . . . . . . . . . . . . . . . . . . . . . . . 24
        PTS. . . . . . . . . . . . . . . . . . . . . . . . . . . . 85
ARROW. . . . . . . . . . . . . . . . . . . . . . . . . . . . 138
ATC clearances. . . . . . . . . . . . . . . . . . . . . . 131
    And procedures. . . . . . . . . . . . . . . . . . . . 129
        ACS. . . . . . . . . . . . . . . . . . . . . . . . . . . . 10
        PTS. . . . . . . . . . . . . . . . . . . . . . . . . . . . 74
ATD, ACS. . . . . . . . . . . . . . . . . . . . . . . . . . . 42
ATIS. . . . . . . . . . . . . . . . . . . . . . . . . . . . . . 112
Attitude
    Indicator. . . . . . . . . . . . . . . 119, 128, 150, 151
        Error. . . . . . . . . . . . . . . . . . . . . . . . . . . 119
        Power source. . . . . . . . . . . . . . . . . . . . 119
    Instrument flying. . . . . . . . . . . . . . . . . . . . 172
Automatic
    Direction finder. . . . . . . . . . . . . . 126, 129, 137
    Terminal Information Service. . . . . . . . . . . 112
Automation management. . . . . . . . . . . . . . . 104
    PTS. . . . . . . . . . . . . . . . . . . . . . . . . . . . . 62
Autopilot. . . . . . . . . . . . . . . . . . . . . . . 104, 127
Avgas. . . . . . . . . . . . . . . . . . . . . . . . . . . . . 117
Aviation training devices. . . . . . . . . . . . . . . . . 42
Avionics master switch. . . . . . . . . . . . . . . . . 151

Basic instrument flight maneuvers. . . . . . . . . 134
Battery. . . . . . . . . . . . . . . . . . . . . . . . . . . . 122
Behavior of student. . . . . . . . . . . . . . . . . . . 155
Blood alcohol content. . . . . . . . . . . . . . . . . . 169
Bracketing. . . . . . . . . . . . . . . . . . . . . . . . . . 137

CAL. . . . . . . . . . . . . . . . . . . . . . . . . . 158, 159
Carbon monoxide. . . . . . . . . . . . . . . . . . . . . 168
Carburetor
    Heat. . . . . . . . . . . . . . . . . . . . . . . . . 116, 117
    Icing. . . . . . . . . . . . . . . . . . . . . . . . . 116, 117
Category
    A approach. . . . . . . . . . . . . . . . . . . . 135, 136
    B approach. . . . . . . . . . . . . . . . . . . . 135, 136
    C approach. . . . . . . . . . . . . . . . . . . . . . . 135
    D approach. . . . . . . . . . . . . . . . . . . . . . . 135
    E approach. . . . . . . . . . . . . . . . . . . . . . . 135
    I ILS approach. . . . . . . . . . . . . . . . . . . . . 124
    II ILS approach. . . . . . . . . . . . . . . . . . . . 124
    III ILS approach. . . . . . . . . . . . . . . . . . . . 124
CDI. . . . . . . . . . . . . . . . . . . . . . . . . . . 123, 137
Center Weather Advisory. . . . . . . . . . . . . . . 107
CFIT. . . . . . . . . . . . . . . . . . . . . . . . . . . 96, 103
    Awareness. . . . . . . . . . . . . . . . . . . . . . . 103
    PTS. . . . . . . . . . . . . . . . . . . . . . . . . . . . . 61
Change of airspeed in straight-and-level and
turning flight. . . . . . . . . . . . . . . . . . . . . . . . 172
    PTS. . . . . . . . . . . . . . . . . . . . . . . . . . . . . 76

179

Changeover point. . . . . . . . . . . . . . . . . . . . . . . 140
Checking instruments and equipment. . . . . . . . . 151
    ACS. . . . . . . . . . . . . . . . . . . . . . . . . . . . . . . . 25
    PTS. . . . . . . . . . . . . . . . . . . . . . . . . . . . . . . . 87
Choose, DECIDE model. . . . . . . . . . . . . . . . 94, 95
Chronic fatigue. . . . . . . . . . . . . . . . . . . . . . . . . . 168
Circling
    Approach. . . . . . . . . . . . . . . . . . . . . . 146, 147
        ACS. . . . . . . . . . . . . . . . . . . . . . . . . . . . . 19
        PTS. . . . . . . . . . . . . . . . . . . . . . . . . . . . . 84
    Minimum altitude. . . . . . . . . . . . . . . . . . . . . 146
Class
    A airspace. . . . . . . . . . . . . . . . . . . . . 105, 131
    B airspace. . . . . . . . . . . . . . . . . . . . . . . . . 130
    C airspace. . . . . . . . . . . . . . . . . . . . . . . . . 130
    D airspace. . . . . . . . . . . . . . . . . . . . . . . . . 130
    E airspace. . . . . . . . . . . . . . . . . . . . . . . . . 130
    G airspace. . . . . . . . . . . . . . . . . . . . . . . . . 130
Clear ice. . . . . . . . . . . . . . . . . . . . . . . . . . . . . . 116
Clearance
    Delivery frequency. . . . . . . . . . . . . . . . . . . 138
    Limit. . . . . . . . . . . . . . . . . . . . . . . . . . . . . . 147
    Void time. . . . . . . . . . . . . . . . . . . . . . . . . . 131
Cleared as filed. . . . . . . . . . . . . . . . . . . . . . . . 138
Climbs. . . . . . . . . . . . . . . . . . . . . . . . . . . 134, 173
Cold front, fast-moving. . . . . . . . . . . . . . . . . . . 98
Collision avoidance. . . . . . . . . . . . . . . . . . . . . 148
Commercial pilots. . . . . . . . . . . . . . . . . . . . . . 105
Communication, effective. . . . . . . . . . . . . 156, 157
Communications, loss. . . . . . . . . . . . . . . . 142, 147
Compass correction card. . . . . . . . . . . . . . . . . 120
Compliance with
    Air traffic control clearances, ACS. . . . . . . . . 10
    Departure, en route, & arrival procedures
        & clearances, PTS. . . . . . . . . . . . . . . . . . 74
Composite flight plan. . . . . . . . . . . . . . . . 129, 131
Computer-assisted learning. . . . . . . . . . . . 158, 159
Congestion. . . . . . . . . . . . . . . . . . . . . . . . . . . . 166
Constant
    Airspeed climbs/descents. . . . . . . . . . . . . . 173
        PTS. . . . . . . . . . . . . . . . . . . . . . . . . . . . . 76
    Rate climbs and descents. . . . . . . . . . . . . . 173
        PTS. . . . . . . . . . . . . . . . . . . . . . . . . . . . . 77
Contact approach. . . . . . . . . . . . . . . . . . . . . . . 141
Controlled flight into terrain. . . . . . . . . . . . . 96, 103
    Awareness. . . . . . . . . . . . . . . . . . . . . . . . . 103
    PTS. . . . . . . . . . . . . . . . . . . . . . . . . . . . . . . 61
Convective
    Outlook chart. . . . . . . . . . . . . . . . . . . . . . . 111
    SIGMET. . . . . . . . . . . . . . . . . . . . . . . 111, 112
COP. . . . . . . . . . . . . . . . . . . . . . . . . . . . . . . . . 140
Course deviation indicator. . . . . . . . . . . . . 123, 137
CRAFT. . . . . . . . . . . . . . . . . . . . . . . . . . . . . . . 138
Criticism, constructive. . . . . . . . . . . . . 156, 162, 164
Critique & evaluation. . . . . . . . . . . . . . 158, 161, 162
    PTS. . . . . . . . . . . . . . . . . . . . . . . . . . . . . . . 69
Cross-country flight planning. . . . . . . . . . . 112, 113
    ACS. . . . . . . . . . . . . . . . . . . . . . . . . . . . . . . . 6
    PTS. . . . . . . . . . . . . . . . . . . . . . . . . . . . . . . 72
Cruise
    Clearance. . . . . . . . . . . . . . . . . . . . . . . . . . 141
    Power settings. . . . . . . . . . . . . . . . . . . . . . 113
Cruising. . . . . . . . . . . . . . . . . . . . . . . . . . . . . . 113
    Altitude. . . . . . . . . . . . . . . . . . . . . . . . 129, 131
CTAF. . . . . . . . . . . . . . . . . . . . . . . . . . . . . . . . 147
Cut-off position. . . . . . . . . . . . . . . . . . . . . . . . 149

CWA. . . . . . . . . . . . . . . . . . . . . . . . . . . . . . . . 107

DA. . . . . . . . . . . . . . . . . . . . . 144, 145, 146, 147
Dead leg, dead engine. . . . . . . . . . . . . . . . . . . 148
Deceleration error. . . . . . . . . . . . . . . . . . . . . . 120
DECIDE model. . . . . . . . . . . . . . . . . . . . . . 94, 95
    One engine inoperative. . . . . . . . . . . . . . . . 150
Decision
    Altitude. . . . . . . . . . . . . . 144, 145, 146, 147
    Height. . . . . . . . . . . . . . . . . . . . . . . . . . . . 145
    Making, one engine inoperative. . . . . . . . . . 150
Decongestant. . . . . . . . . . . . . . . . . . . . . . . . . . 166
Defective equipment. . . . . . . . . . . . . . . . . . . . . 152
Defense mechanisms. . . . . . . . . . . . . . . . 155, 156
Deflection. . . . . . . . . . . . . . . . . . . . . . . . . . . . . 149
Dehydration. . . . . . . . . . . . . . . . . . . . . . . . . . . 169
Deicing. . . . . . . . . . . . . . . . . . . 98, 100, 115, 116
Demonstration-performance
    method. . . . . . . . . . . . . . 158, 160, 161, 170, 171
Departure
    Clearance. . . . . . . . . . . . . . . . . . . . . . . . . . 138
    En route, & arrival procedures & clearances. . . 138
        ACS. . . . . . . . . . . . . . . . . . . . . . . . . . . . . 15
    Procedure. . . . . . . . . . . . . . . . . . . . . . . . . . 138
Descents. . . . . . . . . . . . . . . . . . . . . . . . . 135, 173
Detect, DECIDE model. . . . . . . . . . . . . . . . . 94, 95
Deviate from a clearance. . . . . . . . . . . . . . . . . 148
Deviation. . . . . . . . . . . . . . . . . . . . . . . . . . . . . 120
DH. . . . . . . . . . . . . . . . . . . . . . . . . . . . . . . . . . 145
Dip error. . . . . . . . . . . . . . . . . . . . . . . . . . . . . 120
Direct
    Holding pattern entry. . . . . . . . . . . . . . . . . . 132
    Routes. . . . . . . . . . . . . . . . . . . . . . . . . . . . 141
    Routing clearance. . . . . . . . . . . . . . . . . . . . 112
Distance measuring equipment. . . . . . . . . . . . . 124
    Arc. . . . . . . . . . . . . . . . . . . . . . . . . . . 124, 126
    Fix. . . . . . . . . . . . . . . . . . . . . . . . . . . . . . . 144
DME. . . . . . . . . . . . . . . . . . . . . . . . . . . . . . . . 124
    Arc. . . . . . . . . . . . . . . . . . . . . . . . . . . 124, 126
    Fix. . . . . . . . . . . . . . . . . . . . . . . . . . . . . . . 144
Do, DECIDE model. . . . . . . . . . . . . . . . . . . 94, 95
Documents. . . . . . . . . . . . . . . . . . . . . . . . . . . . 138
Domains of learning. . . . . . . . . . . . . . . . . . . . . 154
DP. . . . . . . . . . . . . . . . . . . . . . . . . . . . . . . . . . 138
Dust storms. . . . . . . . . . . . . . . . . . . . . . . . . . . 111


EFC time. . . . . . . . . . . . . . . . . . . . . . . . . . . . . 147
EFD. . . . . . . . . . . . . . . . . . . . . . . . . . 122, 123, 127
Effect, law of. . . . . . . . . . . . . . . . . . . . . . . . . . 154
Electrical
    Failure. . . . . . . . . . . . . . . . . . . . . . . . . 122, 123
    System. . . . . . . . . . . . . . . . . . . . . . . . . . . . 122
Electronic flight display. . . . . . . . . . . . 122, 123, 127
Embedded thunderstorms. . . . . . . . . . . . . . 99, 112
Emergency. . . . . . . . . . . . . . . . . . . . . . . . . . . . 148
    Operations. . . . . . . . . . . . . . . . . . . . . . . . . 147
        ACS. . . . . . . . . . . . . . . . . . . . . . . . . . . . . 21
        PTS. . . . . . . . . . . . . . . . . . . . . . . . . . . . . 85
Endorsements. . . . . . . . . . . . . . . . . . . . . . 163, 170
Engine failure. . . . . . . . . . . . . . . . . . . . . . . . . . 148
    During straight-and-level flight and turns, PTS. . . 86
En route
    Charts. . . . . . . . . . . . . . . . . . . . . . . . . . . . 140
    Low altitude charts. . . . . . . . . . . . . . . . . . . 140

## Index

Equipment
   Checking. . . . . . . . . . . . . . . . . . . . 151, 152
     Requirements and limitations, ACS. . . . . . . . . 40
Estimate, DECIDE model. . . . . . . . . . . . . . . 94, 95
Estimated time en route. . . . . . . . . . . . . 113, 124
ETE. . . . . . . . . . . . . . . . . . . . . . . . . . . . . . 113, 124
Evaluate
   3P model, ME. . . . . . . . . . . . . . . . . . . . . . . . . 94
   DECIDE model. . . . . . . . . . . . . . . . . . . . 94, 95
Evaluations. . . . . . . . . . . . . . . . . . . . 158, 161, 163
Exercise, law of. . . . . . . . . . . . . . . . . . . . . . . 154
Expect further clearance time. . . . . . . . . . . . . 147
External pressures. . . . . . . . . . . . . . . . . . . . . . 97


FAA charts. . . . . . . . . . . . . . . . . . . . . . . . . . . 114
FAF. . . . . . . . . . . . . . . . . . . . . . . . . . . . . 142, 144
Fast-moving cold front. . . . . . . . . . . . . . . . . . . 98
Fatigue. . . . . . . . . . . . . . . . . . . . . . . . . . . . . . 168
FDC NOTAM. . . . . . . . . . . . . . . . . . . . . . . . . 114
Feather detente. . . . . . . . . . . . . . . . . . . . . . . 149
Feathering the propeller. . . . . . . . . . . . . . . . . 149
Feeder route. . . . . . . . . . . . . . . . . . . . . . . . . 141
Final approach
   Fix. . . . . . . . . . . . . . . . . . . . . . . . . . . 142, 144
   Point. . . . . . . . . . . . . . . . . . . . . . . . . . . . . 142
   Segment. . . . . . . . . . . . . . . . . . . . . . . . . . 141
     One engine inoperative. . . . . . . . . . . . . . 149
Fixation. . . . . . . . . . . . . . . . . . . . . . . . . . . . . 102
Fixed-distance markings. . . . . . . . . . . . . . . . . 144
Flight
   By ref. to instruments. . . . . . . . . . . . . . 134, 171
     ACS. . . . . . . . . . . . . . . . . . . . . . . . . . . . . 12
     PTS. . . . . . . . . . . . . . . . . . . . . . . . . . . . . 75
   Cross-country. . . . . . . . . . . . . . . . . . . . . . . 113
   Instructor characteristics
   and responsibilities. . . . . . . . . . . . . . . 162, 164
     PTS. . . . . . . . . . . . . . . . . . . . . . . . . . . . . 69
   Instruments. . . . . . . . . . . . . . . . . . . . . . . . 150
   Management system. . . . . . . . . . . . . . . . . 127
   Review. . . . . . . . . . . . . . . . . . . . . . . . . . . 163
   Simulation training device. . . . . . . . . . . 106, 107
     ACS. . . . . . . . . . . . . . . . . . . . . . . . . . . . . 42
     Credit, PTS. . . . . . . . . . . . . . . . . . . . . . . . 88
     PTS. . . . . . . . . . . . . . . . . . . . . . . . . . . . . 57
   Simulator. . . . . . . . . . . . . . . . . . . . . . 106, 107
FMS. . . . . . . . . . . . . . . . . . . . . . . . . . . . . . . . 127
Fog. . . . . . . . . . . . . . . . . . . . . . . . . . . . . . . . . 99
Forgetting. . . . . . . . . . . . . . . . . . . . . . . . . . . 155
Freezing
   Level chart. . . . . . . . . . . . . . . . . . . . . . . . 110
   Rain. . . . . . . . . . . . . . . . . . . . . . . . . . . . . . 98
   Temperatures. . . . . . . . . . . . . . . . . . . . . . . 99
Front, fast-moving cold. . . . . . . . . . . . . . . . . . 98
Frost. . . . . . . . . . . . . . . . . . . . . . . . . . . 115, 116
FSS. . . . . . . . . . . . . . . . . . . . . . . . . . . . . . . . 138
FSTD, ACS. . . . . . . . . . . . . . . . . . . . . . . . . . . 42
Fuel. . . . . . . . . . . . . . . . . . . . . . . . . . . . . . . . 129
   Burn. . . . . . . . . . . . . . . . . . . . . . . . . . . . . 113
   Flow. . . . . . . . . . . . . . . . . . . . . . . . . . . . . 113
   Icing. . . . . . . . . . . . . . . . . . . . . . . . . . . . . 117
   Requirements. . . . . . . . . . . . . . . . . . . 113, 114
   Reserves. . . . . . . . . . . . . . . . . . . . . . . 96, 113
Fundamentals of instructing. . . . . . . . . . . . . . 154

Garmin G1000. . . . . . . . . . . . . . . . . . . . . . . . 104
Glass panel. . . . . . . . . . . . . . . . . . . . . . . 100, 151
   Display failure. . . . . . . . . . . . . . . . . . . . . . 151
Glide
   Path. . . . . . . . . . . . . . . . . . . . . . . . . . . . . 144
   Slope. . . . . . . . . . . . . . . . . 123, 124, 144, 145
Go/no-go decisions. . . . . . . . . . . . . . . . . . . . . 97
GPS. . . . . . . . . . . . . . . . . . . . . 100, 126, 127, 129
   Approach. . . . . . . . . . . . . . . . . . . . . . . . . 143
   NOTAM. . . . . . . . . . . . . . . . . . . . . . . . . . 115
   Overlay approach. . . . . . . . . . . . . . . . . . . 127
GPWS. . . . . . . . . . . . . . . . . . . . . . . . . . . . . . 103
GRABCARD. . . . . . . . . . . . . . . . . . . . . . . . . . 105
Graveyard spiral. . . . . . . . . . . . . . . . . . . . . . . 167
Ground proximity warning system. . . . . . . . . . 103
Groundspeed. . . . . . . . . . . . . . . . . . . . . . . . . 113
Guided discussion method. . . . . . . . . . . . 159, 160
Gyroscope. . . . . . . . . . . . . . . . . . . 119, 121, 128
Gyroscopic precession. . . . . . . . . . . . . . . 121, 152


Hail. . . . . . . . . . . . . . . . . . . . . . . . . . . . 111, 112
Hazardous attitudes. . . . . . . . . . . . . . . . . . . . . 95
Haze. . . . . . . . . . . . . . . . . . . . . . . . . . . . . . . 146
Heading indicator. . . . . . . . . . . 120, 121, 150, 152
   Limitation. . . . . . . . . . . . . . . . . . . . . . . . . 121
   Preflight check. . . . . . . . . . . . . . . . . . . . . 128
Holding
   Pattern. . . . . . . . . . . . . . . . . . . . . . . 132, 133
     Entries. . . . . . . . . . . . . . . . . . . . . . 132, 133
   Procedures. . . . . . . . . . . . . . . . . . . . . . . . 132
     ACS. . . . . . . . . . . . . . . . . . . . . . . . . . . . . 11
     PTS. . . . . . . . . . . . . . . . . . . . . . . . . . . . . 80
Homing. . . . . . . . . . . . . . . . . . . . . . . . . . . . . 137
Horiz. situation indic. . . . . . . . . . . . 119, 123, 137
HSI. . . . . . . . . . . . . . . . . . . . . . . . . 119, 123, 137
Human
   Behavior and effective comm. . . . . . . . . . . 155
     PTS. . . . . . . . . . . . . . . . . . . . . . . . . . . . . 68
   Needs. . . . . . . . . . . . . . . . . . . . . . . . . . . 155
Hyperventilation. . . . . . . . . . . . . . . . . . . . . . . 166
Hypothermia. . . . . . . . . . . . . . . . . . . . . . . . . 169
Hypoxia. . . . . . . . . . . . . . . . . . . . . . . . . . . . . 166


IAF. . . . . . . . . . . . . . . . . . . . . . . . . . . . . 141, 143
IAP. . . . . . . . . . . . . . . . . . . . . . . . . . . . . . . . 141
   Chart. . . . . . . . . . . . . . . . . . . . 135, 141, 143
Ice. . . . . . . . . . . . . . . . . . . . . . . 98, 100, 115, 117
   Propeller. . . . . . . . . . . . . . . . . . . . . . . . . . 116
   Severe. . . . . . . . . . . . . . . . . . . . . . . . . . . 111
   Significant weather charts. . . . . . . . . . . . . 109
   Structural. . . . . . . . . . . . . . . . . . . . . . . . . 116
Ident. . . . . . . . . . . . . . . . . . . . . . . . . . . . . . . 125
Identify, DECIDE model. . . . . . . . . . . . . . . 94, 95
IFR
   Clearance. . . . . . . . . . . . . . . . . . . . . . . . . 131
   Departure clearance. . . . . . . . . . . . . . . . . 138
   Flight plan. . . . . . . . . . . . . . . . . . 129, 131, 148
   Pilot in command. . . . . . . . . . . . . . . . . . . 105
   Preferred route. . . . . . . . . . . . . . . . . . . . . 112
   Required instruments and equipment. . . . . . . 105
Illusions. . . . . . . . . . . . . . . . . . . . . . . . . . 146, 167

## Index

ILS. . . . . . . . . . . . . . . . . . . . . . . . . . . . . . . . 124, 129
   Approach. . . . . . . . . . . . . 124, 125, 144, 145, 147
      Critical area. . . . . . . . . . . . . . . . . . . . . . 139
      Glide slope angle. . . . . . . . . . . . . . . . . . 124
Impact icing. . . . . . . . . . . . . . . . . . . . . . . . . . . 117
Impulsivity, hazardous attitude. . . . . . . . . . . . . 95
Induction icing. . . . . . . . . . . . . . . . . . . . . . . . 117
Initial approach
   Fix. . . . . . . . . . . . . . . . . . . . . . . . . . . . 141, 143
   Segment. . . . . . . . . . . . . . . . . . . . . . . . . . 141
Inner marker. . . . . . . . . . . . . . . . . . . . . . . . . 125
Inoperative instrument/equipment. . . . . . . . . . . 152
Inspections, required. . . . . . . . . . . . . . . . . . . 106
Instrument
   Approach
      One engine inoperative (multiengine). . . . . . 149
         PTS. . . . . . . . . . . . . . . . . . . . . . . . . . . . 87
      Procedure chart. . . . . . . . . . . . . 135, 141, 143
      Procedures. . . . . . . . . . . . . . . . . . . . 141, 143
         ACS. . . . . . . . . . . . . . . . . . . . . . . . . . . . 16
         PTS. . . . . . . . . . . . . . . . . . . . . . . . . . . . 81
   Cockpit check, PTS. . . . . . . . . . . . . . . . . . . . 73
   Currency. . . . . . . . . . . . . . . . . . . . . . . . . . 106
   Flight
      ACS. . . . . . . . . . . . . . . . . . . . . . . . . . . . . . 12
      Time. . . . . . . . . . . . . . . . . . . . . . . . . 106, 107
   Flight deck check. . . . . . . . . . . . . . . . . . . . 128
      ACS. . . . . . . . . . . . . . . . . . . . . . . . . . . . . . 9
   Landing system. . . . . . . . . . . . . . . . . . 124, 129
      Approach. . . . . . . . . . 124, 125, 144, 145, 147
      Glide slope angle. . . . . . . . . . . . . . . . . . 124
   Proficiency check. . . . . . . . . . . . . . . . 106, 107
      ACS. . . . . . . . . . . . . . . . . . . . . . . . . . . . . 37
   Rating. . . . . . . . . . . . . . . . . . . . . . . . . . . . 105
Instruments. . . . . . . . . . . . . . . . . . . . . . . . . 150
   Checking. . . . . . . . . . . . . . . . . . . . . . 151, 152
   Failure. . . . . . . . . . . . . . . . . . . . . . . . . . . 150
Integrated Flight Instruction. . . . . . . . . . . . . . . 160
Intensity, law of. . . . . . . . . . . . . . . . . . . . . . . 154
Intercepting and tracking navigational systems and
arcs. . . . . . . . . . . . . . . . . . . . . . . . . . . . . . . 136
Intercepting and tracking navigational systems and
DME arcs
   ACS. . . . . . . . . . . . . . . . . . . . . . . . . . . . . . 14
   PTS. . . . . . . . . . . . . . . . . . . . . . . . . . . . . . 79
Intermediate approach segment. . . . . . . . . . . 141
Invulnerability, hazardous attitude. . . . . . . . . . . 95
I'M SAFE checklist. . . . . . . . . . . . . . . . . . 98, 100


Jeppesen charts. . . . . . . . . . . . . . . . . . . . . . 114
Jet A fuel. . . . . . . . . . . . . . . . . . . . . . . . . . . 117
Judgment assessment matrix, PTS. . . . . . . 55, 90


K index. . . . . . . . . . . . . . . . . . . . . . . . . 110, 111
Known icing conditions. . . . . . . . . . . . . . . . . 116
Kollsman window. . . . . . . . . . . . . . . . . . 118, 128

Landing. . . . . . . . . . . . . . . . . . . . . . . . . 146, 147
   Behind a large aircraft. . . . . . . . . . . . . . . . . 96
   From a(n)
      Circling approach. . . . . . . . . . . . . . . . . . 146
      Instrument approach, ACS. . . . . . . . . . . . . 20
      Straight-in approach. . . . . . . . . . . . . . . . 143
         PTS. . . . . . . . . . . . . . . . . . . . . . . . . . . . 84
LDA. . . . . . . . . . . . . . . . . . . . . . . . . . . . . . 143
Learning
   Curve. . . . . . . . . . . . . . . . . . . . . . . . . . . . 155
   Process. . . . . . . . . . . . . . . . . . . . . . . 154, 155
      PTS. . . . . . . . . . . . . . . . . . . . . . . . . . . . . 68
Lecture method. . . . . . . . . . . . . . . 158, 159, 160
Lesson plan. . . . . . . . . . . . . 157, 158, 164, 165
Letter of discontinuance, PTS. . . . . . . . . . . . . 59
Levels of learning. . . . . . . . . . . . . . . . . . . . . 154
Lifted index chart. . . . . . . . . . . . . . . . . . . . . 110
LOC. . . . . . . . . . . . . . . . . . . . . . . . . . . . . . 143
   Approach. . . . . . . . . . . . . . . . . . . . . . . . . 143
Localizer. . . . . . . . . . . . . . . . . . . . 124, 144, 145
   -Type directional aid. . . . . . . . . . . . . . . . . 143
Logbook
   Aircraft maintenance. . . . . . . . . . . . . . . . . 106
   Entries related to instrument instruction. . . . . . 170
      PTS. . . . . . . . . . . . . . . . . . . . . . . . . . . . 71
   Instrument flight time. . . . . . . . . . . . . . . . . 106
   Simulator/training device. . . . . . . . . . . . . . . 107
Loss of
   Communications. . . . . . . . . . . . . . . . . 142, 147
      ACS. . . . . . . . . . . . . . . . . . . . . . . . . . . . 21
      PTS. . . . . . . . . . . . . . . . . . . . . . . . . . . . 85
   Primary flight instrument indicators. . . . . . . . 150
Low-level significant weather charts. . . . . . . . . 109
Lubber line. . . . . . . . . . . . . . . . . . . . . . . . . 119


Macho, hazardous attitude. . . . . . . . . . . . . . . . 95
Magnetic
   Compass. . . . . . . . . . . . . 119, 120, 121, 128, 152
   Variation. . . . . . . . . . . . . . . . . . . . . . . . . . 120
Maintenance logbook. . . . . . . . . . . . . . . 106, 128
Maneuver lesson. . . . . . . . . . . . . . . . . . . . . . 170
   PTS. . . . . . . . . . . . . . . . . . . . . . . . . . . . . 73
Manufacturer's operating limitations. . . . . . . . . 149
MAP. . . . . . . . . . . . . . . . . . . . . . . . . . 144, 145
Marker
   Beacons. . . . . . . . . . . . . . . . . . . . . . 124, 125
   System. . . . . . . . . . . . . . . . . . . . . . . . . . 125
MDA. . . . . . . . . . . . . . . . . . . . 142, 143, 144, 146
MEA. . . . . . . . . . . . . . . . 113, 129, 135, 140, 141
Medication. . . . . . . . . . . . . . . . . . . . . . . . . . 166
Memory. . . . . . . . . . . . . . . . . . . . . . . . . . . . 155
Microburst. . . . . . . . . . . . . . . . . . . . . . . . . . . 99
Middle marker. . . . . . . . . . . . . . . . . . . . . . . 125
Minimum
   Descent altitude. . . . . . . . . . . . . . 143, 144, 146
      FAF. . . . . . . . . . . . . . . . . . . . . . . . . . . 142
   En route altitude. . . . . . . . . . . . . 135, 140, 141
      Cruise flight. . . . . . . . . . . . . . . . . . . 113, 129
      IFR cross-country. . . . . . . . . . . . . . . . . . 113
   Fuel requirements. . . . . . . . . . . . . . . . . . . 130
   Obstruction clearance altitude. . . . . . . . 140, 141
      Cruise flight. . . . . . . . . . . . . . . . . . . 113, 129
      IFR cross-country. . . . . . . . . . . . . . . . . . 113
   Reception altitude. . . . . . . . . . . . . . . . . . . 140
   Safe/sector altitude. . . . . . . . . . . . . . . . . . 134

# Index

Missed approach. . . . . . . . . . . . . . . . . . . . . 144, 145
   ACS. . . . . . . . . . . . . . . . . . . . . . . . . . . . . . . . 18
   Point. . . . . . . . . . . . . . . . . . . . . . . . . . . 144, 145
   Procedures. . . . . . . . . . . . . . . . . . . . . . . . . 145
   PTS. . . . . . . . . . . . . . . . . . . . . . . . . . . . . . . . 83
   Segment. . . . . . . . . . . . . . . . . . . . . . . . . . . 141
Mitigate. . . . . . . . . . . . . . . . . . . . . . . . . . . . . . . . 94
Mixed ice. . . . . . . . . . . . . . . . . . . . . . . . . . . . . 116
MOCA. . . . . . . . . . . . . . . . . . . . . . . . . . . 140, 141
   Cruise flight. . . . . . . . . . . . . . . . . . . . 113, 129
   IFR cross-country. . . . . . . . . . . . . . . . . . . . 113
Mode C. . . . . . . . . . . . . . . . . . . . . . . . . . . . . . 125
Morse code. . . . . . . . . . . . . . . . . . . . . . . . . . . 137
Motion sickness. . . . . . . . . . . . . . . . . . . . . . . 167
MRA. . . . . . . . . . . . . . . . . . . . . . . . . . . . . . . . 140
MSA. . . . . . . . . . . . . . . . . . . . . . . . . . . . . . . . 134
Multiengine airplane
   Considerations, ACS. . . . . . . . . . . . . . . . . . . 39
   Instrument approach, one engine inoperative. . . 149
   Straight-and-level flight and turns, one engine
      inoperative. . . . . . . . . . . . . . . . . . . . . . . . 148

National Weather Service. . . . . . . . . . . . . . . . 109
NAV mode. . . . . . . . . . . . . . . . . . . . . . . . . . . 104
NAVAID. . . . . . . . . . . . . . . . . . . . . . . . . . . . . 144
Navigation systems. . . . . . . . . . . . . . . . . . . . . 136
   ACS. . . . . . . . . . . . . . . . . . . . . . . . . . . . . . . . 14
   PTS. . . . . . . . . . . . . . . . . . . . . . . . . . . . . . . . 79
Navigational facility. . . . . . . . . . . . . . . . . . . . 137
NDB. . . . . . . . . . . . . . . . . . . . . . . . . . . . . . . . 126
   Approach. . . . . . . . . . . . . . . . . . . . . . . . . . . 143
   Bearing. . . . . . . . . . . . . . . . . . . . . . . . . . . . . 137
Needle valve. . . . . . . . . . . . . . . . . . . . . . . . . . 122
Negative transfer of learning. . . . . . . . . . . . . . 155
No DP. . . . . . . . . . . . . . . . . . . . . . . . . . . . . . . 138
Non-directional beacon. . . . . . . . . . . . . . . . . . 126
   Approach. . . . . . . . . . . . . . . . . . . . . . . . . . . 143
   Bearing. . . . . . . . . . . . . . . . . . . . . . . . . . . . . 137
Nonprecision
   Approach. . . . . . . . . . . . . . . . . . . 127, 143, 144
      ACS. . . . . . . . . . . . . . . . . . . . . . . . . . . . . . 16
      PTS. . . . . . . . . . . . . . . . . . . . . . . . . . . . . . 81
   Runway. . . . . . . . . . . . . . . . . . . . . . . . . . . . 144
NoPT. . . . . . . . . . . . . . . . . . . . . . . . . . . . . . . . 135
North turning error. . . . . . . . . . . . . . . . . . . . . 120
NOTAM. . . . . . . . . . . . . . . . . . . . . . . . . 114, 126
   (D). . . . . . . . . . . . . . . . . . . . . . . . . . . . . . . . 114
Notices to Airmen. . . . . . . . . . . . . . . . . . 114, 126
   Publication. . . . . . . . . . . . . . . . . . . . . . 114, 115
NPA. . . . . . . . . . . . . . . . . . . . . . . . 127, 143, 144
   ACS. . . . . . . . . . . . . . . . . . . . . . . . . . . . . . . . 16
   PTS. . . . . . . . . . . . . . . . . . . . . . . . . . . . . . . . 81
NTAP. . . . . . . . . . . . . . . . . . . . . . . . . . . 114, 115
NWS. . . . . . . . . . . . . . . . . . . . . . . . . . . . . . . . 109

OBS. . . . . . . . . . . . . . . . . . . . . . . . . . . . 123, 136
Obscured thunderstorms. . . . . . . . . . . . . . . . 112
Off-airway routes. . . . . . . . . . . . . . . . . . . . . . 141
Omnibearing selector. . . . . . . . . . . . . . . 123, 136
One engine inoperative
   During straight-and-level flight and turns
      (multiengine). . . . . . . . . . . . . . . . . . . 22, 148
   Instrument approach (multiengine). . . . . . . . 149
      ACS. . . . . . . . . . . . . . . . . . . . . . . . . . . . . . 23

Operating limitations. . . . . . . . . . . . . . . . . . . 149
Operational requirements, limitations and task info,
   ACS. . . . . . . . . . . . . . . . . . . . . . . . . . . . . . . . 40
Outer marker. . . . . . . . . . . . . . . . . . . . . . . . . 125
Outlook briefing. . . . . . . . . . . . . . . . . . . . . . . 107
Over-the-counter drug. . . . . . . . . . . . . . . . . . 166

PA. . . . . . . . . . . . . . . . . . . . . . . . . . . . . . . . . 144
   ACS. . . . . . . . . . . . . . . . . . . . . . . . . . . . . . . . 17
   PTS. . . . . . . . . . . . . . . . . . . . . . . . . . . . . . . . 82
Parallel holding pattern entry. . . . . . . . . . . . . 132
PAR approach. . . . . . . . . . . . . . . . . . . . . . . . 144
PAVE checklist. . . . . . . . . . . . . . . . 94, 96, 97, 98
Perceive, 3P model. . . . . . . . . . . . . . . . . . . . . . 94
Perform, 3P model. . . . . . . . . . . . . . . . . . . . . . 94
Performance. . . . . . . . . . . . . . . . . . . . . . 113, 115
   -Based objectives. . . . . . . . . . . . . . . . . . . . . 158
   Standards. . . . . . . . . . . . . . . . . . . . . . . . . . . 162
PFD. . . . . . . . . . . . . . . . . . . . . . . . . . . . . . . . 123
PIC. . . . . . . . . . . . . . . . . . . . . . . . . 105, 106, 149
Pilot
   In command. . . . . . . . . . . . . . . . . 105, 106, 149
   Qualifications. . . . . . . . . . . . . . . . . . . . . . . . 105
      ACS. . . . . . . . . . . . . . . . . . . . . . . . . . . . . . . 4
   Reports. . . . . . . . . . . . . . . . . . . . . . 99, 107, 108
PIREPs. . . . . . . . . . . . . . . . . . . . . . . 99, 107, 108
Pitch attitude. . . . . . . . . . . . . . . . . . . . . . . . . 171
Pitot
   Heat. . . . . . . . . . . . . . . . . . . . . . . . . . . 117, 128
   -Static
      Check. . . . . . . . . . . . . . . . . . . . . . . . . . . 128
      Instrumentation. . . . . . . . . . . . . . . . . . . . 117
      System. . . . . . . . . . . . . . . . . . . . . . . . . . 118
      Tube. . . . . . . . . . . . . . . . . . . . . . . . . 118, 119
Planning instructional activity. . . . . . . . 164, 165
   PTS. . . . . . . . . . . . . . . . . . . . . . . . . . . . . . . . 70
Position error. . . . . . . . . . . . . . . . . . . . . . . . . 119
Positive
   Exchange of flight controls
      ACS. . . . . . . . . . . . . . . . . . . . . . . . . . . . . . 38
      PTS. . . . . . . . . . . . . . . . . . . . . . . . . . . . . . 62
   Transfer of learning. . . . . . . . . . . . . . . . . . . . 155
Postflight procedures. . . . . . . . . . . . . . . . . . . 151
   ACS. . . . . . . . . . . . . . . . . . . . . . . . . . . . . . . . 25
   PTS. . . . . . . . . . . . . . . . . . . . . . . . . . . . . . . . 87
Power settings. . . . . . . . . . . . . . . . . . . . 113, 151
Powering down. . . . . . . . . . . . . . . . . . . . 151, 152
Practical Test Standards
   Flight instructor–instrument. . . . . . . . . . . . . . 51
Precision
   Approach. . . . . . . . . . . . . . . . . . . . . . . 124, 144
      ACS. . . . . . . . . . . . . . . . . . . . . . . . . . . . . . 17
      PTS. . . . . . . . . . . . . . . . . . . . . . . . . . . . . . 82
      Radar. . . . . . . . . . . . . . . . . . . . . . . . . . . . 144
   Instrument runway markings. . . . . . . . . . . . 144
Preflight
   Checks. . . . . . . . . . . . . . . . . . . . . . . . . . . . . 128
   Inspection. . . . . . . . . . . . . . . . . . . . . . . . . . . 128
   Lesson on a maneuver to be performed in flight. 170
      PTS. . . . . . . . . . . . . . . . . . . . . . . . . . . . . . 73
   Preparation. . . . . . . . . . . . . . . . . . . . . . . . . . 105
      ACS. . . . . . . . . . . . . . . . . . . . . . . . . . . . . . . 4
      PTS. . . . . . . . . . . . . . . . . . . . . . . . . . . 68, 72
   Procedures. . . . . . . . . . . . . . . . . . . . . . . . . . 116
      ACS. . . . . . . . . . . . . . . . . . . . . . . . . . . . . . . 7

Primacy, law of. . . . . . . . . . . . . . . . . . . . . . . 154
Primary
   Flight
      Display. . . . . . . . . . . . . . . . . . . . . . . . 123
      Instruments, loss of. . . . . . . . . . . . . . 150
   Instruments. . . . . . . . . . . . . . . . . . . . . . 134
Prioritizing. . . . . . . . . . . . . . . . . . . . . . . . . . 101
Procedure turn. . . . . . . . . . . . . . . . . 135, 143
Process, 3P model. . . . . . . . . . . . . . . . . . . 94
Prognostic charts. . . . . . . . . . . . . . . . . . . 109
Propeller, feathering. . . . . . . . . . . . . . . . . 149
PT. . . . . . . . . . . . . . . . . . . . . . . . . . . . . . . 135
PTS, Flight instructor–instrument. . . . . . . . . 51

Questioning students. . . . . . . . . . . . . . . . . 161

Radar. . . . . . . . . . . . . . . . . . . . . . . . . . . . 108
   Weather maps. . . . . . . . . . . . . . . . . . . . 107
Radial. . . . . . . . . . . . . . . . . . . . . . . . 136, 137
Radio. . . . . . . . . . . . . . . . . . . . . . . . . . . . 128
   Communication, lost. . . . . . . . . . . . 142, 147
   Magnetic indicator. . . . . . . . . . 124, 126, 137
RAIM. . . . . . . . . . . . . . . . . . . . . . . . . . . . 126
Rain, freezing. . . . . . . . . . . . . . . . . . . . . . . 98
Readiness, law of. . . . . . . . . . . . . . . . . . . 154
Receiver autonomous integrity monitoring. . . . . . . 126
Recency, law of. . . . . . . . . . . . . . . . . . . . 154
Recovery
   From unusual flight attitudes. . . . . . . . . . 136
      ACS. . . . . . . . . . . . . . . . . . . . . . . . . . 13
      PTS. . . . . . . . . . . . . . . . . . . . . . . . . . 78
   Procedure. . . . . . . . . . . . . . . . . . . . . . . 136
References, ACS. . . . . . . . . . . . . . . . . . . . 46
Regulations and publications
   related to IFR operations, PTS. . . . . . . . . 71
REILs. . . . . . . . . . . . . . . . . . . . . . . . . . . . 146
Report radio failure. . . . . . . . . . . . . . . . . . 142
Resignation, hazardous attitude. . . . . . . . . . 95
Resource management. . . . . . . . . . . . . . . 146
Restricted area. . . . . . . . . . . . . . . . . . . . . 113
Reverse sensing. . . . . . . . . . . . . . . . . . . . 123
Rime ice. . . . . . . . . . . . . . . . . . . . . . . . . . 116
Risk management. . . . . . . . . . . . . . . . . 96, 97
   Four fundamental risk elements. . . . . . . . 97
   PTS. . . . . . . . . . . . . . . . . . . . . . . . . . . . 60
RMI. . . . . . . . . . . . . . . . . . . . . 124, 126, 137
Rudder pressure, engine failure. . . . . . . . . 148
Runway
   Centerline lights. . . . . . . . . . . . . . . . . . . 139
   Distance remaining signs. . . . . . . . . . . . 139
   Edge lights. . . . . . . . . . . . . . . . . . . . . . 139
   Hold position
      Markings. . . . . . . . . . . . . . . . . . . . . 139
      Signs. . . . . . . . . . . . . . . . . . . . . . . . 139
   Lights. . . . . . . . . . . . . . . . . . . . . . 139, 146
   Markings. . . . . . . . . . . . . . . . . . . . . . . 146

Safety of
   Flight, ACS. . . . . . . . . . . . . . . . . . . . . . . 38
   Student. . . . . . . . . . . . . . . . . . . . . . . . 163
Sand storms. . . . . . . . . . . . . . . . . . . . . . 111
Scuba diving. . . . . . . . . . . . . . . . . . . . . . 169

SDF. . . . . . . . . . . . . . . . . . . . . . . . . . . . . 143
Severe
   Thunderstorm watches. . . . . . . . . . . . . . 111
   Turbulence. . . . . . . . . . . . . . . . . . . . . . 111
   Weather
      Outlook chart. . . . . . . . . . . . . . . . . . 111
      Watch. . . . . . . . . . . . . . . . . . . . . . . 111
Shut-down process. . . . . . . . . . . . . . . . . . 152
SIGMET. . . . . . . . . . . . . . . . . . . . . . . . . . 111
Significant
   Meteorological Info. . . . . . . . . . . . . . . . 111
   Weather charts. . . . . . . . . . . . . . . . . . . 109
      Low-level. . . . . . . . . . . . . . . . . . . . . 109
Simplified directional facility. . . . . . . . . . . . 143
Single-pilot resource management. . . . . . . . 94
   One engine inoperative. . . . . . . . . . . . . 150
   PTS. . . . . . . . . . . . . . . . . . . . . . . . . . . . 60
Sinuses. . . . . . . . . . . . . . . . . . . . . . . . . . 166
Situational awareness. . . . . . . . . . 97, 101, 103
   PTS. . . . . . . . . . . . . . . . . . . . . . . . . . . . 61
South turning error. . . . . . . . . . . . . . . . . . 120
Spatial disorientation. . . . . . . . . . . . . . . . . 167
Special
   Emphasis areas, PTS. . . . . . . . . . . . . . . 56
   VFR. . . . . . . . . . . . . . . . . . . . . . . 130, 131
      Minimums. . . . . . . . . . . . . . . . . . . . 130
Speed limit. . . . . . . . . . . . . . . . . . . . . . . . 134
Squall line. . . . . . . . . . . . . . . . . . . . . 98, 112
SRM. . . . . . . . . . . . . . . . . . . . . . . . . . . . . 94
   One engine inoperative. . . . . . . . . . . . . 150
   PTS. . . . . . . . . . . . . . . . . . . . . . . . . . . . 60
Stability chart. . . . . . . . . . . . . . . . . . . . . . 110
Standard
   Localizer. . . . . . . . . . . . . . . . . . . . . . . 143
   Minimum climb gradient. . . . . . . . . . . . . 138
   Terminal arrival route. . . . . . . . . . . . 114, 141
   Weather briefing. . . . . . . . . . . . . . . . . . 107
STAR. . . . . . . . . . . . . . . . . . . . . . . . 114, 141
Static port. . . . . . . . . . . . . . . . . 117, 118, 119
Station passage. . . . . . . . . . . . . . . . . . . . 137
Steep turns. . . . . . . . . . . . . . . . . . . . . . . 174
   PTS. . . . . . . . . . . . . . . . . . . . . . . . . . . . 78
Stormscope. . . . . . . . . . . . . . . . . . . . . . . 108
Straight-and-level flight. . . . . . . . . . . . 171, 173
   One engine inoperative. . . . . . . . . . . . . 148
   PTS. . . . . . . . . . . . . . . . . . . . . . . . . . . . 75
Stress. . . . . . . . . . . . . . . . . . . . . . . . . . . 168
Suction relief valve. . . . . . . . . . . . . . . . . . 122
Supercooled water. . . . . . . . . . . . . . . . . . 116
Supporting instruments. . . . . . . . . . . . . . . 134
Surface analysis chart. . . . . . . . . . . . 108, 109

Takeoff minimums. . . . . . . . . . . . . . . . . . . 139
Task management. . . . . . . . . . . . . . . . . . 101
   PTS. . . . . . . . . . . . . . . . . . . . . . . . . . . . 61
TAWS. . . . . . . . . . . . . . . . . . . . . . . . . . . 103
TCAS resolution advisory. . . . . . . . . . 131, 148
Teaching
   Methods. . . . . . . . . . . . . . . . . . . . 158, 160
      PTS. . . . . . . . . . . . . . . . . . . . . . . . . 69
   Process. . . . . . . . . . . . . . . . . . . . 157, 158
      PTS. . . . . . . . . . . . . . . . . . . . . . . . . 68
Teardrop hold pattern entry. . . . . . . . . 132, 133
Technical subject areas. . . . . . . . . . . . . . . 166
   PTS. . . . . . . . . . . . . . . . . . . . . . . . . . . . 70

# Index

Television news weather. . . . . . . . . . . . . . . . . . 108
Temperature inversion. . . . . . . . . . . . . . . . . . . . 99
Terrain awareness and warning system. . . . . . . 103
Threshold. . . . . . . . . . . . . . . . . . . . . . . . . . . . . 146
Thunderstorms. . . . . . . . . . . . . . 99, 108, 111, 112
    Embedded. . . . . . . . . . . . . . . . . . . . . . . 99, 112
    Obscured. . . . . . . . . . . . . . . . . . . . . . . . . . . 112
    Severe. . . . . . . . . . . . . . . . . . . . . . . . . . . . . 111
Timed
    Approaches from a holding fix. . . . . . . . . . . 134
    Turns to magnetic compass headings. . . . . . . 174
        PTS. . . . . . . . . . . . . . . . . . . . . . . . . . . . . . 77
TO/FROM indicator. . . . . . . . . . . . . . . . . . . . . 123
Tornado. . . . . . . . . . . . . . . . . . . . . . . . . . . . . . 112
    Watches. . . . . . . . . . . . . . . . . . . . . . . . . . . . 111
Touchdown zone
    Elevation. . . . . . . . . . . . . . . . . . . . . . . . . . . 125
    Markings. . . . . . . . . . . . . . . . . . . . . . . 144, 146
Tracking. . . . . . . . . . . . . . . . . . . . . . . . . . . . . 137
Traffic alert and collision avoidance system
resolution advisory. . . . . . . . . . . . . . . . 131, 148
Training syllabus. . . . . . . . . . . . . . . . . . . . . . . 164
Transition route. . . . . . . . . . . . . . . . . . . . . . . . 141
Transponder. . . . . . . . . . . . . . . . . . . . . . . . . . 125
    Code. . . . . . . . . . . . . . . . . . . . . . . . . . . . . . 142
Tropical cyclones. . . . . . . . . . . . . . . . . . . . . . . 111
True airspeed. . . . . . . . . . . . . . . . . . . . . . . . . . 113
Turbulence. . . . . . . . . . . . . . . . . . . 99, 107, 108
Turn
    -And-slip indicator. . . . . . . . . . . . . . . . 121, 128
    Coordinator. . . . . . . . . . . . . . . . . . . . . 121, 128
Turns. . . . . . . . . . . . . . . . . . . . . . . . . . . . . . . . 172
    One engine inoperative. . . . . . . . . . . . . . . . 148
    PTS. . . . . . . . . . . . . . . . . . . . . . . . . . . . . . . . 75
    Steep. . . . . . . . . . . . . . . . . . . . . . . . . . . . . . 174
Two-way radio communication failure. . . . . 147, 148

Uncontrolled field. . . . . . . . . . . . . . . . . . . 138, 147
Unusual attitude. . . . . . . . . . . . . . . . . . . . . . . 136

Vacuum
    Pump. . . . . . . . . . . . . . . . . . . . . . . . . . . . . . 122
    System. . . . . . . . . . . . . . . . . 119, 121, 122, 150
VASI. . . . . . . . . . . . . . . . . . . . . . . . . . . . 144, 146
VDP. . . . . . . . . . . . . . . . . . . . . . . . . . . . . . . . 143
Vectors to final. . . . . . . . . . . . . . . . . . . . . . . . 144
Vertical speed indicator. . . . . . . . . . . . . . 118, 119
    Built-in error. . . . . . . . . . . . . . . . . . . . . . . . . 119
    Instrument cockpit check. . . . . . . . . . . . . . . 128
VFR
    Clearance. . . . . . . . . . . . . . . . . . . . . . . . . . 131
    -On-top. . . . . . . . . . . . . . . . . . . . . . . . . . . . 131
        Clearance. . . . . . . . . . . . . . . . . . . . . 105, 131
    Visibility and cloud clearance minimums. . . . . 130
Visual
    Approach. . . . . . . . . . . . . . . . . . . . . . . . . . . 141
        Slope indicator. . . . . . . . . . . . . . . . . 144, 146
    Descent point. . . . . . . . . . . . . . . . . . . . . . . . 143
Volcanic ash. . . . . . . . . . . . . . . . . . . . . . . . . . 111

VOR. . . . . . . . . . . . . . . . . . . . . . . . . . . . . . . . 137
    Accuracy check. . . . . . . . . . . . . . . . . . 123, 129
    Approach. . . . . . . . . . . . . . . . . . . . . . . . . . . 143
    Indicator. . . . . . . . . . . . . . . . . . . . . . . 123, 137
    OBS/CDI type indicator. . . . . . . . . . . . . . . . 123
    Radials. . . . . . . . . . . . . . . . . . . . . . . . 136, 137
    Station. . . . . . . . . . . . . . . . . . . . . . . . 123, 137
VOR/DME. . . . . . . . . . . . . . . . . . . . 124, 136, 137
    Approach. . . . . . . . . . . . . . . . . . . . . . . . . . . 114
VOR/ILS indicator. . . . . . . . . . . . . . . . . . . . . . 123
VORTAC. . . . . . . . . . . . . . . . . . . . . 124, 136, 137
VSI. . . . . . . . . . . . . . . . . . . . . . . . . . . . . 118, 119
    Built-in error. . . . . . . . . . . . . . . . . . . . . . . . . 119
    Instrument cockpit check. . . . . . . . . . . . . . . 128
VYSE. . . . . . . . . . . . . . . . . . . . . . . . . . . . . . . 149

WAAS approach. . . . . . . . . . . . . . . . . . . . . . . 126
Wake turbulence. . . . . . . . . . . . . . . . . . . . . . . 139
Waypoint. . . . . . . . . . . . . . . . . . . . . . . . . . . . . 136
Weather
    Information. . . . . . . . . . . . . . . . . . . . . . . . . 107
        ACS. . . . . . . . . . . . . . . . . . . . . . . . . . . . . 5
        PTS. . . . . . . . . . . . . . . . . . . . . . . . . . . . . 72
    Radar. . . . . . . . . . . . . . . . . . . . . . . . . . . . . 107
Weight and balance. . . . . . . . . . . . . . . . . . . . 114
Wind shear. . . . . . . . . . . . . . . . . . . . . . . . . . . . 99
Windmilling propeller. . . . . . . . . . . . . . . . . . . . 149
Winds and Temperatures Aloft Forecasts. . . . . . 110

185

# Update Service

Visit the **GLEIM**® website for free updates, which are available until the next edition is published.

# GleimAviation.com/updates